BULLYING AMONG
UNIVERSITY STUDENTS

Bullying Among University Students is a pioneering collection of knowledge and evidence exploring the under-researched phenomenon of bullying in universities. Abusive behaviour among young people is a serious and pervasive problem that is exacerbated by the rapid advances in electronic communication, and in this book the authors highlight the problem and proceed to facilitate new practices and policies to address it.

This book brings together an international team of authors from a range of disciplines, encompassing education, psychology, criminology, law and counselling, who have carried out research in the area of university bullying. Addressing critical dialogues and debates, the authors explore peer on peer violence, intimidation and social exclusion before considering the effects on students and making recommendations for action and further research. Key topics include:

- cyberbullying and cyber aggression
- rape culture across the university
- homophobic and transphobic bullying
- the impact of bullying on mental health
- the role of bully and victim across the lifespan
- policies and procedures to address bullying.

International in authorship and scope, this book will be an invaluable resource for students and researchers in fields such as education, psychology, sociology, health studies and criminology. It is also essential reading for university policy-makers and union representatives responsible for the emotional and physical well-being of students.

Helen Cowie is Emerita Professor at the University of Surrey in the Faculty of Health and Medical Sciences where she specializes in strategies to counteract school bullying. She is also visiting professor at Brunel University and visiting researcher at Regent's University London. She has over 100 publications in refereed journals on the subject of mental health in youth, emotional development, cyberbullying and peer support.

Carrie-Anne Myers is a lecturer in Criminology at City University London where she researches and teaches in a number of key areas including Childhood, Youth and Adolescence, School Violence and Bullying, Victims, Victimology and Criminal Justice Policy, Gender and Feminist Criminology, and Media and Youth Cultures of Consumption.

BULLYING AMONG UNIVERSITY STUDENTS

Cross-national perspectives

Edited by Helen Cowie and Carrie-Anne Myers

Routledge
Taylor & Francis Group

LONDON AND NEW YORK

First published 2016
by Routledge
2 Park Square, Milton Park, Abingdon, Oxon OX14 4RN

and by Routledge
711 Third Avenue, New York, NY 10017

Routledge is an imprint of the Taylor & Francis Group, an informa business

British Library Cataloguing in Publication Data
A catalogue record for this book is available from the British Library

Library of Congress Cataloging in Publication Data
Bullying among university students : cross-national perspectives / edited
by Helen Cowie and Carrie-Anne Myers.
pages cm
Includes bibliographical references.
1. Bullying in universities and colleges--Cross-cultural studies. 2.
Cyberbullying--Cross-cultural studies. I. Cowie, Helen editor of
compilation. II. Myers, Carrie-Anne, editor of compilation.
LB2345.3.B85B85 2015
371.5'8--dc23
2015012717

ISBN: 978-1-138-80925-3 (hbk)
ISBN: 978-1-138-80926-0 (pbk)
ISBN: 978-1-315-75013-2 (ebk)

Typeset in Bembo
by Saxon Graphics Ltd, Derby
Printed and bound in Great Britain by Ashford Colour Press Ltd, Gosport, Hampshire

To Spiros for his love and encouragement (HC)
To Constance for her timely arrival (CM)

CONTENTS

PART VI
Reflections   **191**

CONTRIBUTORS

Osman Tolga Arıcak is an associate professor of Educational Psychology. He worked at Trakya University, Indiana University, Tulane University, Fatih University and Harvard University respectively. He is currently associate professor in the Department of Psychology at Hasan Kalyoncu University, Turkey. His main research interest is cyberbullying, cyber victimization, online identity, online privacy, and online safety. Dr Arıcak is also interested in methodological and statistical issues in psychological research.

Rashid Aziz is a lecturer in Applied Criminology at the School of Law, Criminal Justice and Computing, Canterbury Christ Church University, UK. He is currently writing up his PhD thesis on British Asian Muslims and marriage. His research interests lie in the areas of race, ethnicity, culture, masculinity, power and symbolic interactionism.

Sheri Bauman is a professor and director of the Counselling and Mental Health graduate degree program at the University of Arizona, USA. Before earning her doctorate in 1999, Dr Bauman worked in public schools for 30 years, 18 of those as a school counsellor. She is also a licensed psychologist. Dr Bauman conducts research on bullying and cyberbullying. She is the recipient of two grants from the National Science Foundation. She has given presentations on topics related to bullying/cyberbullying at local, state, national, and international conferences. She has published two books: *Special Topics for Helping Professionals* (2007, Pearson); *Cyberbullying: What Counselors Need to Know* (2011, American Counseling Association), and is lead editor of *Principles of Cyberbullying Research: Definition, Measures, and Methods* (with Donna Cross and Jenny Walker 2013, Routledge). Her vita includes over 50 publications in peer-reviewed journals, two training DVDs for counsellors, and numerous other publications.

Katja Björklund is a senior researcher at the National Institute for Health and Welfare in the Child and Adolescent Mental Health Unit in Finland. She is a doctor of criminal psychology, a clinical psychologist and psychotherapist. Her main research interests include stalking, violence and health, the role of the victims of violence in health care settings, socio-emotional skills, and intervention studies. Currently she studies children's social and emotional skills in the school community. She has several years of experience of working within the school mental health settings and university health care services. She has published several research papers on stalking and violence victimization among university students.

Marilyn Campbell is a professor at the Queensland University of Technology. She is a registered teacher and a registered psychologist. Before this, Marilyn supervised school counsellors and has worked in infant, primary and secondary schools as a teacher, teacher-librarian and school counsellor. Her main clinical and research interests are the prevention and intervention of anxiety disorders in young people and the effects of bullying, especially cyberbullying in schools. She has published several papers on cyberbullying and won three national competitive grants to further research in this area.

Helen Cowie is Emeritus Professor at the University of Surrey, UK, in the Faculty of Health and Medical Sciences where she specializes in strategies to counteract school bullying, and Honorary Professor at Brunel University, UK. She is also Visiting Researcher at Regent's University London, UK. She has over 100 publications in refereed journals on the subject of mental health in youth, emotional development, cyberbullying and peer support. She has authored and co-authored a number of influential books. In *Managing School Violence* and *New Perspectives on Bullying* (2007, Open University), she and Dawn Jennifer designed training for a whole-school approach that emphasized the importance of fostering positive relationships in the school community as a whole and provided a wealth of evidence-based good practice for professionals. *Understanding Children's Development* (Smith, P. K., Cowie, H. and Blades, M. (2015), Chichester: John Wiley) now into its sixth edition, remains one of the most popular undergraduate textbooks in the field. Her most recent book *From Birth to Sixteen* (www.routledge.com/cw/cowie) is a useful resource for educators and health care professionals working with children and young people.

Iain Coyne is Associate Professor in Occupational Psychology at the University of Nottingham, UK. He is a Registered Occupational Psychologist, Associate Fellow of the British Psychological Society (BPS) and Senior Editor for the BPS Test Reviews. Iain has been a council member for the International Test Commission, where he co-developed the ITC's Guidelines on Test User and Computer/Internet-based Testing. He has also acted as a work group coordinator for a European COST programme on cyberbullying in educational contexts and a member of a working party for the Chartered Management Institute in their development of a workplace-bullying guide for managers. Dr Coyne's experience lies within bullying/cyberbullying at work and productive/counterproductive work behaviour. He has published peer-reviewed papers, book chapters, edited a book as well as presented at national and international conferences on these areas.

Kristen Cvancara is an associate professor at Minnesota State University, Mankato, USA, in the Department of Communication Studies. Her areas of research include interpersonal communication and social influence. She investigates the socialization and use of verbal aggression in romantic, sibling, and parent-child relationships. As a Fulbright Scholar in 2012 (Finland), she began investigating the relationship between sibling communication patterns and bullying behaviour in schools. Her research is published in *Communication Quarterly*, *Journal of Family Communication*, and *Personal Relationships*.

Ashley DeMartini is a PhD student in the Department of Integrated Studies in Education at McGill University, Canada. She has an interdisciplinary background in Gender Studies, Human Rights, Informal Education, and Genocide Studies. Her current research interests are Human Rights Education and Teacher Education, and she continues to draw from her diverse academic background. Before her PhD studies, Ashley was a Media Educator for the National Film Board in Toronto. She currently teaches a course on Education, Media, and Technology at McGill University.

Theodoros Giovazolias is Assistant Professor of Counselling Psychology at the Department of Psychology, University of Crete, Greece. His main research interests include the examination of bullying in children and adolescents, as well as its effects on adult psychosocial adjustment. More specifically, he tries to understand how both family and school factors are related to the occurrence of the phenomenon. Additionally, he has participated as educator and co-coordinator in various seminars and educational programs (both on a national and European level) on school bullying. His has presented his work in national and international conferences and has published in peer-reviewed scientific journals. His most recent co-authored book is Giovazolias T. and Malikiosi-Loizos M. (Eds.) (2014), *Counselling Psychology: Current Issues in Research and Practice*, Athens Pedio (in Greek).

Johanne Ives is Assistant Dean of Students and Director for Fraternity and Sorority Programs at the University of Arizona, USA, and a doctoral student in the Center for the Study of Higher Education at the University of Arizona.

Esta Kaal holds a Master of Arts in Media and Communication and is a lecturer in research methods at the Institute of Communication, Tallinn University, Estonia. She is an experienced research practitioner and consultant, having 10 years of research experience in a leading marketing and opinion research company, TNS. She was also a member of AQR (Association for Qualitative Research) from

2000–09. She has been working at Tallinn University since 2011. Her main research interests include environmental and health communication in university.

Maria Luca holds a PhD in Psychotherapy Studies, is Reader in Psychotherapy and Counselling Psychology and the Head of the Reflections Research Centre at Regent's University London, UK. She has taught modules on sexual dynamics in therapy, assessment and formulation, embodied grounded theory, therapeutic relationships and Medically Unexplained Symptoms, both at UK and other universities abroad. She has extensive clinical experience as a psychotherapist in the British National Health Service and has a small private practice in London. Maria gained her PhD from the University of Kent at Canterbury and is a registered psychotherapist with the United Kingdom Council for Psychotherapy and an accredited supervisor with the British Association for Counselling and Psychotherapy. She is editor of the 2014 book, *Sexual Attraction in Therapy: Clinical Perspectives on Moving Beyond the Taboo – A Guide for Training and Practice*, London: Wiley; and (2004) *The Therapeutic Frame in the Clinical Context – Integrative Perspectives,* London: Brunner-Routledge; and author of book chapters and articles in refereed journals. Among other publications, she is the author of (2003) Containment of the Sexualized and Erotized Transference, *Journal of Clinical Psychoanalysis*, Vol. 11, No. 4. Maria is chief editor of the journal *Psychotherapy and Counselling Psychology Reflections*.

Maria Malikiosi-Loizos is Professor Emeritus of Counselling Psychology at the University of Athens, Greece. Her main research interests include student temperament, personality and attitudes, as well as applications of counselling and peer support programs in higher education. Additionally, she has participated as educator and co-coordinator in various seminars and educational programs concerning the applications of counselling in primary, secondary and higher education. She has presented her work at national and international conferences and has published books and articles in peer-reviewed scientific journals. She established the first peer-counselling centre at the University of Athens in 1995 and has been directing it since then. Back in the 1980s, she co-authored the first nationwide study on students' personality and attitudes ever to be conducted in Greece: Anderson, L. R. and Malikiosi-Loizos, M. (1980). *Personality and Attitudes of Students of the Greek Higher Education Institutions.* Athens: National Centre of Social Research (in Greek).

Carrie-Anne Myers is a lecturer in Criminology at City University London, UK, where she researches and teaches in a number of key areas including: childhood, youth and adolescence, school violence and bullying, victims, victimology and criminal justice policy, gender and feminist criminology, and media and youth cultures of consumption. She has had a number of articles published in refereed journals such as *Pastoral Care in Education* and *Emotional and Behavioural Difficulties* focusing on young people bullying, cyberbullying and violence.

Toni Pearce is the National President of the National Union of Students (NUS) and, as such, represents over 600 students' unions and seven million students. Toni is the first NUS President who has not been to university. She believes in shaping the future of education to help create a fairer society and is passionate about the power of students to drive change. Having studied at Cornwall College before serving as President of Cornwall College Students' Union from 2009 to 2011, Toni was elected NUS Vice-President (Further Education) in 2011 and re-elected for a second term in 2012 where she won £41m for student parents through Care to Learn and £50m in bursaries for adult FE student support. She also held the position of NUS Deputy President between 2011 and 2013. The bodies on which Toni has represented NUS and the student voice include the Further Education and Skills Ministerial Advisory Panel, the Skills Funding Agency Advisory Board, the Institute for Learning Advisory Council, the LSIS Board, NIACE Policy Committee, the FE Guild Steering Group, the Further Education Reputation Strategy Group and the National Improvement Partnership Board.

Maili Pörhölä is Adjunct Professor and University Researcher in the Department of Communication at the University of Jyväskylä, Finland. Her research focuses on bullying at school, in higher education, and in the workplace, including examining aspects of peer relationships, peer community integration, and psychosocial well-being. She has also worked in steering committees of two development projects focusing on prevention of bullying in kindergartens. She has published a number of research articles in peer-reviewed journals as well as authoring several book chapters. Among other publications, she has co-edited with Terry A. Kinney the book *Anti and Pro-Social Communication: Theories, Methods, and Applications* (2009, Peter Lang Publishing Inc.) and co-authored with Terry A. Kinney the book *Bullying: Contexts, Consequences, and Control* (2010, Aresta), which has been translated into Spanish (El Acoso: Contextos, Consecuencias y Control) and Catalan (L'assetjament: Contextos, conseqüències i control).

Ian Rivers is Professor of Human Development at Brunel University, UK, Visiting Professor in Psychological Sciences and Health at the University of Strathclyde, UK, and Visiting Professor of Education at Anglia Ruskin University, UK. He is an HCPC registered health psychologist and developmental psychologist. Previously he was Professor of Community Psychology at Queen Margaret University Edinburgh and before that he was Professor of Applied Psychology at York St John College, UK. Ian has also been a visiting fellow at the Centers for Disease Control and Prevention (CDC) in Atlanta, USA, and recently served on two American Federal expert panels to develop a uniform definition of bullying to inform public health surveillance in schools across the USA, and to explore the relationship between bullying behaviour and suicide in American youth. Between 2006 and 2008, Ian served on the Scottish Government's, *LGBT Heart and Minds Forum* to develop LGBT inclusive legislative agenda for the next decade in terms of workplaces and public services, religion and belief, education and family, media and leadership, and citizenship and social capital.

Shaheen Shariff is an associate professor and expert on legal issues that have emerged in relation to online social communications such as cyberbullying, free expression, privacy, libel and criminal harassment. Professor Shariff has developed guidelines for policymakers, school administrators, teachers and parents regarding the extent of their legal responsibilities to address cyberbullying in various contexts. She currently holds grants from the Social Sciences and Humanities Research Council of Canada that focus on human rights, constitutional and tort law as they inform institutional responsibilities to provide safe and productive school and work environments, and censorship and diversity in schools. She was invited to participate on a United Nations panel on cyber-hate chaired by Secretary General Ban Ki Moon. She is also one of four recipients globally of Facebook's Inaugural Digital Citizenship Grant. Her fifth book on cyberbullying is *Sexting and Cyberbullying: Defining the Lines for Digitally Empowered Kids* (2014, Cambridge University Press) (www.mcgill.ca/definetheline). She received the Queen's Diamond Jubilee Medal in 2013 and contributed as expert witness to the Senate Standing Committee of Human Rights investigation on cyberbullying in Canada.

Jessica Simmons is a doctoral student with Sheri Bauman, professor in the Department of Disability and Psychoeducational Studies.

Keith Sullivan is the Statutory Professor of Education at the National University of Ireland, Galway. He has researched and written extensively about school bullying in the real and the cyber worlds, and also concerning workplace bullying. His major concern has been to translate our understandings about the nature of bullying in its many forms in order to find humane, inclusive and practical solutions to neutralize bullying so that individuals can live happier lives. Keith has taught at secondary schools and been a counsellor in England, Canada and New Zealand, and has taught at universities in England, New Zealand, the South Pacific and Ireland. He has held the Charter Fellowship in Human Rights at Oxford University and has presented his bullying work to many international audiences. His first book, the first edition of *The Anti-Bullying Handbook* (2000, Oxford University Press) was nominated for New Zealand's prestigious Montana Book Awards.

Kaja Tampere graduated with a PhD degree in Organizational Communication and Public Relations from Jyväskylä University, Finland in 2003. She has been working in government communication and in big infrastructure business companies as a communication consultant for many years. Currently she is a professor and Head of the Communication Institute at Tallinn University, Estonia. In addition, she has been teaching Organizational Communication and PR since 1996. Her courses include: Introduction to Public Relations, History of Public Relations, PR Theories, PR Case Studies and Communication Strategy. Her research interests are: history of public relations, communication effectiveness, propaganda, environmental and health communication, and communication strategy research.

Maria Beatriz Torres is Associate Professor of Communication Studies at Gustavus Adolphus College, USA. She has been working in the communication field for 30 years. She was awarded Mexico's National Council of Science and Technology, and Fulbright scholarships. She consults and trains healthcare organizations on effective cross-cultural communication. Her scholarship looks at the intersection between culture and health communication. She is involved in several community based participatory action research projects developing entertainment education media to promote the health of Latino, Hmong and Somali immigrants in Minnesota. Dr Torres also serves as Gustavus Sexual Misconduct Complaints investigator and harassment officer.

PERMISSIONS

PART I
Overview

1

WHAT WE KNOW ABOUT BULLYING AND CYBERBULLYING AMONG UNIVERSITY STUDENTS

Helen Cowie and Carrie-Anne Myers

In recent years, university students themselves have become concerned about the growing culture of violence and bullying on campus with disturbing accounts of the long-term damage to self-esteem, academic achievement and emotional well-being experienced by some students. The bullying behaviour appears to be embedded in a culture that glorifies violent, disrespectful attitudes towards women – a sexualized 'laddish' culture often expressed through misogyny and homophobia that 'normalizes' such behaviour and attitudes and shames bystanders into apathy.

Jackson *et al.* (2014) suggest that there are strong parallels between laddish behaviour at university and at school. They note that women students (like girls at school) are often viewed as having a 'civilizing' influence on males and their research also showed that the 'lads' at university tended to be 'weeded out' at the end of the first year. However, to date, research into bullying in educational settings has mainly focused on nursery, primary and secondary school levels, with only a very small number of studies (e.g. Isaacs *et al.* 2008; Pörhölä, 2011) addressing aspects of bullying in higher education colleges and universities. (For a review, see Cowie *et al.* 2013.) At the same time, although some research explores bullying in the university *workplace*, very little addresses the problem of peer-on-peer violence, intimidation and social exclusion as it impacts on the students themselves. University students, as young adults, who are neither children in need of protection nor employees in the workplace, seem to be largely overlooked, with some notable exceptions, in the research literature on bullying and sexual violence. Furthermore, many students who are targets of bullying report that they do not know of any policies, systems or avenues to help them.

Bullying at university takes many forms and includes such behaviour as:

- spreading nasty rumours on the grounds of age, race, sex, disability, sexual orientation and religion or belief;

- ridiculing or demeaning someone;
- social exclusion;
- unwelcome sexual advances;
- threatening someone, either directly or anonymously online.

Definitions tend to be operational and typically focus on bullying as hostile behaviour that can be physical or psychological, usually sustained or repeated within an unbalanced power relationship. This is in line with the prominent and widely used definition of school bullying proposed by Olweus (1993) that encompasses three core components:

- there is an intent to harm or upset another student;
- the harmful behaviour is done repeatedly and over time;
- the relationship between bully/bullies and victim/victims is characterized by an imbalance in power.

Coleyshaw (2012) points out the lack of theory to explain bullying at university, despite the fact that some models have been applied to workplace bullying, such as disempowerment theory and attribution theory. We explore some theoretical models later in the book. For example, in chapter 4, Maili Pörhölä considers peer-community integration theory and positioning theory; in chapter 8, Jessica Simmons, Sheri Bauman and Johanne Ives consider social identity theory; and in chapter 15, Iain Coyne discusses the relevance of the victim-perspective model, which includes aspects of organizational culture as well as individual characteristics as antecedents of bullying in the workplace.

The recent emergence of cyberbullying as a new form of bullying (Bennett *et al.* 2011; Sourander *et al.* 2010) also indicates distress among university students; Schenk and Fremouw (2012) found that college student victims of cyberbullying scored higher than matched controls on measures of depression, anxiety, phobic anxiety and paranoia. Common types of cyberbullying include the following:

- harassment: e.g. sending insulting or threatening messages;
- denigration: spreading rumours on the Internet;
- outing and trickery: revealing personal information online about a person which was shared in confidence (Willard 2006); posting embarrassing material online;
- exclusion: preventing a person from taking part in online social activities, such as games or chats;
- Bennett *et al.* (2011) found evidence of hostility, humiliation, exclusion and intrusiveness by means of electronic victimization in friendship and dating relationships.

Bullying and cyberbullying among university students

In one large survey of 2,805 Finnish university students, Lappalainen *et al.* (2011) found that around 5 per cent reported being bullied either by a fellow student or by a member of staff. Around half of the bullies and half of the victims in this survey reported that they had been involved in bullying incidents before they left school. This continuum from school to university was especially prevalent among men in the study. Curwen *et al.* (2011) speculate that decreases in the use of verbal and physical bullying methods by university students may be caused by fewer opportunities to bully than there are at school and by the possibility that the values of most university students may be more strongly opposed to bullying behaviour. At the same time, they note that bullies at university continue – unchallenged – to target peers who are vulnerable in some way. Similarly, in a retrospective study, Chapell *et al.* (2006) found a positive relationship between being a child and adult bully and between being an adolescent and adult bully. In this study, it was found that 54 per cent of the adult bully participants had also bullied during childhood and adolescence. Curwen *et al.* (2011) surveyed 159 female and 37 male undergraduates who admitted to having bullied a fellow student at least once since coming to university. The survey revealed that most of those who were bullies at university had a history of bullying at school. Although again the incidence was lower than at school, bullies tended to target victims who were passive and less likely to retaliate. As the researchers speculate, the fact that many of these young adults had stable bullying characteristics suggests that there are strong benefits to them arising from this kind of behaviour. Furthermore, victims may remain silent through embarrassment, and bystanders may reinforce the aggressive behaviour by remaining detached from the target.

Studies of nursing and medical students report significantly higher than average rates of bullying. For example, Farley *et al.* (2015, in press) found in their survey of 158 trainee doctors (104 females and 54 males) that cyberbullying acts were experienced by nearly half of the sample during their training, with fellow students as the main perpetrators. These experiences were significantly linked to ill health and job dissatisfaction; those individuals who blamed themselves appeared to be more at risk of developing ill health. The authors support recommendations that professional training should heighten students' awareness on how their online interactions may affect their future careers. For example, the American Medical Association has issued guidelines on the use of social media with regard to posting sensitive information, maintaining professional boundaries and using privacy settings where appropriate.

Similarly, Mukhtar *et al.* (2010) investigated bullying among medical students in a private medical college in Pakistan. They identified 'horizontal' (that is, from fellow students) and 'hierarchical' (that is, from colleagues in positions of power) bullying, which included verbal insults, written abuse, physical bullying or coercion, and social exclusion. The researchers found that such negative behaviour was passed on from one cohort of students to the next leading to long-term consequences with regard to the target students' mental health, professional practice and career aspirations. In this study, 70 per cent of the bullied students were female. Factors including a history of feeling lonely or sad, and not having any close friends were significantly associated with being bullied. Importantly, too, lack of knowledge about support services at the medical college was significantly associated with experiences of bullying. The authors strongly recommend the introduction of mentoring programmes and peer support, as well as education on the adverse effects of bullying.

Although anti-bullying policies do exist in some universities, research indicates that the students' perception is that university authorities appear to provide very little protection from bullying. Kenworthy (2010) carried out an online survey of 452 American university students inviting those who had experienced cyberbullying to respond. In this sample, the majority did not report it to anyone and only 14 per cent indicated that their formal complaints had resulted in disciplinary action against the perpetrator. The more effective coping strategies were limiting exposure and accessibility online; less effective coping strategies were characterized by aggressive or vengeful contact with the perpetrator. Those who coped least well were students for whom the bullying met the legal definition of *cyberstalking* and those who were being bullied by a former dating/intimate partner. One aspect concerned students' confusion about the seriousness of cyberbullying, since some considered it to simply be a prank rather than a crime. The lack of research into the nature and incidence of bullying and the piecemeal approach to dealing with the problem means that this is an aspect of student life that is neglected. One argument, Coleyshaw (2012) proposes, is that the university environment may resist such investigations since this could be counterproductive in terms of recruiting new students and promoting a positive image of university life. So, it is safer to pathologize bullying and view it as an individual problem, not an organizational one. Coleyshaw (2012) argues that there needs to be more focus on universities as organizations – an idea that we explore throughout this book. Furthermore, we argue that a policy consistent across universities needs to be designed and implemented along the lines of whole school policies adopted across the school sector.

By focusing purely on individual bullies and victims, the wider social context in which bullying occurs is often overlooked; most importantly the role of the majority who are witnesses, reinforcers and assistants to bullying are not taken into account. To explore this wider context, Myers and Cowie (2013) investigated views from university students on peer group bullying from three standpoints: bully, victim and bystander. Building on the participant role approach (Salmivalli *et al.* 1996), the researchers adopted role play, which is defined as 'participation in simulated social situations that are intended to throw light upon the role/rule contexts governing "real life" social episodes' (Cohen *et al.* 2007, p. 448). Role-play methods are widely used in educational settings, because they focus attention on the ways in which people interact with one another (Goldenberg *et al.* 2005; van Ments 1983). By stimulating the imagination of participants, these methods have the potential to express or arouse emotion as well as to address cognitive and behavioural domains (Tolan and Lendrum 1995). In the context of bullying, they give rich insights into understanding the effect of group affiliation on how participants behave (for example, whether they resist or support the aggressive intentions of the bully), and on the emotions (for example, group-based emotions of pride, shame and anger) experienced as a consequence (Jennifer and Cowie 2012). Although this research was based on a fictional case study, the findings suggest that the power of the peer group and wider networks need to be fully understood if bullying/cyberbullying is to be tackled efficiently. The bystanders tended to blame the victim and were reluctant to intervene, the victim felt let down and marginalized by peers' indifference and hostility, and the bullies failed to realize or understand the consequences of their actions. The findings confirm Salmivalli's (2010) proposition that bystanders are 'trapped in a social dilemma'. Although they understand that bullying is wrong, and may wish that they could do something to stop it, they are acutely aware of their own needs for security within the peer group. Their inaction supports the bully and undermines the victim. Their feelings of shame and guilt are overridden by the need to belong in the group and keep the bully onside.

Young people who spontaneously defend the victim are to be found in all social groups. However, it must be remembered that even at university level these individuals remain a minority and are easily overruled by the majority. The study by Myers and Cowie (2013) indicated no demonstration of altruism in the bystander group until they were required to reach a resolution of the problem, at which point some recognition of the psychological distress to the victim became apparent. Furthermore, it is essential to recognize the complexity of bullying as well as the interactions among such factors as social class, culture, gender, ethnicity and sexual orientation. As Zhang *et al.* (2014) argue in the context of schools, bullying has many facets with wide variation in its impact on students and, therefore, potentially different implications for policy and practice. Jackson *et al.* (2014) provide a new angle on the bullies in their study of laddishness at university by exploring the idea that the 'lads' are often working-class male students from families with no history of higher education. Their disruptive behaviour may signal their alienation from a system in which they feel deeply insecure. The fact that these lads often drop out at the end of the first year may actually demonstrate a form of discrimination on the part of the university authorities against young people who do not know the unwritten rules of the higher education game.

Clearly, we need to understand bullying in different contexts – individual, year group, social group and institutional level – within the university if we are to develop effective interventions and policies. This book aims to present current knowledge about the phenomenon and to address the complex dialogues and debates that are involved. The aims are to:

- collate in one volume current knowledge and evidence about this under-researched phenomenon;

- identify the nature and extent of bullying/cyberbullying at university and its impact on students;
- investigate continuities and discontinuities between school bullying and bullying at university;
- explore the social contexts where bullying flourishes;
- explore current interventions to prevent and reduce bullying at university and to alleviate its negative effects on students;
- discuss the implications for policy-makers, lawmakers, practitioners and researchers in this important field.

Themes in this book

Following on from this overview, the book explores five overlapping themes: *the student experience*; *the nature of bullying at university*; *the social context of bullying at university*; *interventions and policies* to prevent it; *reflections* on the issues raised.

The student experience

In chapter 2, Toni Pearce, the president of the National Union of Students (NUS) at the time of writing, presents disturbing material on the topic of bullying among undergraduate university students from the most recent research commissioned by NUS. Traditional forms of bullying continue to feature as an element of many students' experiences of study in the UK. Current data suggest that cyberbullying now forms a significant proportion of the bullying reported and presents a number of challenges to students' unions and institutions whose policies and procedures tend to have been designed to deal with non-technological forms of bullying. This chapter reports on the extent of bullying in UK universities and explores how far the cultural milieu of higher education is exacerbating and normalising behaviours of harassment. The National Union of Students (2013, p. 6) points out that there is no mention of women's issues in current higher education policy in the UK and the most recent government framework around violence against women makes no mention of risks to university students. NUS also assesses the strategies that students' unions and institutions can use to tackle the novel problem of cyberbullying and the apparent anonymity it gives to perpetrators.

In chapter 3, Rashid Aziz describes the vulnerability of PhD students by focusing on their exploitation by tenured staff. As he argues, many postgraduate students have an idealistic perspective of academia and believe that by becoming research students they will have a unique opportunity to broaden their knowledge and experience as academics. Too often, however, the experience is one of exploitation, discrimination and over-work, even theft of original ideas, as indicated in the new interview material gathered by Rashid Aziz for this chapter. Although undergraduate and postgraduate experiences differ, one common element is the abuse of power and the silencing of victims through direct or indirect threats.

The nature of bullying at university

Under the second theme, the authors explore the roles of bully, victim and bystander and elaborate on the impact of bullying on the students' health and well-being, providing illustrative examples of sexism, sexual harassment, objectification and homophobia. This section also assesses some of the equality aspects of the challenges that cyberbullying presents. In chapter 4, Maili Pörhölä explores whether there are continuities in bullying from school contexts to university contexts, and provides a discussion about the possible reasons why some people remain in the role of bully or victim over time, and through various social contexts, whereas others find a way to escape these roles. Research conducted among university students in Finland indicates that the roles of bully and victim can continue, not only from primary school to secondary school, but also to higher education; around half of those who bullied their fellow students during their higher education had previously bullied their schoolmates. Correspondingly, around half of those who were bullied during their higher education had previously been subjected to school bullying. Maili Pörhölä reviews theories that might explain these role continuities, and explores important questions about individual qualities of vulnerability and resilience, as well as the nature of the social contexts where this bullying behaviour takes place. She also includes a discussion about the reasons why some people continue to be bullies or victims over time and why some are able to escape.

In chapter 5, Ian Rivers discusses the latest research on lesbian, gay, bisexual and transgendered (LGBT) inclusion in higher education. Drawing upon large-scale quantitative studies, as well as case study material, the chapter explores the prevalence and correlates of homophobia in university contexts focusing particularly upon LGBT student inclusion and the challenges that universities face in promoting equality on campus.

In chapter 6, Katja Björklund explores the nature of stalking from social, psychological, behavioural, as well as clinical and public policy perspectives in the light of related theory, research, and practice. Stalking is a large-scale social problem across both adult and student populations. It has been argued that prevalence rates among college students are even higher than in the general population. NUS (2013) provide alarming statistics from the USA indicating that between 14 per cent and 27.5 per cent of women university students experienced rape and attempted rape. In fact, in the USA, university women students are more at risk of rape and sexual assault than women in the general population. A broad range of negative social, economic, psychological, and psychiatric effects on victims has been well documented in the past 20 years. Katja Björklund discusses victim reactions and coping with stalking. This chapter ends by analysing how to help victims of stalking and educate professionals working with the victims in order to improve public policy, practices and behaviour towards stalking and violent victimization.

In chapter 7, Tolga Arıcak focuses on the impact of bullying on students' mental health, whether they are targets or perpetrators, and considers whether mental health difficulties are the *cause* of bullying or one of its *outcomes*. In this chapter, he explores the relationship between mental health and bullying (online and offline) and proposes that the problem has two facets. One is the negative effect that bullying has on the mental health of those involved, especially on the victims. The other is that individuals with mental health problems may be more vulnerable to becoming the targets of bullying. This can be seen as a classical chicken and egg debate, and the chapter considers aspects of cause and effect in this context. Tolga Arıcak discusses ways in which these concepts, derived from research into school bullying, could potentially apply to the phenomenon of bullying among university students.

The social context of bullying at university

In chapter 8, Jessica Simmons, Sheri Bauman, and Johanne Ives report on a series of studies (quantitative and qualitative) that examine bullying and cyberbullying behaviour in the context of sororities and fraternities in American universities. The roles and functions of those organizations are described as they relate to the increased risk of involvement in bullying, and the implications for university policies and practices are discussed.

In chapter 9, Theodoros Giovazolias and Maria Malikiosi-Loizos investigate bullying in Greek universities at a time of particular economic and social hardship for young people. Research on students' well-being often reveals links with their exposure to some form of peer rejection and victimization. The absence of systematic research on bullying in the university context impedes the effort to capture the students' experience during this transformative age phase. To the authors' knowledge, this is the first attempt to study the phenomenon in the Greek university context and they examine such variables as the nature of bullying (traditional and cyberbullying), the profile of the perpetrators and the victims and the role of peer support and bystanders, as well as the relationship with students' memories of parenting, self-esteem, resilience and emotional well-being. The implications of the findings are discussed within the current socio-political situation in Greece and recommendations are made about tailoring such interventions as counselling to the particular needs of Greek university students at a time of social crisis.

Chapter 10 presents findings from a large cross-cultural study of bullying at universities in Argentina, Estonia, Finland and the USA. Here Maili Pörhölä, Kristen Cvancara, Esta Kaal, Kaja Tampere and Beatriz Torres examine the social and cultural aspects of bullying at university and explore possible explanations for commonalities and differences among the different countries represented. They indicate that contrasts among the four countries in terms of geography, culture, politics, history and education may be reflected in the bullying experiences of students. The authors consider ways in which learning environments might be developed in order to support pro-social behaviour among students and staff.

Interventions and policies

This section concerns interventions and policies to counteract and prevent bullying at university. As indicated throughout the book, there are many negative consequences of bullying, such as long-term psychological problems, including increased levels of anxiety, depressive symptoms, poor self-worth, social isolation and loneliness, psychosomatic complaints, suicidal ideation and suicide attempts for students who have been victimized. Perpetrators of bullying have also been found to be at heightened risk of experiencing problems such as anxiety, depression, psychosomatic symptoms and eating disorders, psychosocial adjustment, externalising behaviours and anti-social behaviour. Here the authors address the problem at different levels: face-to-face counselling and support; policies and education; and legal frameworks to inform practice and policy.

In chapter 11, Maria Luca discusses the crucial role of counselling services in supporting student victims of bullying. There are times when sexual bullying among university students remains undetected, unreported or even romanticized as part of a normal and growing sexualized culture. This creates a climate of fear of exposure with the implication that the person bullied suffers in silence. Such climate may also induce guilt and shame, both compromising the individual's self-esteem and sense of relational belonging to the peer group, perpetuating feelings of being an 'outsider', as well as self-blame. The trauma associated with sexual bullying often remains elusive until the habitual coping mechanisms in the individual break down, with negative consequences and an adverse impact on psychological health, compromising the individual's studies. The extreme manifestation of what appears to be benign sexual innuendo among university students but is in fact malign, presents itself in student counselling services, if indeed the person sexually bullied is able to seek help. This chapter explores the types of sexual bullying among university students, especially where trust is betrayed, and the impact on mental health. A vignette of a sexually bullied individual highlights the lived experience in being sexually bullied and the benefits of appropriate psychological interventions. The chapter concludes with a discussion on how universities could play a part in supporting victims of sexual bullying and implications for student counselling services.

In chapter 12, by contrast, Marilyn Campbell discusses the need for strong action at institutional level in order to change attitudes and behaviour. Drawing on wide experience of effective interventions to tackle school bullying, she notes that the most effective prevention and intervention strategy is the provision of anti-bullying policies and procedures (Ttofi and Farrington, 2011). Clear policies and procedures provide a valuable framework for schools to show commitment to the prevention and intervention of bullying, including cyberbullying, and to demonstrate and communicate its procedural response to the whole school community. In the context of bullying at university, Marilyn Campbell presents research into policies and procedures and what they mean to students at one Australian university. Implications for practice for other universities and future research are discussed.

In chapter 13, Shaheen Shariff and Ashley DeMartini discuss the legal framework for addressing online abuse at university level and explore the dilemmas that face legislators. Although a significant amount of attention has been paid to cyberbullying among children in elementary and high schools, less research is available on the extent of sexting and online abuse among university students. This chapter presents research addressing this issue in the light of the introduction of legislation at the federal and provincial levels in Canada. The *Protecting Canadians from Online Crime Act* updates the *Criminal Code* to make the non-consensual distribution of intimate images a crime punishable with a five-year prison term. Young adults at the post-secondary level have grown up immersed in digital media and often defend their actions as unintentional and 'just for fun'. Shariff and DeMartini discuss the implications of posting such material and argue that there is an urgent need for legal literacy at university level. She also addresses the challenge for those who develop public policies of balancing free expression, privacy, safety and regulation, or over-regulation.

Reflections

Finally, we present two commentaries from different perspectives. In chapter 14, Keith Sullivan discusses ways in which extensive knowledge about interventions in schools to address bullying might be adapted to the university setting and proposes the potential of student power in addressing the issue. In chapter 15, Iain Coyne discusses what universities can learn from existing research and practice in the workplace about how to deal with bullying on campus. In the *Epilogue*, chapter 16, the editors discuss the implications for policy and practice, the need for further research and the implications of current knowledge about bullying at university for deepening understanding of bullying in forms not covered directly in the book, for example, peer discrimination on the grounds of disability, religion and belief. They also discuss the dearth of literature on bullying of university staff by students, a topic that is introduced by Rashid Aziz in the context of the experience of PhD students who are both students and staff members. The three final chapters provide a commentary written after completion of the main body of the book including the perspective of experts on interventions to counteract school bullying and workplace bullying. They explore the implications for university senior management, policymakers and staff in developing new practices to address the problem. They also identify areas of particular importance for future research.

References

Bennett, D. C., Guran, E. L., Ramos, M. C. and Margolin, G. (2011). College students electronic victimization in friendships and dating relationships: Anticipated distress and associations with risky behaviours. *Violence and Victims*, 26(4): 410–29.

Chapell, M. S., Hasselman, S. L., Kitchin, T., Lomon, S. N., MacIver, K. W. and Sarullo, P. L. (2006). Bullying in elementary school, high school, and college. *Adolescence*, 41: 633–48.

Cohen, L., Manion, L. and Morrison, K. (2007). *Research Methods in Education* (6th ed.) London: Routledge.

Coleyshaw, E. (2012). The power of paradigms: a discussion of the absence of bullying research in the context of university student experience. *Research in Post-Compulsory Education*, 15(4): 377–86.

Curwen, T., McNichol, J. S. and Sharpe, G. W. (2011). The progression of bullying from elementary school to university. *International Journal of Humanities and Social Science*, 1(13): 47–54.

Cowie, H., Bauman, S., Coyne, I., Myers, C-A, Pörhölä, M. and Almeida, A. (2013). Cyberbullying amongst university students: an emergent cause for concern? In P. K. Smith and G. Steffgen (Eds.) *Cyberbullying Through the New Media*. London: Psychology Press. pp. 165–77.

Farley, S., Coyne, I., Sprigg, C., Axtell, C. and Subramanian, G. (2015, in press). Exploring the impact of workplace cyberbullying on trainee doctors. *Medical Education*.

Goldenberg, D., Andrusyszyn, M-A. and Iwasiw, C. (2005). The effects of classroom simulation on nursing students' self-efficacy related to heath teaching. *Journal of Nurse Education*, 44: 310–14.

Isaacs, J., Hodges, E. and Salmivalli, C. (2008). Long-term consequences of victimization: A follow-up from adolescence to young adulthood. *European Journal of Developmental Science*, 2: 387–97.

Jackson, C., Dempster, S. and Pollard, L. (2014). 'They just don't seem to really care, they just think it's cool to sit there and talk': laddism in university teaching-learning contexts. *Educational Review*, 9(10): 1–15.

Jennifer, D. and Cowie, H. (2012). Listening to children's voices: moral emotional attributions in relation to primary school bullying. *Emotional and Behavioural Difficulties*, 17: 3–4, 229–41.

Kenworthy, A. (2010). One goal, one community: moving beyond bullying and empowering for life. Bond University Centre for Applied Research in Learning, Engagement, Andragogy and Pedagogy, Available at http://www.bond.edu.au/research/university-research-centres/centre-for-applied-research-in-learning-engagement-andragogy-and-pedagogy/one-goal-one-community/index.htm. [Accessed on 16 February 2012].

Lappalainen, C., Meriläinen, M., Puhakka, H. and Sinkkonen, H-M. (2011). Bullying among university students – does it exist? *Finnish Journal of Youth Research*, 29(2): 64–80.

Miles, M. B. and Huberman, M. (1994). *Qualitative Data Analysis*. London: Sage Publications.

Mukhtar, F., Daud, S., Manzoor, I., Amjad, I., Saeed, K., Naeem, M. and Javed, M. (2010). Bullying of medical students. *Journal of the College of Physicians and Surgeons Pakistan*, 20(12): 814–18.

Myers, C-A. and Cowie, H. (2013). University students' views on bullying from the perspective of different participant roles. *Pastoral Care in Education*, 31(3): 251–67.

Olweus, D. (1993). *Bullying at School: What We Know and What We Can Do*. Oxford: Blackwell Publishers.

National Union of Students (2013). *That's What She Said: Women Students' Experiences of 'Lad Culture' in Higher Education*. London: National Union of Students.

Pörhölä, M. (2011). Kiusaaminen opiskeluyhteisössä [Bullying in university community]. In K. Kunttu, A. Komulainen, K. Makkonen and P. Pynnönen (Eds.), *Opiskeluterveys*. Helsinki, Finland: Duodecim. pp. 166–68.

Salmivalli, C. (2010). Bullying and the peer group: A review. *Aggression and Violent Behaviour*, 15: 112–20.

Salmivalli, C., Lagerspetz, K., Björkqvist, K., Österman, K. and Kaukiainen, A. (1996). Bullying as a group process: Participant roles and their relations to social status within the group. *Aggressive Behavior*, 22: 1–15.

Schenk, A. M. and Fremouw, W. J. (2012). Prevalence, psychological impact, and coping of cyberbully victims among college students. *Journal of School Violence*, 11(1): 21–37.

Smith, P. K., Cowie, H., Olafsson, R. and Liefooghe, A. (2002) Definitions of bullying: a comparison of terms used, and age and gender differences, in a fourteen-country international comparison. *Child Development*, 73(4): 1119–33.

Sourander, A., Brunstein Klomek, A. B., Ikomen, M., Lindroos, J., Luntamo, T., Koskelainen, M., Ristkari, T. and Helenius, H. (2010). Psychosocial risk factors associated with cyberbullying among adolescents. *Archives of General Psychiatry*, 67(7): 720–8.

Tolan, J. and Lendrum, S. (1995). *Case Material and Role Play in Counselling Training*. London: Routledge.

Ttofi, M. M. and Farrington, D. P. (2011). Effectiveness of school-based programs to reduce bullying: a systematic and meta-analytic review. *Journal of Experimental Criminology*, 7: 27–56.

van Ments, M. (1983). *The Effective Use of Role Play: a Handbook for Teachers and Trainers*. London: Kogan Page.

Willard, N. (2006). *Flame Retardant. School Library Journal*, 52(4), 55–6.

Zhang, L., Osberg, L. and Phipps, S. (2014). Is all bullying the same? *Archives of Public Health*, 72(19): 1–8.

PART II

The student experience

2

THE STUDENT VOICE

Toni Pearce

When we hear the word bullying, our minds often jump to the school playground. Big kids ganging up on little kids, finding the thing that makes them different, and not letting them forget it. We like to think that universities are free of this kind of behaviour; that our seats of learning are places where everyone is accepted for who they are. Unfortunately, this just isn't the case. Our research over the past few years has shown that many students' experience of higher education is one that is characterized by an environment where bullying and harassment are not only tolerated, but also expected. In 2010, the NUS conducted the first UK-wide study of 2058 women in further and higher education with regard to their experiences of harassment, stalking, violence and sexual assault (NUS 2010). The survey found that one in seven respondents had experienced a serious physical or sexual assault during their time as a student. While at university or college, 12 per cent had been stalked, and 68 per cent had been a victim of one or more kinds of sexual harassment. Fellow students were the major perpetrators. Furthermore, only a minority of students who had been seriously sexually assaulted reported it to their institution (4 per cent) or to the police (10 per cent).

The NUS became so concerned about what the media have termed 'laddishness' in university culture that in 2012 we commissioned Dr Alison Phipps and Isobel Young of the Centre for Gender Studies at Sussex University to conduct a literature review and qualitative study of 40 UK women students' experiences through four focus groups and 21 interviews. The participants were aged between 18 and 25 years and included women of different ethnicities, sexual orientation and social class status; six participants self-identified as having a disability.

The resulting report (Phipps and Young 2013) demonstrated just how pervasive laddism and the behaviour that goes with it is on our campuses. In the report, 'laddishness' was defined as: A 'pack' mentality evident in activities, such as sport, and heavy alcohol consumption and 'banter', which were often sexist, misogynist and homophobic. It was also thought to be sexualized and to involve the objectification of women and, at its extremes, rape supportive attitudes and sexual harassment and violence (Phipps and Young 2013, p. 53).

The bullying behaviour appeared to be embedded in a culture that glorifies violent, disrespectful attitudes towards women. The literature review revealed widespread sexist and misogynist behaviours in some student communities, to include such activities as initiation ceremonies, 'geeks and sluts' parties, 'slag and drag' parties, the sexual pursuit of female freshers (sometimes termed 'seal clubbing') and 'slut drops' where male students offer female students a lift home but leave them miles from their destination. There were also websites such as Uni Lad, True Lad and The Lad Bible that provide space for online 'banter'.

The women students reported being exposed on a daily basis to sexist, misogynistic and homophobic comments, commonly termed 'banter'. Although often considered harmless, this can have a significant impact on how safe women feel. It often spills over into sexual harassment and humiliation. And it's important to recognize that this behaviour affects not only women students, but anyone who is seen not to comply or 'get it', creating social pressures and in some cases causing exclusion for anyone who does not engage in or accept this kind of behaviour.

Many of the participants referred to derogatory attitudes towards women, as well as towards lesbian, gay, bisexual and trans (LGBT) students and the normalisation of sexual violence. Participants commented that people who challenged such attitudes were made to feel like 'kill-joys' who lacked a sense of humour: As one student put it: 'Facebook has a Uni Lad group which regularly posts demeaning things about women and rape jokes which I and my fellow female students find appalling. I have seen many male university Facebook friends have "liked" this page.' (Phipps and Young 2013, p. 38)

Laddism had a particularly strong influence on the social side of university life with sports and extra-curricular activities being singled out. Participants reported that women students were often sexually harassed on nights out. As one reported:

> 'It was the rugby night initiation and they stood on either side of the pavement so you had to walk through them, they were creating like a bridge thing with their hands, and they started shouting really loudly in the main street, "U.G.L.Y. – she's ugly, she's ugly" and I was just stood there, I was on the phone. I just didn't expect it, and maybe if I had been dressed like I was today, but I was dressed up, and maybe that's what they had to do, pick out the girl who was on her own.'
>
> (Phipps and Young 2013, p. 45)

Sexual violence appeared to be commonplace:

> 'I don't know anyone, any of my female friends who haven't had some kind of encounter that was harassment whether it be verbal or physical since they've been at university.'
>
> (Phipps and Young 2013, p. 50)

In some instances, verbal harassment became violent:

> 'I've been pushed down the stairs of a bus before because I stood up for a girl that a pack of lads were picking on in quite a sexually violent way and then no one did anything and then all the guys started chanting, "she doesn't want to have sex with you" about me because I was standing up for this woman who they got their penises out on the bus [in front of whom] and started being "wahaay" and I was like "I'm sorry, fuck off! That's not okay," and then they pushed me down the stairs and then I had to get off the bus. I can't really do anything!'
>
> (Phipps and Young 2013, p. 50)

In 2014, NUS undertook a national survey of over 4000 students from 80 UK universities about the experiences of LGBT students. The survey used the term 'LGB+' to refer to respondents who defined their sexuality as lesbian, gay, bisexual or in another way (including queer, asexual, pansexual or 'unsure'). The term 'trans' referred to respondents who said that their gender identity did not correspond to the identity they were assigned at birth. 'LGBT' refers to students who self-define as either LGB+ or trans.

The resulting report (NUS 2014) indicated that one in five LGB and one in three trans respondents had experienced at least one form of bullying or harassment on their campus. The most commonly cited issue reported in the survey concerned the pejorative meaning associated with the term 'gay'. Passing as 'straight' seemed to be a strategy used by a substantial proportion of LGBT students to protect themselves from homophobia and transphobia. For example:

> 'The general attitude on our campus is one [that is] extremely anti-gay or bi and I would not feel comfortable coming out to anyone about my liking for guys as well as women.'
>
> (NUS 2014, p. 23)

> 'Making jokes about transgender people, either to poke fun or say they're "disgusting" is completely socially acceptable.'
>
> (NUS 2014, p. 23)

The experiences included name-calling, physical assault, harassment and threats or intimidation. Consequently, those who had experienced a form of homophobic or transphobic harassment were two to three times more likely to consider leaving their course than those who did not experience any bullying. Most of the trans students in the survey reported that they did not know whom to talk to about transphobic abuse. As a result, they felt 'distressed', 'isolated' and 'lonely'. For instance one student who identified as trans said: 'I felt invisible, stupid, misgendered, and there was nothing they could do about it, nor was there any staff who fully understood my situation on site.' (NUS 2014, p. 30)

As the survey showed, this can have a devastating impact on students in terms of their mental health and their feelings about their studies as a whole. This research followed on from our previous work on hate crime (NUS 2011/2012), which showed that students were vulnerable to acts of hate focused around a range of identity factors including race and ethnicity, religion and belief, and disability, as well as sexual orientation and gender identity.

It is important to recognize that as we enter a new era of communication, so too must we recognize the new media and spaces in which bullying can occur. In recent years we have seen the rise of web-based campus gossip sites; from *Spotted* pages, where students can anonymously post what they think about their classmates' appearance, through to *Rate Your Shag*, which encourages students to publicly and humiliatingly rate the performance of their sexual partners. It is vital that universities take their responsibilities seriously and ensure that their policies and practices are fit for purpose for the current generation of students, where bullying can just as easily take place from a smartphone in a student's home as in a physical space on a campus.

I, along with my fellow student representatives, welcome this book's important contribution to this little examined topic, and hope that it will help to bring the higher education sector's understanding of what we mean by bullying forward. It is only through improving this understanding that we will be able to work together to create campuses and communities which are truly inclusive spaces, free from bullying and harassment.

References

Phipps, A. and Young, I. (2013). *That's what she said: women students' experiences of 'lad culture' in higher education.* London: NUS.

National Union of Students (2010). *Hidden marks: a study of women students' experiences of harassment, stalking, violence and sexual assault.* London: NUS.

National Union of Students (2014). *Education beyond the straight and narrow; LGBT students' experience in higher education.* London: NUS.

National Union of Students (2011–12). *No place for hate: hate crimes and incidents in further and higher education summary reports.* London: NUS.

3

THE RESEARCH STUDENT EXPERIENCE

Rashid Aziz

Introduction

This chapter looks at the often-ignored group of research students in academia and their experiences of bullying and intimidation. The results of an exploratory research project are presented in this chapter. The main aim of this study was to determine whether or not bullying was evident among this group of students from supervisors and others in their respective departments. In order to achieve this, a series of questions was asked about the research student experience.

For many, becoming a full-time research student means the opportunity for reflection, intellectual stimulation and to broaden the knowledge of a field that they are passionate about. Teaching is a wonderful way of generating and testing ideas. It also enables the research student to experience what life might be like post-PhD as a full-time lecturer or researcher. Yet, many research students at the start of their journey do not realize one important fact: they are vulnerable. Supervisors have the power to control a research student's destiny. This chapter attempts to answer to what extent is this power being abused? I have been very lucky to have had two brilliant advisors during my time as a PhD student. I am given guidance when required and always feel I can contact them when needed. Others I have been on the journey with have not been so lucky. From being forced into changing topics, given extra teaching hours for no extra pay, doing endless hours of marking and having to deal with sexist senior members of staff, a research student can be made to feel powerless. The situation for some has escalated to the point where they have either dropped out of the process completely, or have changed supervision teams. Neither considered as 'colleagues' nor as 'students', research students can be left in a situation where they do not feel as if they belong, or do not know what they can and cannot be asked to do whilst being a research student.

Olweus (1993) argues that bullying encompasses three core elements: (i) an intent to harm or upset another student; (ii) the harmful behaviour is done repeatedly and over time; and (iii) the relationship between bully/bullies and victim/victims is characterized by an imbalance in power. It is the third element that we focus on in this chapter. The study demonstrates that the unequal balance of power between research students and their supervisors, as well as others in the department, can and has led to bullying-type behaviour and thus satisfies the first two elements in the given definition.

Literature

It is difficult to locate research students within the framework that surrounds the bullying literature. On the one hand, they are not employees or colleagues, but on the other hand, they are expected to teach, and in the cases of funded students, receive money in order to carry out their research. An important question remains as to whether or not PhD students should be considered as 'workers' or students.

Chapter 1 outlined what we know about bullying at universities; there is an obvious gap in the academic literature concerning research students, whose experiences at university will differ from that of undergraduate and postgraduate students. Studies conducted by Marsh, Rowe and Martin (2002) and by Heath (2002) in Australia and by Salmon (1992) in the United Kingdom, appear to be the only ones that consider the experience of research students and their relationship with their supervisors (outside of 'how to' guides). However, these studies were not conducted under the framework of power relations or bullying. They were designed to discuss research provisions in order to improve the facilities and supervision of these students. The research and literature mentioned in the overview (pages 3–14) is referenced to establish where research students sit in the academic literature around bullying.

Methods

To conduct this study, ten former PhD students were contacted to conduct a self-completion survey based on their experiences. They were asked to consider both the time it took to conduct and write up their research and the experience of the viva voce examination. The sample was conducted through already established research networks. The majority of respondents were from social science backgrounds and two were from backgrounds in natural science. Four of the sample were male and six were female. This is represented in the table opposite.

Open questions were used so that respondents could elaborate on their thoughts and were not constrained by any answers given to them. Davies, Francis and Jupp (2011) argue that this type of question is particularly relevant when asking about people's experiences and perceptions. Given that this was a small pilot study to gauge the existence of the problem, using open-ended surveys was an adequate choice of data collection. It allowed me to establish the nature of the problem and reach a wide sample from across the country over a relatively short period.

TABLE 3.1 Depicting the age and gender of respondents

Age	Male	Female
25–29	0	2
30–34	2	2
35–39	1	0
40–44	1	1
45–49	0	0
50–54	0	0
55–59	1	0

As the respondents were former PhD students, this research asked them to recall their experiences. Rivers (2001) found that asking respondents to recall incidents of bullying retrospectively did not harm their ability to recall the events. Respondents were asked to comment on time spent with their supervisors, how long it took for work to be read, their teaching and marking loads, their positions within the department, and whether or not they had been bullied during their time as a research student.

Findings

This section discusses the findings of this exploratory study. It is divided into five sections which discuss the expectations and reality of the experience, the relationship with other members of the department, supervision, workload and bullying.

The expectations of the research experience

To begin, respondents were asked about why they wanted to conduct research and how they saw the academic process before they began, they were then asked if this was what they experienced.

Before undertaking the PhD, many of the respondents had a positive view of what the experience would entail, often talking about how they thought they would enjoy the process and the sense of belonging among the academic community it would bring. This was all the more evident if the student had been at the institution during their time as an undergraduate and postgraduate student, given that they had built up a relationship with their supervisors and others in the department:

> Because I had already been an undergraduate and Masters student at the institution where I went on to do my PhD I had a fairly good idea of what the academic community in that setting would be like. I knew some people who were already undertaking PhDs so I knew what was involved in terms of being paired up with supervisors, the various student led workshops that went on and had some general ideas about what doing a PhD would be like.
>
> (Respondent 1)

On the whole, respondents reported positive reviews of the experience post-PhD. Those that did tended to report a structure to the programme, and ample contact time with others who were doing the PhD and their supervisors:

> Largely yes. In our first year, we had a lot of contact time with our supervisors and with other staff who coordinated the doctoral research programme within our school. We had weekly meetings throughout our first year, but as time went on there was very little overall structure to the PhD and we really only had contact with our supervisors, although I don't think this was a bad thing as by that point I was more engaged with my individual project and doing empirical work.
>
> (Respondent 1)

However, there were incidents where the expectations of the research experiences were not met. The respondent below recounts his time as a PhD student and tries to give reasons as to why his experience was one that he did not enjoy:

> I think I had a bit of a romanticized notion of academia that was pretty much squashed by my experiences of it. I thought it would be dusty libraries and long intellectual chats with a supervisor. The period of undertaking my PhD was perhaps the worst in my life. I found the university ... had no interest in supporting research students. I think as well, because my subject area was in a disciplinary area that did not really sit well with the orientation of the department, this may have been a contributory factor.
>
> (Respondent 2)

The respondent below talks of her expectations of the process and how these were not met. She describes her surprise at the attitudes of those whom she was working with.

> Oh I had lots of ivory tower type imaginings, thought it would all be terribly collegial, with lots of intellectual discussions, open minds, very reasonable people etc. Because I would be working with people who were very highly educated I didn't expect them to be quite as narcissistic, petty or childish as quite a few of them turned out to be.
>
> (Respondent 3)

Power relations became evident very quickly throughout the research and many respondents commented on this throughout:

> Realising that what most people were doing was putting most of their time into power games, not doing much substantively but trying to hide that (especially re teaching etc.) not all like that though.
>
> (Respondent 3)

These power games became a theme found throughout the research and it became clear that supervisors, in some cases, would abuse that power for their own gain.

Position within the department

Research students are in a situation where they are both students and in many cases, employees as they receive payment for teaching and other activities. Respondents were asked to comment on their position within the department and many commented positively. However, there were some that felt this was not the case: 'My position was lowest of the low. Relationships with other members of staff were minimal. The other PhD students were similarly of the mind that they were being unsupported.' (Respondent 2)

With a range of bursaries and scholarships available, research students are often 'paid' to do their research. This leaves the possibility that research students do not view themselves as students, but academics at the beginning of their careers. The respondent below felt welcome within the department but the question of identity arose, as he felt as though he should have been treated like a member of staff at the beginning of his career, rather than as a student:

> I generally felt welcome in the department and had a good relationship with other staff members. However, I sometimes thought there was an invisible barrier between PhD researchers and lecturers. I would have preferred to be treated more like a young academic rather than a student.
>
> (Respondent 4)

As well as an invisible barrier between research students and other members of staff, some respondents felt that there was also a physical barrier, with research student offices being located away from the department, which created a sense of isolation:

> It would have been better to be more embedded in the department. There was quite a separation between research students and other staff, which was made worse by a physical separation in terms of office space. This added to the sense of isolation during the PhD.
>
> (Respondent 5)

It appears as though research students, in some instances, are not valued as members of the department, that their contribution is not considered worthy. Perhaps this is because they have not yet achieved a PhD and been awarded with a permanent lectureship, thus they are viewed as being beneath other members of staff. It could also be due to other factors, which have not been uncovered by this research, such as age and gender.

Supervision

The majority of respondents reported a good relationship with their PhD supervisors and believed their level of supervision to be adequate. However, there were instances where the research student felt the supervision they were receiving was not adequate. The following respondent changed supervision after being unsatisfied with her initial supervisor:

> I had more frequent contact time with my first supervisor however I found this time was often misused and unproductive. In the latter stages of my PhD when I was working with the second supervisor the contact time was less but the quality of the project improved. Feedback was mostly in writing (and that was very useful), phone calls and where possible meetings. All these options were made available to me on request.
>
> (Respondent 6)

There are well-documented examples of the abuse of power in the form of theft, that is, a supervisor stealing the work of a student. There are many examples of this found online. For example, an anonymous letter posted by a former student entitled *After Finding Evidence of Plagiarism, PhD Student Fights Back,* details the experiences of a student who discovered her PhD supervisor had stolen portions of her work without permission:

> In May 2007, I found a paper on PubMed that seemed very familiar. One third of this paper (1200 words), including one table, was copied almost paragraph for paragraph from Chapter 3 of my PhD dissertation. I was astonished as I saw scientific omissions, contradictions, and even false statements. Looking up, I recognized the name of the sole author—none other than my former PhD advisor.
>
> (Anon 2007)

Another example found on an online forum, The Grad Café (2012), sees a PhD student asking for advice after their supervisor had published a manuscript without including the student as a co-author. This also came up in the research:

> Yes. Quite a bit really but I was quite gobby back! PhD supervisor definitely, she just seemed to want to use me to reinforce her status as professor, the other one just wanted me to write publications for her to put her name on.
>
> (Respondent 3)

These examples show clearly how supervisors have abused their powers. These cases illustrate not only a form of bullying but also plagiarism, which is unethical, and if copyright has been infringed can carry legal penalties.

There was also an indication that PhD supervisors could be competitive among themselves regarding their supervisees. The respondent below highlights this issue:

> PhD supervisors used to play top trumps with their students in a sort of my student is better than yours type thing, so I often found myself in the middle of power games I had no idea about.
>
> (Respondent 3)

This suggests that the student would feel pressure to outperform other research students in the department.

For Respondent 2, who considered his PhD experience to be the worst time in his life, a contributing factor could have been that his supervisor, who had been allocated to him, through no choice, had a limited knowledge of the area of study:

> He was a nice guy, but overall the experience wasn't very good. He had very limited knowledge of the subject area that I was investigating and had no qualitative research experience.
>
> (Respondent 2)

From these findings, it is clear that whilst on the whole, supervision seems adequate among this sample, there are problems around the use of publications, knowledge of the subject area and competitiveness between supervisors.

Teaching, marking and other work outside of the project

In my experience, an important part of being a research student was finding work in order to support my studies, such as teaching. As an unfunded student, it was crucial that I had paid work. This left me vulnerable, as not receiving enough teaching time would mean I would need to find work elsewhere. The research indicates that, generally, no formal training is given to research students who are asked to teach.

From the research, the allocation of teaching hours came up as a source of conflict among staff members and teaching. This is similar to my own experiences: 'It varied: sometimes yes, but at other times, I felt certain people were favoured in the teaching allocation.' (Respondent 7)

Whilst this does not necessarily equate to bullying behaviour, it does reinforce the fact that there is a power imbalance between research students and others in the department.

Another theme that emerged from the research concerning teaching was that senior members of staff were worried about their reputations if research students were better teachers than them:

Head of department used to tell me not to be so good at teaching because it was making others look bad. He got worse as time went on because I resisted being part of his 'clique'.

(Respondent 3)

The respondents of the study did not raise any concerns with the amount of teaching they were asked to do, given that in most cases, they were paid extra to do it. When they were not paid extra, this was because the teaching was a part of the bursary they were receiving in order to complete the PhD. However, marking came up as a problem in many of the responses. Respondents often felt that the marking share was unfair and they often did not receive any extra payment for the task. The hourly wage for teaching appeared to be attractive, but once marking was taken into consideration, the pay was deemed unfair.

In my second year of teaching, lecturers were only involved in second marking and since I was the only seminar tutor at the time, I had to do all the first marking by myself. This means that I had to mark about one hundred 2,500-word essays that year... My teaching load was fair. As I explained in my previous answer, I think my marking load could have been fairer.

(Respondent 4)

I didn't mind the teaching load, partly because I liked it and I needed the money. The marking wasn't fair, not enough sharing the load between class tutors and those giving lectures... it looks like a lot per hour but once you've done all admin, answering emails, prep etc then it can quickly be below minimum wage.

(Respondent 3)

It appears as though the research students who were unhappy with their level of marking did not speak up against this. This may indicate a lack of policy in place that dictates how much marking a research student can be asked to do. This may also indicate that the research student is unaware of the procedures in place to raise such issues.

Outside of marking and teaching some respondents were asked, as part of their bursary, to complete other tasks, without training. In the example below, the student who did not know how to complete the task, and thought the situation was resolved, soon learned that his failure to complete the task would have consequences for his time with the university:

I was a social scientist doing a PhD in a law school on a bursary. Part of the bursary was a condition that I did a certain amount of hours of departmental tasks. I was told once that a professor needed me to photocopy some law reports, or something that only a law student would understand how to access. I told the secretary that I didn't know how to access these. Nothing more was said for a week and then I was hauled in front of the Head of Department who wanted to know why I had refused to undertake this task.

(Respondent 2)

The respondent was asked what the consequences of this were:

Just a growing distancing between me and the department. I just had a cumulative issue with the department fed into by so many issues. No pastoral support, limited supervisor support, no idea of students being supported, criminology students being treated like second-class citizens in the law school. I was made to feel that my value to the department was negligible. In the end, I stopped using library facilities and only came into Uni when I had to. I actually moved to the other side of London.

(Respondent 2)

The lack of support that this student received is an example of bullying. This student was bullied to the extent that he created a large physical distance between himself and the university in order to avoid his aggressors. Another respondent backs up the fact that the subject she studied had an effect on the way in which she was treated. Here, a female student talks of the way in which the head of department treated her after moving from sociology to criminology:

To him I was a traitor I think because I went over to criminology. He used to go at me a lot after that. But I got my own back. I had a rep that one of them told me about as being someone who 'looked after herself'.

(Respondent 3)

By 'rep' the student is stating that she has a 'reputation' for not putting up with behaviour she deemed was inappropriate. This does not only demonstrate a difficulty for the student, but reinforces the fact that staff members are competitive among themselves, even competing across different subject areas in the department. From this quote, it appears as though the competitive nature had created 'camps' within the department. This is consistent with the views of Willard (2006), who proposed that exclusion from online activities was a form of cyberbullying. This is being paralleled in the real world in the form of research students being distanced from the department they are working in. Coleyshaw (2012) highlights that this type of bullying has not been applied to student on student bullying, but it has also not been applied to supervisor and student bullying.

Bullying

The respondents were asked directly if they had been bullied during their time as a research student. Here, we consider their responses. Revisiting Olweus's definition of bullying, which includes the intent to harm or upset an individual, this was something that was evident in the findings. The following respondent talks of a time when a senior member of staff physically assaulted her:

> One quite senior staff member had some mental health issues, she got it in her head that I was trying to undermine her and get her out of a job, she ended up punching me on the arm one time when she lost it.
>
> (Respondent 3)

It is interesting that she claims the staff member had 'mental health' issues, which is in some way neutralising the offending behaviour. Perhaps this was used as an excuse by other members of staff, or a conclusion that was derived from the respondent herself given the staff member's behaviour. Either way, the evidence for physical assault is clear.

> There were significant issues that were entirely overlooked (almost laughed off), by senior members of staff in the early stages. Some of the concerns that were raised around the PhD included: bullying conduct, research ethics problems, inadequate supervision and an absence of feedback, tensions between two supervisors. I was not supported on the whole as a response to these issues. Ultimately, the situation became damaged beyond repair and the university secured me a new supervisor.
>
> (Respondent 6)

When asked directly about bullying, this respondent mentions power and how it leads to the PhD experience being unfavourable for the student:

> I didn't feel 'bullied' in a traditional sense. I just felt that I was dealing with people who were self-centred, arrogant and, on occasion, liked wielding power unwisely. There was little evidence of consideration of the experiences of PhD students.
>
> (Respondent 2)

There was also evidence that verbal bullying was present among this sample.

> Basically there was the odd member of staff who would make undermining comments at any opportunity, often more in how they said things rather than what they actually said. All very Machiavellian and they seemed to think that made them clever!
>
> (Respondent 3)

Only one respondent reported taking action against her supervisors at more than a department level. This could indicate a number of things. First, that PhD students are resigned to their fate, they believe they must finish the PhD under adverse conditions or otherwise drop out. Second, they are frightened of the consequences if they complain; the online forums mentioned earlier are fraught with these feelings. Students may feel that they would be asked to leave university and that they would be unable to find a place elsewhere. Third, because of a lack of proper policy or procedure, research students are unable to report such incidences or formally complain about their supervisors.

Ultimately, it has been shown that the research student experience can be either one that is extremely enjoyable and lives up to the expectations of the student, or one that is fraught with difficulties. The following respondent sums this up:

> Ultimately, my situation illustrates the two sides of the spectrum in academia. In the first instance, I have seen the most unprofessional of characteristics and experienced a highly challenging and unsatisfying situation. In the second instance, I was lucky enough to encounter a highly professional and skilled academic. I have a good relationship long term with my second supervisor and I still turn to them for advice now (most recently several weeks ago), so in the end my experience was satisfying.
>
> (Respondent 6)

It is clear from the findings of the study that the research student experience is one that is controlled by the senior members of staff in the department. It is also clear that the bullying experienced by research students is similar to that experienced by undergraduate students, those in the workplace and those at school, either in the real world, or by electronic means. The findings of this chapter are consistent with the literature outlined in chapter 1 of this reader.

Conclusion

The experience of the research student is one that has been ignored in academia. A larger study investigating the bullying of this group and among this group is required. This small, pilot study is a glimpse into what one might find if a more in-depth study was undertaken..

It is clear from this research that research students can be faced with physical, emotional and mental bullying. Based on the findings of this research, a larger scale study into the experiences of bullying among research students is recommended. Questions regarding the policies in place in order to protect PhD students from this behaviour should be investigated and policies should be derived which consider the research student experience. PhD students who did not complete the process should be contacted in order to establish the reasons why they failed to do so. A theme that did not emerge during the course of this research was that of research students being bullied by the undergraduates they teach. A larger study may help to identify this problem.

Policies regarding the recording of supervision, the allocation of marking and teaching, and reporting incidences of verbal, physical, mental and emotional bullying of research students should be put in place. These policies should take into consideration the fact that the PhD student is often not just a student, but an employee who is fearful of his or her place in academia.

What this research inevitably shows is that there is potentially a large cohort of research students who are gaining doctorates, but are left with the impression that academia is an unfriendly and hostile environment.

References

Anon (2007) After Finding Evidence of Plagiarism, PhD Student Fights Back, *Plagiary*, Available at http://quod.lib.umich.edu/p/plag/5240451.0002.016?view=text;rgn=main. [Accessed 10 September 2014].

Coleyshaw, E. (2012) The power of paradigms: a discussion of the absence of bullying research in the context of university student experience. *Research in Post-Compulsory Education*, 15(4): 377–86.

Davies, P., Francis, P. and Jupp, V. (2011) *Doing Criminological Research* (2nd ed.). London: Sage.

Heath, T. (2002) A Quantitative Analysis of PhD Students' Views of Supervision. *Higher Education and Research Development* 21(1): 41–53.

Olweus, D. (1993) *Bullying at School: What We Know and What We Can Do*. Oxford: Blackwell Publishers.

Marsh, H. W., Rowe, K. J. and Martin, A. (2002). PhD Students' Evaluations of Research Supervision: Issues, Complexities, and Challenges in a Nationwide Australian Experiment in Benchmarking Universities. *The Journal of Higher Education*, 73(3): 313–48.

Salmon, P. (1992) *Achieving a PhD – Ten Students' Experiences*. Sterling VA, Stylus Publishing.

Rivers, I. (2001) Retrospective reports of school bullying: Stability of recall and its implications for research. *British Journal of Developmental Psychology*, 19(1): 129–41.

The Grad Café (2012) *My PhD-advisor Stole my Manuscript and Published it Himself*. Available at http://forum.thegradcafe.com/topic/32627-my-phd-advisor-stole-my-manuscript-and-published-it-himself. [Accessed on 10 September 2014].

Willard, N. (2006). *Flame Retardant. School Library Journal*, 52(4): 55–6.

PART III

The nature of bullying at university

4

DO THE ROLES OF BULLY AND VICTIM REMAIN STABLE FROM SCHOOL TO UNIVERSITY?

Theoretical considerations

Maili Pörhölä

This chapter explores the continuities in bullying from school contexts to university contexts, and discusses the possible reasons why some people remain in the role of bully or victim over time and through various social contexts, whereas others find a way to escape these roles. Two theories – *peer community integration theory* and *positioning theory* – are reviewed to examine the ways in which engagement in bullying processes at school is associated with the development of individuals' peer relationships and their position within the peer group; the impact of bullying on their perceptions of themselves and others; and how bullying affects the establishment of future peer relationships through which these individuals integrate into social communities in later life. The chapter concludes by discussing the impact that supportive peer relationships have for an individual who has been engaged in bullying. The significance of the social cognitive processes in which individuals make sense of their bullying experiences are emphasized, as they are able to re-determine their peer group position and change their role as bully or victim.

Introduction

Individuals integrate into groups and communities through their interpersonal relationships. It is the quality of our interpersonal relationships that often promotes or prevents us from succeeding in the integration process. Hence, becoming an equal and accepted member of one's social community is important for our individual well-being and success. Bullying is widely identified as a pervasive social problem, which can prevent individuals from becoming equal and accepted members in groups and social communities in which they need or wish to integrate (Pörhölä and Kinney 2010).

As schoolmates comprise the most important peer community for children and adolescents for a number of years, successful integration into this peer community becomes crucial for the psychosocial well-being and development of individuals, and forms the foundation for their ability to integrate into other communities, such as campus life during the undergraduate years. Being engaged in bullying at school therefore poses a severe developmental risk for individuals, whether they are in the role of bully, victim, or act in dual roles. In addition to causing several kinds of psychosocial and physical health problems (Due *et al.* 2005; Hawker and Boulton 2000; Houbre *et al.* 2006; Kaltiala-Heino *et al.* 2000), being engaged in bullying can prevent individuals from becoming integrated into their peer communities during childhood and adolescence, and even in young adulthood.

This chapter first reviews research on the continuities of abusive peer relationships in individuals' lives, focusing on repeated bullying and victimization experiences. The chapter continues by providing theoretical perspectives to help understand why these continuities tend to persist in individuals' peer relationships from one social context to another, hampering their integration into their peer communities.

Continuities of bullying and victimization

The studies examining the continuity of abusive peer relationships suggest that the roles of bullies and victims remain quite stable from elementary to middle school and high school (Boulton and Smith 1994; Salmivalli *et al.* 1998; Schäfer *et al.* 2005; Sourander *et al.* 2000). For example, Schäfer *et al.* conducted a six-year longitudinal study following German second and third graders through to the seventh and eighth grades, and found that bullying behaviour in elementary school was likely to continue at the later age, although being victimized by peers did not have similar continuity. However, in their eight-year longitudinal study among Finnish students, Sourander *et al.* found that bullying at age eight was associated with bullying at age 16, and being bullied at age eight was associated with being bullied at age 16.

Evidence also exists to suggest that the roles of bully and victim tend to remain stable from childhood to adulthood and from school settings to higher education and workplace contexts. For example, in a retrospective study by Chapell *et al.* (2006) in the United States, it was found that 54 per cent of individuals who admitted to having bullied as adults had also bullied during childhood and adolescence. In Canada, Curwen, McNichol, and Sharpe (2011) examined 159 female and 37 male undergraduates who had bullied a fellow student at least once since coming to university and detected that most of the bullies at university had a history of bullying at school. Bauman and Newman (2013) examined a sample of 709 university students in the USA and found that 3.7 per cent of the students had been bullied at university at least occasionally. Of those who were bullied at university, 84.6 per cent reported that they had been bullied in junior high school as well, and 80.8 per cent reported that they had been victimized in high school; 73 per cent had been victims of bullying at both school levels. Being a stable victim from junior high school to high school and then to university was more characteristic for male than female students (100 per cent of males, 64.7 per cent of females).

Furthermore, a nationally representative sample of 5,086 university students in the University Student Health Survey 2008 in Finland revealed that 51 per cent of those individuals who had bullied their fellow students during higher education had also bullied their schoolmates. While 47 per cent of those who had been victimized during their higher education had previously been subjected to school bullying (Pörhölä 2011a). It is worth noting that those who bully at school are most likely to continue to engage in various kinds of abusive behaviours in their social relationships. Particularly males who bully at school have been shown to have a heightened risk for sexual harassment (DeSouza and Ribeiro 2005; Pellegrini 2002), and dating violence (Connolly et al. 2000; Pepler et al. 2002).

Preliminary research also exists to link experiences involving bullying at school with continued exposure in the workplace. Smith, Singer, Hoel and Cooper (2003) conducted a retrospective study in which 5,288 British working adults reported on whether they had been bullied at school and whether they were being bullied in their workplace, and found a clear relationship between having been bullied at school and being bullied in their workplace. Those who had been in both roles at school, bullying others and simultaneously being victimized, were even more likely to be bullied as adults at work.

As a social problem, taking place between individuals in their interaction processes, bullying can have serious negative effects on the developmental courses of the involved individuals' peer relationships. Being victimized by the majority of one's classmates and having only a minority of defenders among them, which is often the case (Hodges and Perry 1996; Salmivalli et al. 1996), can result in an inability to trust any of one's peers and, consequently result in difficulty in establishing and sustaining friendships with them. Indeed, evidence shows that during their school years, victims of bullying tend to avoid social contacts and events (Crick and Grotpeter 1996; Slee 1994) and suffer from loneliness (Kochenderfer and Ladd 1996). For example, in a cross-cultural comparison in seven countries conducted in primary and secondary schools, Eslea et al. (2003) found that victims of bullying reported having the fewest friends and being left alone at playtimes most often, and those who occupied dual roles (bully-victims) reported similar experiences on a less frequent basis. Furthermore, a meta-analysis of 18 longitudinal studies conducted by Reijntjes et al. (2010) revealed significant associations between peer victimization and internalizing problems including anxiety, depression, withdrawal and loneliness among primarily middle school students over time.

However, those who bully also tend to have a range of difficulties in their peer relationships. Recent studies have indicated that children who bully consistently at a moderate or high rate from elementary through high school have peer relationship problems, including high conflict with peers, association with similarly aggressive peers, and susceptibility to negative peer pressure (Pepler et al. 2008). Further, a cross-cultural, cross-sectional survey including nationally representative samples from 25 countries indicated that bullies, victims and bully-victims report higher levels of health problems and poorer school adjustment than non-involved youth.

Victims and bully-victims reported poorer emotional adjustment and relationships with classmates, whereas bullies and bully-victims reported greater alcohol use (Nansel *et al.* 2004). The nationally representative sample of Finnish university students also revealed significantly higher levels of substance abuse among those university students who had a history of bullying their schoolmates, as compared to victims and those without a history of being engaged in bullying processes during their schooling (Pörhölä 2011b).

In another study in Finland among seventh and eighth graders (Pörhölä 2008, 2009b), it was found that victimized students reported the most peer-relationship problems (e.g. having fewer or no close friends; not feeling valued and being actively disliked by peers; having few contacts with classmates; being unsuccessful in the establishment of peer relationships; and being afraid of peers in general). These problems occurred less for bullies, who usually had a group of close friends and companions, felt highly respected and valued by their peers, and found it easy to establish social relationships with equals, although they were also simultaneously afraid of losing their friends and, except for their best friends, were also poorly integrated with the rest of their schoolmates. Finally, individuals uninvolved in bullying reported the highest quality in their peer relationships and acceptance in peer communities.

Previous studies have revealed that even in their later lives, former victims of school bullying tend to have difficulties in maintaining friendships, suffer from loneliness and display lowered levels of self-esteem (Schäfer *et al.* 2004). Further, victims of bullying have been found to have a tendency to anticipate negative evaluation and experience high levels of anxiety in social situations (Storch *et al.* 2003; Storch and Masia-Warner 2004). Young people victimized by their peers in adolescence also still tend to have negative perceptions of their peers' behaviour toward them in young adulthood (Salmivalli and Isaacs 2005). This set of peer relationship problems might partly explain formerly victimized individuals' lower levels of trust and satisfaction in their friendships during young adulthood (Jantzer *et al.* 2006). In the following sections, two theories will be discussed to examine how individuals' interpersonal relationships with other peer group members in childhood, adolescence and young adulthood affect their success in peer integration processes and determine their current position, and direct their future position, in peer communities, enabling the continuities of abusive peer relationships into the university years.

Bullying and peer community integration

The peer-community integration theory (Pörhölä 2009a, 2009b) describes how interpersonal peer relationships either promote or prevent individuals from integrating into their peer communities. While peers are usually understood as people who are at the same level with an individual in their cognitive, emotional and social development, *peer community* refers here to the crowd of peers with whom an individual has, or could, have an interpersonal relationship (Pörhölä 2009a).

During childhood and adolescence, school peers, and particularly the student's own class, form an important peer community. In their school class, students tend to develop some sort of interpersonal relationship with each of their classmates. In addition to their school and classmates, children and adolescents might establish peer relationships, for example, with individuals living in their neighbourhood, with relatives of the same age, or peers who get together because of their shared leisure-time activities, or peers who communicate only virtually, for example, via the Internet. Successful integration into one's peer community is a reciprocal process which can be defined as the individual feeling accepted, liked and valued by peers; as well as showing acceptance, care and respect for peers; and, consequently, feeling an equal member of the peer community (Pörhölä 2009b; Pörhölä and Kinney 2010).

The basic assumption in the peer-community integration theory is that individuals become integrated into the surrounding peer community through their interpersonal peer relationships. In the integration process, different kinds of dyadic peer relationships have different impacts or *weights*. Five kinds of relationships are distinguished on the basis of the impact these relationships have on the integration process: (i) *friendships* in which partners show mutual commitment, trust, support, valuation, love and care, are assumed to have the highest value, +2; (ii) *companionships*, which are characterized by a substantial amount of time spent in shared activities, also hold positive value, +1; (iii) *neutral relationships,* which can be characterized by a mutual lack of interest in the company of the other, are considered neutral in value, 0; (iv) mutually hostile *enemy relationships* carry negative value, −1; and (v) *abusive relationships*, such as bullying relationships, which carry the most negative value, −2, for both perpetrator and victim (Pörhölä 2008, 2009b).

While enemy relationships can be characterized by mutual verbal, non-verbal or physically hurtful behaviour, manifested as repeated conflicts and fights, an abusive relationship is characterized by an imbalance of power, unilateral subjection and hurtful behaviour, and the victim's inability to affect the nature of the relationship. As compared with the mutually hostile enemy relationship, an abusive relationship, such as a bullying relationship, can be presumed to be more devastating for both parties. In this relationship, the victim, as the less powerful party, can only lose without being able to terminate or change the nature of the relationship. However, as the winner of each confrontation with their victims, bullies have only positive outcomes from their behaviour, which increases their tendency to continue this kind of behaviour, and even extend adopting it in various peer relationships. In the end, this would result in these individuals failing to achieve integration into their peer community.

The peer-community integration theory (Pörhölä 2009a, 2009b) suggests that the nature of individuals' peer relationships determines how well they succeed in integrating into the peer community. While friends and companions pull an individual toward the centre of the peer community, enemy relationships and abusive relationships operate in the opposite direction, pushing individuals away from the centre of the peer community. Each relationship affects the integration process in accordance with its weight. The more enemy relationships, and particularly abusive relationships, a person has, the less successful the integration process will become for him or her, and vice versa: the more supportive relationships, like friends and companions a person has, the more successful he or she will be in integrating into the surrounding peer community.

Furthermore, the peer-community integration theory assumes that the level of an individual's integration into their peer community during childhood and adolescence is reflected in later life in their ability to integrate into other peer communities. Individuals who have failed to integrate into their peer community because of being bullied by their schoolmates, and who move on to the next educational level (university), are likely to see the new peer community as a threat rather than as a positive challenge. They may be frightened of their new peers, have difficulty trusting them, feel insecurity in their presence, and expect that they will not be approved of, valued and liked by their new peers, and that their peers will not want to be in their company. After having had only limited opportunities to practice their communication skills with their peers, and having received mostly negative feedback from their interactions with peers, they may also have deficiencies in peer interaction skills, which could help in establishing and maintaining rewarding peer relationships. Suffering from long-lasting and severe problems in their psychosocial well-being and health can further lower their ability to integrate into the new peer community at university.

Individuals who have bullied others for several years at school, and have therefore failed to integrate into their peer community, may also lack peer interaction skills because of their previous experiences of biased peer feedback, which may have prevented them from being able to practise their skills as an equal member of the peer community. After having bullied their schoolmates, they might also experience being disliked by most peers, and therefore see the new peer community at university as a threat. In this situation, they might end up gathering a group of trusted companions, but ignore the rest of the peer community or even start bullying some of them. Hence, both the roles of victims and bullies may transfer from one social context to another (Pörhölä 2009b; Pörhölä and Kinney 2010).

To conclude, the theory of peer community integration aims to explain how engagement in bullying is related to the development of the relationships of individuals within a group of peers, eventually forming a peer group position, which tends to remain stable for quite a long time in the individuals' lives. While this theory operates on interpersonal relationship and group dynamics levels, it does not yet offer explanations to the question *why* these developmental courses take place in individuals' lives, enabling the continuities of bullying and victimization from one social context to another. The following section will provide theoretical perspectives on some social, cognitive-level phenomena, which, in turn, could explain why these developmental courses take place.

Bullying and positioning

Applying the positioning theory by Harré and colleagues (Harré and van Langenhove 1999; Harré and Moghaddam 2003b), to examine the continuities of bullying experiences in individuals' lives can extend our understanding of the ways in which engagement in bullying processes might affect the development of individuals' social positions within a peer group, and also have an impact on their self-positioning. Self-positioning, in particular, can further explain the ways in which peer group positions, being embedded in group structures and internalized by individuals, have a tendency to remain stable from one social context to another.

The positioning theory (Davies and Harré 1999; Harré and van Langenhove 1999; Harré and Moghaddam 2003a) focuses on the ways in which identities, social positions and the meanings related to them are constructed in the course of interaction. Positioning can be seen as a way of building and rebuilding one's own and others' social positions and identities through interaction. Positions exist as patterns of beliefs in the members of a relatively coherent social community, and they are shared in the sense that the relevant beliefs of each member are similar to those of others in the community. Positions are relational – meaning that adopting a particular position for oneself assumes a position for other interaction partners as well. Although positions are jointly produced and reproduced, a person can either appropriate a particular position within a social group or community, or it can be given to him or her. Once having taken up, or been given, a particular position, the person inevitably sees the world from the vantage point of that position.

One of the essential facets of position theory is the power dynamics, which shapes and is shaped, by interaction in positioning processes. A position can be seen as a set of rights and duties that delimit the possibilities of behaviour. Hence, a position implicitly delimits how much and what the person in that position can say and do, in a particular context and to particular interaction partners (Davies and Harré 1999; Harré and Moghaddam 2003a). For example, individuals in more legitimate positions are presumed to produce more relevant and worthy ideas, and, therefore, are more entitled to speak and to be heard. In each social community, individuals can adopt a realm of positions: they can strive to locate themselves in, be pushed into, be displaced from or be refused access to, or recess themselves from, in dynamic ways in their interaction processes.

In the positioning theory (e.g. Harré and Moghaddam 2003a; van Langenhove and Harré 1999), there are different categories of positioning, including the distinction between self-positioning and the positioning of others, both of which can be either deliberate or forced. Deliberate self-positioning takes place when someone intends to portray a particular identity, usually in pursuit of a particular goal (for example, by using social or physical power to raise one's own status in a peer group). Forced self-positioning occurs as an obligatory response to the request of an external power (for example, the victim of bullying withdrawing from others' company, or responding with counter violence as self-defence). Deliberate positioning of others can take place in the presence (for example, by selecting persons to be included and excluded in a sports team or group work) or absence (for example, by gossiping and mocking someone behind the target person's back) of those to be positioned. The forced positioning of others can occur in cases when bystanders are required to position others, for example, bystanders in bullying situations can feel themselves being forced to turn their back on the victim, for fear of becoming bullied themselves if they refuse.

Applying the positioning theory, we can visualize what would happen in bullying processes in terms of positioning, to individuals in different bullying roles, and, in particular, how the ways of being positioned within a peer group could affect the peer group integration of victims later in life. In interaction processes, in which the role of bully is both taken by particular persons and given to them by the peer group, the bullies learn to position themselves as the authority above others. Through their communication, behaviour and physical acts, they appropriate the right to choose other people to be included in and excluded from the group, and decide which rights and duties others in the peer group have.

Positioning oneself as this kind of authority would not be possible without the approval of the majority of the peer group. Again, in interaction processes within the peer group, the members of the group approve a particular person to have the right to use power, give orders, choose other members of the group and decide on their rights and duties. Hence, the right to be believed, obeyed and followed must be given by others to the person who strives to appropriate the position of authority. For example, by bullying and excluding some of their peers, these individuals succeed in convincing others of their extensive rights, thus further strengthening their position of authority in the peer group.

The position of the victims is determined in the bullying processes. For example, by mocking the target person's personal qualities (e.g. by calling the person dumb, stupid or an idiot), the bully shows others that the target person has characteristics which mean that individual does not have the right to be heard and valued in the peer group. By accusing the victim of lying or something that they deny having done – which is quite typical in bullying situations – the bully would show that this person has lost the right to be believed. As the bullying continues, the victim's rights are usually taken away while their duties are increased. Eventually, the victim's position can be made so low that they barely have the right to talk at all in the peer group, or even join the group. By means of physical forms of bullying (e.g. physical violence, stealing or destroying their property or plagiarising their university assignments), the bullies can show that the target person no longer has the right to physical integrity, or to keep their own property, money or acknowledge their achievements. Victims can even lose the right to their own intellectual capacity, for example, by being told to do the bully's university work.

Due to their lack of rights within the peer group, victims usually find it very difficult to affect the position that they have been given. However, bullies have also taken and been given the right to reposition the victim with respect to others, thus being able to re-determine their victims' rights and duties. Sometimes this right can be used to return at least some of the rights to the victim, or releasing the person from their duties. This kind of repositioning could result, for example, at school level, from an intervention by teachers, parents or other classmates, or, at university level, by an event or change in the peer group dynamic that would motivate a re-evaluation of the victim's position and generate a repositioning process.

So, how does the theory of positioning increase our understanding of the tendency for victims to be revictimized later in life? Although the theory includes the assumption that repositioning is possible, and empirical findings exist to suggest that some victims of school bullying do succeed in escaping their roles as victims (Smith *et al.* 2004), the experiences of bullying victimization may have a long-term impact on the self-positioning of victims in peer groups. After having learned to position themselves as a person with only duties and without any rights in the peer group, the victims may have created quite a permanent way to see themselves among peers. This perception can probably affect the ways in which they expect and accept to be positioned by new peers in new social contexts.

Positioning oneself as an outsider, without the right to be heard, believed, valued or cared about, would presumably result in avoiding or defensive behaviour in a new peer group. Instead of eagerly joining others, making friends with them, and displaying the self-disclosure that is needed for building social relationships, these people would most likely withdraw from social interaction, limit their self-closure, and hesitate, or even show defensiveness, in situations where peer relationships are established. Due to this behaviour, they would increase the risk of again being positioned as outsiders with duties but no rights. In turn, this kind of peer group position would put them at risk of further victimization and abuse.

Those who have occupied the bully's position have learned to see peer relationships as social battlefields on which individuals must fight for their rights, in order to gain social power over others and to avoid being given the position and duties of the victim. As the establishment of new peer relationships is not difficult for this group of individuals (Pörhölä 2008, 2009b), they would quickly be able to gather a new group of peers around them, and, with the assistance of these companions, take on a leading position within the new peer community at university. As they have previously gained social power by bullying others, the risk of them repeating the same strategy is high.

The impact of friends on stopping the continuities of peer victimization and bullying

Friends can play a significant role in peer community integration processes, by affecting the positioning and self-positioning of individuals. For example, Hodges *et al.* (1999) found that aggressively behaving children avoided bullying children who had friends. They suggested that, in addition to serving a physically protective function, friends may improve the self-esteem and social skills of the victims of bullying, and provide emotional and cognitive support. It has even been shown that some victims have managed to escape their role as victim by acquiring new friends (Smith *et al.* 2004).

Having friends can also reduce the negative consequences of bullying. Evidence shows, for example, that having pro-social relationships with some classmates moderates the relationship between victimization and loneliness felt by the victim (Storch and Masia-Warner 2004). Correspondingly, Newman *et al.* (2005) found that victimization by peers during high school damaged most those who also felt isolated, whereas those who were bullied frequently in high school, but received social support from peers, reported fewer stress symptoms in college. Hence, the benefits of peer support for coping with victimization seem obvious. Storch and Masia-Warner (2004) suggest that supportive peer relationships may provide an arena in which negative beliefs about oneself and others can be corrected, thereby reducing the loneliness and enhancing the self-esteem of the victimized person.

Why do friendships have such an important meaning to the victims of bullying? Can friends contribute to the positions of victims in the peer group and their prospect of being revictimized in the future? The peer-community integration theory (Pörhölä 2009a, 2009b) assumes that friendships in which partners show mutual commitment, trust, support, valuation, love and care, are the most powerful relationships to pull individuals towards the centre of the peer community. Having peer relationships, in which a person shares mutual rights and duties with their partner, can have a significant impact on that individual's peer group positioning. Even though friends might not be able to prevent the person from being bullied by other peers, they are able to affect the victimized person's self-positioning and, in this way, can contribute to the future peer group positioning of that person. When the victimized person perceives that they can have equal rights and duties in a peer relationship, this perception can change their expectations of future peer relationships. It can encourage a more positive self-positioning as a potential insider of a peer group, which in turn, would affect their behaviour when entering a new peer group. Having friends would also provide opportunities for the victims of bullying to practice their peer interaction skills, which would further help them to be able to establish rewarding peer relationships and to integrate them into new peer communities, for example, when moving from school to university.

Regarding those who bully, friends can contribute by changing the course of their behaviour and preventing their bullying behaviour. With feedback from their friends, bullies can be helped to re-determine their own position in the peer group and give up the rights they have appropriated and been given to determine the positions of others in the peer group. In this way, the bullies would also have a better chance of having balanced peer relationships and success in integrating into the peer community at university, and have due respect for the rights of others to study and socialize in harmony with their peers.

References

Bauman, S. and Newman, M. L. (2013). Testing assumptions about cyberbullying. Perceived distress associated with acts of conventional and cyber bullying. *Psychology of Violence,* 3: 27–38.

Boulton, M. J. and Smith, P. K. (1994). Bully/victim problems in middle-school children: Stability, self-perceived competence, peer perceptions and peer acceptance. *British Journal of Developmental Psychology,* 12: 315–29.

Chapell, M. S., Hasselman, S. L., Kitchin, T., Lomon, S. N., MacIver, K. W. and Sarullo, P. L. (2006). Bullying in elementary school, high school, and college, *Adolescence,* 41: 633–48.

Connolly, J., Pepler, D., Craig, W. and Taradash, A. (2000). Dating experiences of bullies in early adolescence. *Child Maltreatment,* 5: 299–310.

Crick, N. R. and Grotpeter, J. K. (1996). Children's treatment by peers: Victims of relational and overt aggression. *Development and Psychopathology,* 8: 367–80.

Curwen, T., McNichol, J. S. and Sharpe, G. W. (2011). The progression of bullying from elementary school to university. *International Journal of Humanities and Social Science,* 1(13): 47–54.

Davies, B. and Harré, R. (1999). Positioning and personhood. In R. Harré and L. van Langenhove (Eds.), *Positioning Theory: Moral Contexts of Intentional Action.* Oxford: Blackwell. pp. 32–52.

De Souza, E. R. and Ribeiro, J. (2005). Bullying and sexual harassment among Brazilian high school students. *Journal of Interpersonal Violence,* 20(9): 1018–38.

Due, P., Holstein, B. E., Lynch, J., Diderichsen, F., Gabhain, S. N., Scheidt, P. and Health Behaviour in School-Aged Children Bullying Working Group (2005). Bullying and symptoms among school-aged children: International comparative cross-sectional study in 28 countries. *European Journal of Public Health,* 15(2): 128–32.

Eslea, M., Menesini, E., Morita, Y., O'Moore, M., Mora-Merchan, J., Pereira, B. and Smith, P. K. (2003). Friendship and loneliness among bullies and victims: Data from seven countries. *Aggressive Behavior,* 30: 71–83.

Harré, R. and Moghaddam, F. (2003a). Introduction: The self and others in traditional psychology and in positioning theory. In R. Harré and F. Moghaddam (Eds.), *The Self and Others: Positioning Individuals and Groups in Personal, Political, and Cultural Contexts.* Westport, CT: Praeger. pp. 1–11.

Harré, R. and Moghaddam, F. (Eds.) (2003b). *The Self and Others: Positioning Individuals and Groups in Personal, Political, and Cultural Contexts.* Westport, CT: Praeger.

Harré, R., and van Langenhove, L. (Eds.), (1999). *Positioning Theory: Moral Contexts of Intentional Action.* Oxford: Blackwell.

Hawker, D. S. J. and Boulton, M. J. (2000). Twenty years' research on peer victimization and psychosocial maladjustment: A meta-analytic review of cross-sectional studies. *Journal of Child Psychology and Psychiatry and Allied Disciplines,* 41: 441–55.

Hodges, E.V., Boivin, M., Vitaro, F. and Bukowski, W. M. (1999). The power of friendship: Protection against an escalating cycle of peer victimization. *Developmental Psychology,* 35: 94–101.

Hodges, E. V. E. and Perry, D. G. (1996). Victims of peer abuse: An overview. *Journal of Emotional and Behavioral Problems,* 5: 23–8.

Houbre, B., Tarquinio, C., Thuillier, I. and Hergott, E. (2006). Bullying among students and its consequences on health. *European Journal of Psychology of Education,* 21: 183–208.

Jantzer, A. M., Hoover, J. H. and Narloch, R. (2006). The relationship between school-aged bullying and trust, shyness and quality of friendships in young adulthood: A preliminary research note. *School Psychology International,* 27: 146–56.

Juvonen, J., Nishina, A. and Graham, S. (2000). Peer harassment, psychological adjustment, and school functioning in early adolescence. *Journal of Educational Psychology,* 92: 349–59.

Kaltiala-Heino, R., Rimpelä, M., Rantanen, P. and Rimpelä, A. (2000). Bullying at school – an indicator of adolescents at risk for mental disorders. *Journal of Adolescence,* 23: 661–74.

Kochenderfer, B. J. and Ladd, G. W. (1996). Peer victimization: Cause or consequence of school maladjustment? *Child Development,* 67: 1305–17.

Nansel, T. R., Craig, W., Overpeck, M. D., Saluja, G., Ruan, W. J. and the HBSC Bullying Analyses Working Group (2004). Cross-national consistency in the relationship between bullying behaviors and psychosocial adjustment. *Archives of Pediatrics and Adolescent Medicine,* 158(8): 730–36.

Newman, M. L., Holden, G. W. and Delville, Y. (2005). Isolation and the stress of being bullied. *Journal of Adolescence,* 28(3): 343–57.

Pellegrini, A. D. (2002). Bullying, victimization, and sexual harassment during the transition to middle school. *Educational Psychologist,* 37(3): 151–64.

Pepler, D., Craig, W., Connolly, J. and Henderson, K. (2002). Bullying, sexual harassment, dating violence, and substance use among adolescents. In C. Wekerle and A. M. Wall (Eds.), *The Violence and Addiction Equation: Theoretical and Clinical Issues in Substance Abuse and Relationship Violence.* Philadelphia: Brunner/Mazel. pp. 153–68.

Pepler, D., Jiang, D., Craig, W. and Connolly, J. (2008). Developmental trajectories of bullying and associated factors. *Child Development,* 79: 325–38.

Pörhölä, M. (2008). Koulukiusaaminen nuoren hyvinvointia uhkaavana tekijänä. Miten käy kiusatun ja kiusaajan vertaissuhteille? [School bullying as a risk factor for the well-being of an adolescent. What happens to the peer relationships of bullies and victims?] In M. Autio, K. Eräranta, and S. Myllyniemi (Eds.), *Polarisoituva nuoruus? Nuorten elinolot -vuosikirja 2008.* Finland: Nuorisotutkimusverkosto/Nuorisotutkimusseura, Nuorisoasiain neuvottelukunta, and Sosiaali- ja terveysalan tutkimus- ja kehittämiskeskus Stakes. pp. 94–104.

Pörhölä, M. (2009a). Kiusaamiskokemukset yhteisöön kiinnittymizen esteenä [Bullying experiences preventing integration into one's peer community]. In T. Valkonen, P. Isotalus, M. Siitonen, and M. Valo (Eds.), *Prologi. Puheviestinnän vuosikirja 2009 .* Finland: Prologos ry. pp. 84–89.

Pörhölä, M. (2009b). Psychosocial well-being of victimized students. In T. A. Kinney and M. Pörhölä (Eds.), *Anti and Pro-Social Communication: Theories, Methods, and Applications (Language as Social Action).* New York: Peter Lang Inc. pp. 83–93.

Pörhölä, M. (2011a). Kiusaaminen opiskeluyhteisössä (Bullying in the university community). In K. Kunttu, A. Komulainen, K. Makkonen, and P. Pynnönen (Eds.), *Opiskeluterveys.* Finland: Duodecim. pp. 166–8.

Pörhölä, M. (2011b). Kouluaikaisten kiusaamiskokemusten vaikutus nuoressa aikuisiässä [Consequences of previous school-bullying experiences in young adulthood]. In K. Kunttu, A. Komulainen, K. Makkonen, and P. Pynnönen (Eds.), *Opiskeluterveys* Helsinki: Duodecim. pp. 46–8.

Pörhölä, M. and Kinney, T. A. (2010). *Bullying: Contexts, Consequences, and Control.* Barcelona, Spain: Editorial Aresta.

Reijntjes A., Kamphuis, J. H., Prinzie, P. and Telch, M. J. (2010). Peer victimization and internalizing problems in children: A meta-analysis of longitudinal studies. *Child Abuse and Neglect,* 34(4): 244–52.

Salmivalli, C. and Isaacs, J. (2005). Prospective relations among victimization, rejection, friendlessness, and children's self- and peer-perceptions. *Child Development,* 76: 1161–71.

Salmivalli, C., Lagerspetz, K., Björkqvist, K., Österman, K. and Kaukiainen, A. (1996). Bullying as a group process: Participant roles and their relations to social status within the group. *Aggressive Behavior,* 22: 1–15.

Salmivalli, C., Lappalainen, M. and Lagerspetz, K. M. J. (1998). Stability and change of behavior in connection with bullying in schools: A two-year follow-up. *Aggressive Behavior,* 24: 205–18.

Schäfer, M., Korn, S., Brodbeck, F. C., Wolke, D. and Schulz, H. (2005). Bullying roles in changing contexts: The stability of victim and bully roles from primary to secondary school. *International Journal of Behavioral Development,* 29: 323–35.

Schäfer, M., Korn, S., Smith, P. K., Hunter, S. C., Mora-Merchán, J. A., Singer, M. M. and van der Meulen, K. (2004). Lonely in the crowd: Recollections of bullying. *British Journal of Developmental Psychology,* 22: 379–94.

Slee, P. T. (1994). Situational and interpersonal correlates of anxiety associated with peer victimization. *Child Psychiatry and Human Development,* 25: 97–107.

Smith, P. K., Singer, M., Hoel, H. and Cooper, C. L. (2003). Victimization in the school and the workplace: Are there any links? *British Journal of Psychology,* 94: 175–88.

Smith, P. K., Talamelli, L., Cowie, H., Naylor, P. and Chauhan, P. (2004). Profiles of non-victims, escaped victims, continuing victims and new victims of school bullying. *British Journal of Educational Psychology,* 74: 565–81.

Sourander, A., Helstelä, L., Helenius, H. and Piha, J. (2000). Persistence of bullying from childhood to adolescence: A longitudional 8-year follow-up study. *Child Abuse and Neglect,* 24: 873–81.

Storch, E. A., Brassard, M. R. and Masia-Warner, C. L. (2003). The relationship of peer victimization to social anxiety and loneliness in adolescence. *Child Study Journal,* 33: 1–18.

Storch, E. A. and Masia-Warner, C. L. (2004). The relationship of peer victimization to social anxiety and loneliness in adolescent females. *Journal of Adolescence,* 27: 351–62.

van Langenhove, L. and Harré, R. (1999). Introducing positioning theory. In R. Harré and L. van Langenhove (Eds.), *Positioning Theory: Moral Contexts of Intentional Action.* Oxford: Blackwell. pp. 14–31.

5

HOMOPHOBIC AND TRANSPHOBIC BULLYING IN UNIVERSITIES

Ian Rivers

> All of us in the academy and in the culture as a whole are called to renew our minds if we are to transform educational institutions – and society – so that the way we live, teach, and work can reflect our joy in cultural diversity, our passion for justice, and our love of freedom.
>
> (bell hooks, Teaching to Transgress, 1994, p. 34)

Introduction

In this chapter the focus is on the issue of homophobic and transphobic bullying in higher education. The fact that there is a body of research on this issue is a cause for concern. As bell hooks says in her book, *Teaching to Transgress*, our teaching should reflect our joy in the diversity that surrounds us. However, as the following pages will demonstrate 'joy' is not always a feature of university life. So, why has homophobia and transphobia taken hold in university and college environments? To answer this question it is necessary to recognize that, as in all things, universities work from a very basic and heterosexual binary position – male or female. The issue of whether a student or member of staff is lesbian, gay, bisexual or trans (LGBT) often does not feature in the development or implementation of policies and practices that promote equality. In the United Kingdom (UK) for example, initiatives such as the Athena SWAN Charter Mark assume that the lack of opportunities faced by women in the pursuit of careers in science are uniform and universal. Indeed there is little acknowledgement in this scheme that women of different sexual orientations face different levels of discrimination and career challenges. The assumption that all women are alike shows a fundamental lack of understanding in the ways in which discrimination works at multiple levels. It is important to recognize that gender can and often does intersect with sexual orientation, disability, pregnancy, childcare, age, gender reassignment, race, and/

or faith and belief, and this is lost in these simplistic approaches to enhancing the role of women in science and academia. Indeed, the fact that eligibility to receive research council funding is linked to university compliance suggests a tacit acknowledgement by the Government of a reticence by our institutions of higher education to sign up to this initiative willingly. In a similar vein, the assumption that all men are and have been privileged in academia also demonstrates a fundamental lack of awareness of the discrimination that has existed within higher education for decades. In his book *Academic Outlaws*, William G. Tierney relates his own and others' experiences of being a gay academic within the American higher education system. In the United States of America (USA), as in many other countries at the time, the failure to recognize same-sex relationships at university, state and national levels meant that same-sex partners of LGBT academics did not share in the health care benefits that were extended to the wives and husbands of their heterosexual colleagues. While Tierney is forgiving of the university and recognizes that the machinery of change can be slow, he also points out that recognising the existence of LGBT staff in academia (and, by extension, students) is a matter of social justice and not one of politics. As he points out, universities, more than any other public or private institution, should embrace dialogue about these issues and be willing to have difficult conversations that challenge the status quo:

> Our colleges and universities need to be noisier – in the sense that honest dialogue that confronts differences is good. To be sure, we must not drown out other voices. Yet it is of concern to me when we assume that we cannot argue or disagree with one another. We must work harder at developing dialogues of respect.
>
> (Tierney 1997, p. 176)

For LGBT students, past research has suggested that universities can be daunting institutions where the issue of disclosing one's sexual orientation can be fraught with anxiety and, in some cases, danger. For example, in early research looking at the issue of living in halls of residence or dormitories, Taulke-Johnson and Rivers (1999) asked a small group of LGB students attending a UK university about their experiences of shared accommodation. The majority of the students advised caution in telling others when they first arrive on campus:

> I wouldn't let onto anyone that you were LGB until you'd sussed out your flat mates... Don't tell them until you feel confident and until you're sure that they won't beat you up basically.
>
> (p. 81)

While some students acknowledged that their flatmates and fellow students were protective and supportive of them when they disclosed their sexual orientation, this was not always the case:

When you come into my flat it's like 'So who've you shagged today then?'...
'What's it like having it up the shit box?'...I've had foam sprayed on my
door stating 'Hello gay boy'...and something sprayed on my window – 'Gay
boy lives here'.

(p. 82)

Much of the early research on homophobia conducted in the USA focused more
generally on LGB experiences across educational contexts – including schools –
and involved young people up to the age of 21 years, some of whom had gone on
to university or college (D'Augelli 1989, 1992; D'Augelli and Rose 1990; D'Emilio
1990; Slater 1993; Evans and D'Augelli 1996).

In his review of data collected from three cross-sectional studies undertaken at
universities in the USA, Comstock (1991) found that 22 per cent of the 560 lesbian
and gay students that were surveyed reported having been followed or chased by
other undergraduates on campus. Fifteen per cent said that they had objects thrown
at them, 11 per cent said that they had been the victims of arson or one or more
acts of vandalism, 4 per cent had been physically assaulted, 3 per cent had been spat
upon, and 1 per cent had been assaulted with a weapon. Based upon these findings,
Comstock estimated that students from sexual minority groups were four times
more likely to be victims of assault or harassment than any other group on a USA
university or college campus.

Although Comstock's (1991) results show that reports of victimization by
lesbian, gay and bisexual young people were much less frequent within the college
or university context when compared with data on school-based aggression,
concerns relating to the increased likelihood of young people being assaulted or
harassed because of their sexual orientation were invariably highlighted by the
murder, in October 1998, of Matthew Shepard, a political science undergraduate
at the University of Wyoming. On the evening of 6 October, Matthew met two
men (Aaron McKinney and Russell Henderson) at a bar called The Fireside Lounge
in Laramie. McKinney and Henderson offered Matthew a ride home. However,
they took Matthew to a remote spot where he was robbed, tortured, tied to a fence
and left to die. Although Matthew was discovered by a passerby, his injuries were
so extensive that he died six days later. While some researchers believe that such
stories should be consigned to history and have ably demonstrated how schools and
university campuses can be places where LGBT young people thrive (Savin-
Williams 2005; McCormack 2012), there remain occasional incidents that focus
our attention on the needs and safety of LGBT students and staff at university and
college.

For example, concerns about LGBT student safety and well-being on campus
have been intensified more recently following the suicide in 2010 of Rutgers
student, Tyler Clementi, who was secretly filmed kissing another man in his dorm
room by his room-mate Dharun Ravi. While Ravi was ultimately sentenced to 30
days in prison, three years' probation, 300 hours community service, a $10,000
fine, and counselling on cyberbullying and alternative lifestyles, the fact that he felt

it was appropriate to stream his room-mate with another man is perhaps an index of the lack of compassion and understanding that many LGBTs experience in higher education, and particularly the license some heterosexual students feel they have to pry into or make fun of their personal lives.

In their ground-breaking study of LGB students at university, Evans and D'Augelli (1996) noted that many of the LGB undergraduates in their study felt that they had to negotiate their sexual identities while on campus. Not only did they have to decide whether or not to disclose their sexual orientation to others – particularly where they shared accommodation or decided to join a fraternity or sorority – but they also had to decide how they were going to 'manage' their lives on and off campus in order to avoid threatening people and/or situations. Indeed, Tyler Clementi's suicide suggests that this is still an issue on many campuses today. In one particular study conducted at a large state university in the USA, D'Augelli (1992) demonstrated the difficulties 121 LGB students faced living day-to-day on campus. He found that most hid their sexual orientation from their room-mates (70 per cent) and fellow students (80 per cent), and that 57 per cent also made specific changes to their lives to avoid harassment on campus. These changes included avoiding LGB clubs and venues, avoiding other well-known LGBs on campus, or pretending to have a romantic interest in a member of the opposite sex. Ultimately, studies carried out in the 1990s demonstrated that universities and colleges were not safe environments for LGB students. It should be noted that, at this time, very little was understood about the experiences of trans students on campus and this is an area where we remain woefully under-informed. So, the question arises, how do universities today support their LGBT students and staff?

The university in the twenty-first century

In the UK in 2009, the Equality Challenge Unit commissioned a report on the experiences of LGBT students and staff (academic and support) in higher education institutions (Valentine *et al.* 2009). Based upon responses from 2,704 LGBT students, 781 support staff and 720 LGBT academic staff, the picture Valentine and her colleagues painted was, alas, not a healthy one and bore many similarities to the studies conducted two decades earlier. For example, only 50 per cent of LGB staff and students said they would disclose their sexual orientation if given the opportunity to self-identify via an institutional monitoring process, and only 40 per cent trans staff and students said they would do so too.

The study indicated that, among LGB students, 49.5 per cent reported having been treated negatively by other students at university and 10.4 per cent reported having been treated negatively by their lecturers. In terms of having received homophobic comments, 46.8 per cent said they had received them from other students and 8.9 per cent from academic staff. For trans students, similar results emerged. Nearly 50 per cent of those who responded to the survey had been treated negatively by other students, and 28.5 per cent by staff. In terms of transphobic comments, 42.5 per cent reported having received them from other students and 19.4 per cent from staff. However, when it came to serious incidents of physical and sexual assault, 6.7 per cent of LGB and 11.3 per cent of trans students said they had experienced physical abuse at the hands of peers with 3.7 per cent of LGB students and 8.6 per cent of trans students experiencing sexual assault. While the data indicated that very few LGB students reported experiencing physical abuse (1.0 per cent) or sexual assault (1.1 per cent) at the hands of lecturers, rates were noticeably higher for trans students – 4.8 per cent and 5.4 per cent respectively. Overall, one-fifth of LGB students reported suspending their studies at university with one-third of trans students reporting having taken time out.

Among LGBT academic and support staff a similar picture to that of LGBT students emerged. Only 38.6 per cent of staff were 'out' to everyone in their institution. One-third of LGB staff said that they had been treated in a negative way by colleagues because of their sexual orientation, with 18.9 per cent reported having been treated negatively by students. Additionally, 31.7 per cent reported receiving homophobic comments from colleagues and 19.2 per cent from students. Eleven per cent had received verbal abuse from colleagues with 1 per cent and 1.5 per cent having been subjected to physical or sexual abuse respectively at the hands of colleagues. In terms of recruitment, one trans academic recounted how difficult it can be to be appointed to posts:

> What I have found is, in academia generally, I cannot get shortlisted for a job, never mind appointed for a job. I have seen people get jobs with CVs that don't compare with mine and I've not even been shortlisted for it. I've had direct responses from senior staff at other universities ... the Vice-Chancellor really doesn't want the university associated with you. I actually got some compensation this year from one university whose V-C threw my application in the bin. I'd been headhunted for the post. Threw it in a bin and made a filthy joke about bearded ladies and cunnilingus. And I happen to know that because someone at another university was on the appointment committee and rang me up ... I really didn't want to go to an employment tribunal with it, though I could have done and the person concerned was willing to give the evidence [on my behalf]. But I felt it would damage any chance of me ever moving on.
>
> (Valentine *et al*. 2009, p. 34)

In many respects, the experiences of these students and staff members are not adequately represented by the term 'bullying'– it is abuse. It is not only abuse in the physical sense, but also in terms of the trust and power that both students and staff place in an institution to support and protect them. As Tierney (1997) points out, there is an academic contract: a contract to provide a safe and effective environment in which to learn and a contract to provide a safe and effective environment in which to work. If neither of these contracts is upheld and if there are disparities in the opportunities offered to students and staff because of their sexual orientation or trans status then, ultimately, those universities will find themselves facing compensation claims and external scrutiny via public investigations by regulatory authorities.

The failure of UK universities to respond adequately to the needs of LGBT students was demonstrated aptly by the National Union of Students (NUS) in their 2014 report entitled *Educating Beyond the Straight and Narrow* (National Union of Students 2014). This report detailed the experiences of over 4,000 students attending 80 universities. The findings indicated that 20 per cent of LGB+ students ('+' refers to those who described themselves as 'queer', 'questioning' or 'unsure') and one-third of trans students had experienced at least one form of bullying or harassment on campus. Over half (51 per cent) of trans students had seriously considered dropping out of their course, and this was found to be significantly more than gay students (27.7 per cent) or those who identified as lesbian (26.6 per cent) or bisexual (30 per cent). Only one-in-five trans students said that they felt completely safe on campus.

In one focus group with trans students, the issue of gender-neutral toilets and facilities arose, together with expressions of frustration at the lack of university guidance relating to the changing of names and gender status on student registers and records. Additionally, concerns were expressed about the attitudes of those responsible for university security.

However, it is the issue of not providing gender-neutral lavatories that has been consistently raised in the research of trans students' experiences at university. It was highlighted in 2013, when a trans microbiology student was assaulted by two other women in the female toilets at the University of Leeds Students' Union. While the student chose not to pursue the issue further, a response from the students' union indicated that the issue of gender-neutral lavatories had been raised and agreed upon as early as 2010 but it seems that the university and the union had not taken any further action (McCormick 2013). In their report for the Equality Challenge Unit, Valentine *et al.* (2009) recounted the response one trans student received following an enquiry about gender-neutral lavatories on campus:

> I've complained about the toilet situation, I've felt, like, intimidated to go into the men's toilet, and I didn't feel comfortable in the women's toilet either. You know, nothing's ever really done. They just say, oh, use the disabled toilet.
>
> (p. 26)

Using the 'disabled toilet' is not an adequate solution to this student's discomfort. Firstly, there is a principle to address: being trans does not constitute an impairment to motor function, or any form of impairment for that matter. Secondly, while using the disabled toilet may be seen by some as a practical solution for this particular student, it sends the wrong message about how trans people (students and staff) are viewed by a university. It sends out a message of 'otherness' and harks back to what we might describe as 'less-enlightened times' when being trans was considered to be something akin to an impairment.

But the issue is not just one about the physical space within a university to be trans, the issue is also about being able to pursue a career as a trans person. The example quoted by Valentine *et al.* (2009) of the trans academic unable to get a job because of prejudice is just one part of the story. Some academics, who have transitioned while holding substantive academic posts within universities, have also found it difficult to remain as a result of their uncertainty about changes in line management and changes in the culture of the university. In the following excerpt one trans academic recalls how difficult it was for her to deal with changes, not only in her immediate manager as she transitioned, but also physical changes to the university environment which she felt prohibited her from being fully herself:

> My institution was very good at producing policy documents and all of them apparently with the best intentions. Some really mattered: it was hugely important to be told by my HR representative that as I transitioned I was not at risk of dismissal. Which is not, of course, a lot to ask of an institution: but a basic right that so many of trans people in so many countries completely lack. I also suspect that one reason why I believed this particular reassurance was to do with the quality of the individual concerned. Just as I believed my first line manager when she told me the step I was taking had her full support. The next line manager was one of those who did his best with the directives: but was actually pretty uncomfortable about it all. Another directive laid out the institution's anti-bullying policy. The fact I had witnessed my line manager being bullied by both superiors and colleagues made me doubt his capacity for implementing it – particularly as my whole department was being bullied out of one campus, where we had the resources we needed, and forcibly removed to a new campus where we had no suitable facilities at all. That may well be one reason why I never felt safe or at ease in this horrible new open plan open space which was designed to cut us off from direct access to our students. Quite apart from the fact I was trans. I never felt safe enough to fully come out; never felt safe enough to wear a skirt, for instance, or use the women's toilets. But then bullying was endemic on that campus at that time; and being trans certainly did not help me find the strength to combat it. It was just one vulnerability too much. I left that institution; and I left academia – never to return.
>
> (Personal communication 2 November 2014)

While the above extract indicates that this academic experienced a great deal of anxiety around the substantial changes in the physical as well as organizational structure of the university in which she worked, it was also clear from this extract that, in designing the physical space of the new campus, simple solutions such as gender-neutral lavatories were never considered. The fact too that support was perceived to be less than effective following a change in line manager is also indicative of failure of this institution to ensure that he was aware of his obligations and had the skills necessary to support this member of staff. Within this extract there is also an underlying narrative of a more generalized bullying culture within this university, which is increasingly featuring in academic and policy literature internationally (see, for example, American Educational Research Association, 2013). Universities and colleges are losing valuable resources by driving out their LGBT academic staff through an inability to live up to the policies they write and purport to enact. However, it is possible for these institutions to change and acknowledge, support and celebrate their LGBT students and staff members. Sometimes this requires action; other times it requires the ability and willingness to pay attention to what is going on around them.

A more accepting campus?

Increasingly, there is evidence that there has been change in the ways students are viewing issues of sexuality. Among young men in particular, new forms of masculinity are being talked about where there is a recalibration of what it means to be male. For example, in one study, Anderson *et al.* (2013) looked at the phenomenon of men kissing on university and college campuses in the UK. Their study showed that same-sex kissing or, indeed, other expressions of affection that were once considered inappropriate among men are now quite common. While this study focused primarily on heterosexual male students in sports associations kissing and showing affection towards other heterosexual male students, the significance of this finding in terms of the acceptance of same-sex expressions of affection should be considered. In their analysis of the findings, Anderson *et al.* (2013) noted that same-sex kissing did not take place in private, team-only spaces, it took place in the social spaces that other students occupy (night clubs, classrooms, and pubs). Thus, while these sportsmen had a certain caché in terms of their heterosexual and 'heteromasculine' social capital, they also usualised such expressions of affection in these student-centred contexts. Indeed, Anderson (2009) noted that by usualising such behaviour in these generally accessible contexts, same-sex kissing no longer became a marker of being gay and was thus less likely to attract the opprobrium of peers.

In terms of promoting LGBT inclusion, Anderson *et al.*'s (2013) study introduces the element of doubt into the mix as to whether or not two male students kissing are indeed gay, but this study does not affirm that it is safe to be gay on university and college campuses. Indeed, Anderson *et al.* (2013) do not consider the experiences of lesbian students or indeed trans students, though research is ongoing into the experiences of bisexual students. In other academic selective environments such as sixth form and further education colleges in the UK, McCormack (2012) found that there is not only acceptance but also pride in LGBT students, with one school electing an openly gay candidate as student union president.

While McCormack's (2012) study certainly suggests that there has been a shift in the way in which LGBT students are viewed by their peers, he has also argued that there has been a concomitant shift in language and that terms such as 'that's so gay', are not homophobic, rather they represent a new, alternative gay discourse that exists among young people. In environments where there is little evidence of overt homophobia, 'that's so gay' becomes a form of expression where 'gay' infers something that is imperfect. While a negative connotation remains, within LGBT-friendly environments its stigma has gone; it becomes part of *pro-gay language* where heterosexual friends can call one another 'lover' or 'boyfriend' and do not face ridicule by peers (McCormack 2013).

Though this research is very encouraging, it remains to be seen how we reconcile heterosexual engagement with pro-gay language or behaviour with LGBT inclusion on campus. Ultimately, heterosexual males can play the 'gay game' without a loss of social and cultural status or capital, but what does this mean for students and staff who are LGBT? Undoubtedly many LGBT students and staff have had positive and fruitful experiences at university and the negative experiences highlighted within the various reports cited in this chapter will be alien to them. However, there are so few publications highlighting such achievements and experiences, it is all too easy to assume that university is no place to be LGBT.

Monitoring sexual orientation and trans status

> You see a lot of information on the university's website about the first woman professor in such and such, and that kind of thing, and that's valid. But you don't see any acknowledgement about the first, you know, gay professor, you know. Maybe that's not ... maybe that's not appropriate, but that kind of acknowledgement would be good really.
>
> (Valentine *et al.* 2009, p. 49)

Undoubtedly one of the reasons why there is such a dearth in the positive stories of LGBT students and staff rests with the fact that very often universities do not monitor sexual orientation or trans status in the recruitment, selection, appointment or annual monitoring. While human resources departments are happy to send out forms that ask about disability, ethnicity and citizenship, few universities ask whether a job applicant or prospective student is LGBT, or consider the implications of someone identifying as LGBT in terms of providing accommodation or ensuring that equality training reflects the diversity of the student and staff population.

In their survey, Valentine *et al.* (2009) found that while less than 20 per cent of universities monitored sexual orientation in recruitment process for staff, less than 10 per cent did so in the recruitment of students. When it came to trans staff, less than 10 per cent of universities specifically monitored the recruitment of trans applicants, and less than 5 per cent monitored the recruitment of trans students. One student from an LGB focus group said:

> I wouldn't declare it, I would be afraid ... that people like admission tutors are going to look at my UCAS form ... I'd think, well, I know he's *[sic]* not meant to judge, but would it really ... you never really know the truth behind these things ... some would declare it, but I think s lot of people

would hide it, so they'd never truly know the numbers of gay people at university.

(p. 47)

One member of an LGB staff focus group was clearly concerned with the way in which the data would be used by the university and questioned whether the ethos was one that really welcomed sexual minority staff:

> It depends, doesn't it, whether it's kind of anonymized and separated off ... and whether it's used for monitoring purposes, or whether it's something to do with staff records. And I think at the moment I would feel ... not suspicious of why they did it, but not as comfortable. I applied for another job a couple of years ago that was a fairly small, not-for-profit, charitable type of organization ... it was the first time actually on the equal opps monitoring form that it did talk about civil partnership, blah-d – blah, kind of thing. And I thought, okay, I'll tick that ... I was happy to do that 'cause it gave you a positive feel about the ethos of that organization. I don't have the same feel about the university as an institution, of thinking ... they really know this stuff.

(p. 47)

If a university – a place of learning and enquiry – cannot deal effectively with the issues relating to sexual orientation and gender diversity or chooses to ignore them, then that is often reflected in the materials they produce, such as equal opportunities monitoring forms. Valentine *et al.* (2009) noted that positive representations of LGBT staff and students affected 14.7 per cent of LGB students' choices in terms of the universities to which they wished to apply to read for a degree, and 23.7 per cent of trans students' choices:

> The reason why I chose this uni was because it was the only university that I could find that had a specific page on the website about trans people, and that they were inclusive, and this, that and the other. And I thought, oh well, I'll go there and I'll start my transition there.

(p. 49)

In terms of staff experience, the appointment of chancellors and vice-chancellors has also been seen as something that has made life difficult for LGBT academics and staff. As one LGBT member of staff said:

> We have a Chancellor ... I find that very hard because he's been very vocal about, you know, against gay couples adopting and things. So I find it hard being, having him as my Chancellor.

(p. 50)

It is unclear whether even today, prospective chancellors (honorary posts usually offered to leading citizens, business people, or celebrities) or vice-chancellors are quizzed on their knowledge of and appreciation of equality and diversity in all its forms before being offered an appointment. However, it was clear from Valentine *et al.*'s report that less than one-third of respondents said their university had an LGBT group for staff, and just over 10 per cent reported that their trade union supported an LGBT group for staff.

What should universities and colleges do?

In the UK, following the Equality Act of 2010, all public authorities, including universities and colleges, are required to ensure equality of opportunity and protect those in their care from all forms of discrimination, and support and employ those who also have one or more protected characteristics. These protected characteristics include those with sexual orientations other than heterosexual, those who undergo or have undergone gender reassignment, and those in marriage and civil partnerships. Other protected characteristics include age, disability, pregnancy and maternity, race, religion and belief (including atheism), and sex. All public authorities also have a single equality duty to eliminate all forms of unlawful discrimination, harassment and victimization, advance equality of opportunity between different groups, and foster good relations between those groups. Currently, some universities are also faith community foundations having originally been established as diocesan colleges for the training of teachers and clergy. While they are also subject to the single equality duty, often the vice-chancellor or principal of such an institution is required to be a communicant member of the Church to which the institution is affiliated. While there is no evidence to suggest that LGBT students and staff are treated any less fairly than in secular institutions of higher education, it does mean that some LGBT academics may still be barred from taking up the most senior post in these institutions because their home life or background is not in keeping with precepts of that faith. While there should be no other bar in terms of recruitment and selection of students or staff, today such institutions are funded principally by the state and not by the Churches to which they are affiliated. Thus, in selecting vice-chancellors or principals, the skills and standing of the applicants should take precedence over their observance of a particular faith.

If British universities are going to live up to the expectations of the single equality duty then, as Tierney (1997) said, they need to be 'noisier' places, and tackle the issue of diversity within a dialogue of respect. Indeed, it is incumbent upon all universities to widen the horizons of their students and staff and not limit their view to one way of living or one way of being. After all the term 'university' derives from the Latin word *universitas* meaning 'the whole'. In this way, universities build a rich and vibrant seam of academic discourse that also offers students an opportunity to explore the whole world they inhabit in multiple and interdisciplinary ways.

In promoting equality for LGBT staff, Tierney (1997) states there are five requirements for a university to be inclusive (these have been adapted to apply to multiple contexts):

1   That an institution's statement about non-discrimination explicitly refers to sexual orientation (and by extension trans status);
2   That accommodation contracts do not discriminate;
3   That any benefits universities negotiate for family members of academic staff also apply to those in same-sex relationships;
4   That universities institute an office and/or a senior officer to ensure implementation of these policies;
5   That an institution makes explicit to the outside world its non-discrimination policies.

More widely, universities have to recognize and celebrate their LGBT students and staff. One way in which this can be achieved is to celebrate LGBT History Month (October in the USA and February in the UK) annually through open lectures, seminars, and events that highlight the contributions LGBT students and staff not only make to the university but also the contribution LGBTs have made to society as a whole.

While there will be those who will disagree with LGBT inclusion or indeed any celebration of LGBT lives, a university provides a forum wherein those disagreements can be explored without resorting to violence or intimidation. The existence of bullying, victimization and discrimination in universities and colleges is shaming. It ultimately demonstrates that bigotry exists even in those places where intellect and insight are in abundance. In changing such damaging cultures we must first ensure that policies are in place, but in changing hearts and minds we have to also ensure that we value the contribution LGBTs make to our communities as we do the contributions of many other groups.

References

American Educational Research Association (2013). *Prevention of Bullying in Schools, Colleges and Universities: Research Report and Recommendations.* Washington, DC: American Educational Research Association.

Anderson, E. (2009). *Inclusive Masculinity: The Changing Nature of Masculinities.* New York: Routledge.

Anderson, E., Adams, A. and Rivers, I. (2013). 'I kiss them because I love them': The emergence of heterosexual men kissing in British institutes of education. *Archives of Sexual Behavior,* 41: 421–30.

Comstock, G. D. (1991). *Violence Against Lesbians and Gay Men.* New York: Columbia University Press.

D'Augelli, A. R. (1989). Lesbians' and gay men's experiences of discrimination and harassment in a university community. *American Journal of Community Psychology,* 17: 317–21.

D'Augelli. A. R. (1992). Lesbian and gay male undergraduates' experiences of harassment and fear of campus. *Journal of Interpersonal Violence*, 7: 383–95.

D'Augelli, A. R., and Rose, M. L. (1990). Homophobia in a university community: attitudes and experiences of heterosexual freshmen. *Journal of College Student Development*, 31: 484–91.

D'Emilio, J. (1990). The campus environment for gay and lesbian life. *Academe*, 76: 317–21.

Evans, N. J. and D'Augelli, A. R. (1996). Lesbians, gay men, and bisexual people in college. In R. C. Savin-Williams, and K. M. Cohen (Eds.), *The Lives of Lesbians, Gays and Bisexuals: Children to Adults*. Fort Worth: Harcourt-Brace, pp. 201–26.

hooks, b. (1994). *Teaching to Transgress: Education as the Practice of Freedom*. New York: Routledge.

McCormack, M. (2012). *The Declining Significance of Homophobia: How Teenage Boys Are Redefining Masculinity and Heterosexuality*. New York: Oxford University Press.

McCormack, M. (2013). Mapping the boundaries of homophobic language in bullying. In I. Rivers, and N. Duncan (Eds.), *Bullying: Experiences and Discourses of Sexuality and Gender*. London: Routledge, pp. 91–104.

McCormick, J. P. (2013). *Trans woman student abused and shoved out of toilets at Leeds University*. Available at http://www.pinknews.co.uk/2013/02/08/trans-woman-student-abused-and-shoved-out-of-toilets-at-leeds-university. [Accessed on 31 October 2014].

National Union of Students (2014). *Educating Beyond the Straight and Narrow: LGBT Students' Experiences in Higher Education*. London: National Union of Students.

Savin-Williams, R. C. (2005). *The New Gay Teenager*. Cambridge: Harvard University Press.

Slater, B. R. (1993). Violence against lesbian and gay male college students. *Journal of College Student Psychotherapy*, 8: 177–202.

Taulke-Johnson, R. J. and Rivers, I. (1999). Providing a safe environment for lesbian, gay and bisexual students living in university accommodation. *Youth and Policy*, 64: 74–89.

Tierney, W.G. (1997). *Academic Outlaws: Queer Theory and Cultural Studies in the Academy*. Thousand Oaks: Sage.

Valentine, G., Wood, N. and Plummer, P. (2009). *The Experience of Lesbian, Gay, Bisexual and Trans Staff and Students in Higher Education*. London: Equality Challenge Unit.

6

STALKING AND VIOLENCE AMONG UNIVERSITY STUDENTS

Katja Björklund

This chapter explores the nature of stalking from social, psychological, behavioural, and clinical and public policy perspectives in the light of related theory, research and practice. It presents the key issues of stalking from the university student perspective by discussing the prevalence and definition of stalking, stalking behaviour and violence, victim-stalker relationships, stalking duration, victim reactions on stalking, and coping.

The nature of stalking

Stalking is well recognised as a large-scale social problem across both adult and student populations especially in the English-speaking part of the world as most of the studies have been conducted in these countries (Bartol and Bartol 2008; Mullen *et al.* 2001; Sheridan *et al.* 2003). Stalking has gradually received more of both academic and public attention. Recent studies conducted in continental Europe have shown that stalking seems also to be a wide-spread, serious social and health problem in many European countries (Björklund *et al.* 2010a; Dovelius *et al.* 2006; Dressing *et al.* 2007).

Even if stalking is often referred to as an 'old' behaviour, it is still a relatively new offence, which has been recognized as illegal only for the past three decades, the first anti-stalking laws appearing in the USA in 1990 (Meloy 2007). In Europe, many countries have managed to stipulate specific anti-stalking legislation, which currently are: Austria, Belgium, Denmark, Finland, Germany, Ireland, Italy, Malta, the Netherlands, Sweden, and the United Kingdom. In those European member states without a specific anti-stalking legislation, it is possible to take legal action against stalking only when the behaviour amounts to a crime, which can then be prosecuted under other existing legal norms (De Fazio 2009).

Defining stalking

Stalking is often defined as 'the wilful, malicious, and repeated following and harassing of another person that threatens his or her safety', as Meloy and Gothard (1995, p. 258) first defined it. Later victim-related factors have been included to the definition, i.e. the stalking behaviour has to be *unwanted* by the target to constitute stalking (Pathé and Mullen 1997).

Defining stalking has, however, been a multifaceted and difficult task. Definitions still vary depending on the perspective. From a legal perspective, there is often a requirement that the stalker has a criminal intent and that the stalking should evoke fear in the victim. However, most stalkers do not have criminal intentions or intentions to hurt the victim. On the contrary, as stalking tends to emerge from close relationships, the stalker's intention is often to build or re-establish a relationship with the victim. However, if these intentions are not met or turned down, the initially harmless forms of communication might progress to more intensive and intimidating, fear-evoking behaviour. Sometimes it is not necessarily the behaviour itself but the way of pursuit and the course of conduct as a whole, which causes distress to the victim (Mullen and Pathé 2001; Rosenfeld 2000; Spitzberg 2002). Consequently, it is how stalking is *experienced* by the victims which is central to understanding and criminalizing stalking, which is also the reason why stalking is often referred to as a victim-defined crime (Mullen *et al.* 1999; Pathé and Mullen 2002).

Other important issues in defining stalking are: the type and minimum number of behaviours required and the duration of stalking. Even if there is still no clear consensus regarding these issues, most definitions share certain key elements, labelling stalking as behaviour that is repetitive, unwanted contact that is perceived by the victim as intrusive and/or threatening (Rosenfeld 2004; Sheridan *et al.* 2003). However, even if there has been much debate over the elements constituting stalking, researchers refer to the same phenomenon and literature. Furthermore, even if defining stalking has been difficult, the studies show that most people have quite a clear picture of what constitutes stalking (Sheridan *et al.* 2003).

Prevalence of stalking

Community studies on stalking in the population show a lifetime prevalence of 12 to 16 per cent for females and 4 to 7 per cent for males (Sheridan *et al.* 2003). However, the prevalence rate of stalking is very much dependent on the definition employed. Furthermore, the prevalence rates also depend on, for example, the study sample (female and/or male samples, representative versus non-representative, convenience versus population based), research design, and the time frame (e.g. one year, life-time prevalence: Jordan *et al.* 2007; Sheridan *et al.* 2003; Tjaden *et al.* 2002). Nonetheless, as shown in Table 6.1, studies on stalking among university students have shown relatively high prevalence rates, ranging from 11 per cent to approximately 40 per cent (Björklund 2010). In line with the studies on student samples, the literature on stalking from community studies and research suggest that young educated people are at greater risk (Fisher *et al.* 2002; Jordan *et al.* 2007; Ravensburg and Miller 2004). However, a review across studies and study populations shows that the mean prevalence rate is only slightly higher in student samples (21 per cent) compared to general population (18 per cent) studies (Spitzberg and Cupach 2007).

TABLE 6.1 Summary of previous studies regarding stalking among university students

Author(s)	Prevalence	Victim-stalker relationship	Definition
Amar 2006 N=601; F	25% Lifetime	Partner Ex-partner Date	A definition of stalking was not provided. The stalking screening question was 'Have you ever been stalked or harassed by a partner, date, or someone important to you?'
Bjerregaard 2002 N=788 F=512, M=276	21% Lifetime	Stranger vs stalker known (e.g. acquaintance, friend, co-worker, boyfriend, husband, family)	The respondents were provided with a general definition of stalking and asked if they believed that they had ever been stalked. The definition of stalking was not reported in the study.
Björklund *et al.* 2010 N=615 F=533, M=82	Lifetime	Strangers Acquaintances Ex-partners	Stalking was defined as 'Persistent unwanted behaviour consisting of several attempts to approach, contact, or communicate that the recipient didn't want and did not encourage' and followed by a question: 'Have you ever experienced persistent, unwanted attention (stalking) from a man/woman?'
Fisher *et al.* 2002 N=4,446; F	13% Within an academic year (in the study, on average a 7-month period)	Stranger vs stalker known (e.g. acquaintance, friend, co-worker, boyfriend, husband, family)	Stalking was asked and defined as 'The same person exhibiting repeated pursuit behavior that seemed obsessive and made the respondent afraid or concerned for her safety.'

TABLE 6.1 (*continued*)

Author(s)	Prevalence	Victim-stalker relationship	Definition
Fremouw *et al.* 1997 N=593 F=319, M=275	24% Lifetime	Strangers Acquaintances Intimate partners	Stalking and stalking victimization were defined as 'Have you ever been stalked, defined as having someone knowingly, and repeatedly following, harassing or threatening you?'
Haugaard and Seri 2003 N=631 80% female 20% men	20% Following a breakup in a relationship	Dating or intimate relationship	The study focuses on stalking and other forms of intrusive contact. Intrusive behaviours were defined as any unwanted behaviour perceived as intrusive. While responding to the questionnaire the participants were asked to refer to a relationship which had begun during high school or college and which one of the persons involved wanted to end.
Jordan *et al.* 2007 N=1,010; F	40% Lifetime 18% While at university 11% Within the past year	Strangers Acquaintances Intimate partners	Stalking and stalking related victimization was defined by responses to behaviourally specific screening questions (e.g. spying, unsolicited emails, phone calls, property damage). A definition of stalking was not provided, however the respondents were asked if they perceived their experience as stalking and how frightened they were by their reported stalking experiences.
Logan *et al.* 2002 N=130 F=84, M=46	27% Following a difficult breakup in a relationship	Intimate partner	A definition of stalking was not provided. While responding to the stalking behavior checklist the participants were asked to refer to a situation following a breakup.

Author(s)	Prevalence	Victim-stalker relationship	Definition
Mustaine and Tewksbury 1999 N=861; F	11% Within six months	Not specified/not reported in the study as routine activity research only uses victim measures	A definition of stalking was not provided. The respondents were asked whether they had been a victim of behavior they defined as stalking.
Spitzberg et al. 1998 N=162 F=93, M=69	27% Lifetime	Not specified/not reported in the study, instructions however refer to intimate relationships	The respondents were provided with some general information regarding relational intrusion and the obsessive relational intrusion/stalking was asked and defined in the questionnaire as follows 'In your lifetime, how often, if at all, has anyone ever obsessively pursued (stalked) you over a period of time for the purpose of establishing an intimate relationship that you did not want by doing any of the following…?'

N = sample size, F = number of female students, M = number of male students

Source: Björklund (2010)

Victim-stalker relationship

Contrasting the public stereotype of a stranger stalker harassing celebrities, stalking tends to emerge from close relationships. Research has shown that most victims (approximately 80 per cent) know their stalkers. Thus, the stalker is usually a former partner, an acquaintance (co-worker, fellow student) or a friend (Spitzberg and Cupach 2007). Similar findings have also been reported among university students. However, while the stalker in most cases is a former partner, the university student population tends to be exposed to *acquaintance* stalkers (Amar 2006; Jordan *et al.* 2007; Spitzberg and Rhea 1999). For example, in a Finnish study on university students, a clear majority (55 per cent) of stalkers were acquaintances, often related to studies (e.g. fellow student) or work (e.g. co-worker, client). Only 25 per cent of the stalkers were ex-partners, and approximately 20 per cent strangers (Björklund *et al.* 2010a). Most stalkers are men (approximately 80 per cent), and the vast majority of the victims are women (Spitzberg and Cupach 2007). Thus, this means that in 10 to 20 per cent of the cases women are the perpetrators and men the targets.

Stalking behaviour

Stalking is composed of a series of actions, which when taken individually, can be seen as legitimate courtship behaviour. Yet in stalking, normal courtship behaviour is taken to an excessive level by, for example, frequently sending dozens of flowers, gifts or emails to a person who experiences the behaviours as unwanted, intrusive and potentially fear-inducing. Certain stalking behaviours are clearly fear-inducing, harmful and illegal, while others are not. However, feelings of fear are warranted as stalking, in many cases, also includes threatening behaviours that can escalate to violence. All in all, stalking includes a broad range of behaviours such as frequent phone calls, emailing, and other electronically-based tactics (cyberstalking), physical approaches, loitering near the victim's school, home or work, driving or walking by, following, contacting third parties, invading the victim's privacy in various ways, breaking in, threats, physical violence, to name just a few. As many as 400 different stalking behaviours have been found across studies and grouped into seven categories in meta-analysis: hyperintimacy; pursuit proximity or surveillance; invasion of privacy; third party pursuit; proxy; intimidation or harassment; psychological manipulation (Spitzberg 2002; Spiztberg and Cupach 2007).

Taken together, stalking can be broadly grouped into three categories: communication/contacting, following/surveillance, and violence/threats (Nadkarni and Grubin 2000). These were also the three stalking behaviour dimensions found in a Finnish study among university students (Björklund *et al.* 2010). These dimensions overlap, i.e. stalking behaviour often includes a mixture of several types of stalking behaviours. The students in the Finnish study for example reported having experienced on average ten of 47 stalking behaviours measured in the study (see also Sheridan *et al.* 2001, for the stalking questionnaire measure). Most common stalking behaviours found across studies are phone calls, personal appearances and contact, following and surveillance (Spitzberg 2002). These are in line with the most frequently reported stalking behaviours by university students (e.g. Amar 2006; Fisher *et al.* 2002; Jordan *et al.* 2007).

Stalking violence

Stalking often begins with relatively harmless forms of contact. Nevertheless, as mentioned above, one of the major causes of concern over stalking is the fear that relatively mild forms of harassment might escalate into potentially dangerous behaviour (Rosenfeld 2000). Meta-analysis across a wealth of studies has shown that the risk of being physically injured or threatened during the course of stalking is justified as approximately one-third of the stalking cases involve physical violence, and one in ten involves sexual violence, and one half some form of threat (Spitzberg and Cupach 2007). Similar rates have been reported in student populations, the prevalence rate ranging from 13 per cent to 36 per cent (Björklund 2010). The risk for violence is considered especially high if the stalker is a former partner (McEwan *et al.* 2007; Mohandie *et al.* 2006; Rosenfeld 2004). Thus, stalking is often referred to as a relationship-centred phenomenon, a variant of intimate violence (Spitzberg 2007). However, it is important to bear in mind that in some recent studies on student samples, acquaintance stalkers were also responsible for a considerable proportion of violence and threats (Björklund *et al.* 2010a). All stalkers groups tend to engage in a relatively broad range of stalking behaviours including behaviours from all above mentioned stalking categories, including contact seeking, following and violence (Björklund *et al.* 2010). Apart from violence, stalking also includes other factors, potentially affecting the victim's health and wellbeing. However, it was the linkage with violence, which led to the criminalization of stalking (Mullen *et al.* 2006).

Stalking duration

The risks in stalking do not only include the risk of violence. It is also the prolonged duration of the stalking which affects the victims. Thus, the persistence and the unknowing of when, and if the stalking is going to stop can lead to severe psychological and social damage (Blaauw *et al.* 2002a). Therefore, it is somewhat surprising that even if stalking duration is one of the key concepts and concerns, it has been relatively underreported and understudied. The mean duration of stalking is approximately two years, while a median stalking case continues for a year or less (Mullen *et al.* 1999; Spitzberg and Cupach 2007). Among college students the reported mean duration has varied from been somewhat lower, i.e. five to ten months (Fisher *et al.* 2002; Björklund *et al.* 2010a). However, more information on stalking duration among university students is needed as not all studies regarding this specific population have reported the duration. The relationship between the stalker and the victim has been shown to be the best predictor of the duration of stalking. Ex-intimates tend to be the most persistent stalkers, while strangers stalk for the shortest period of time. Also acquaintances have been found to be persistent stalkers (McEwan *et al.* 2007, 2009; Mullen *et al.* 2006). Thus, in a recent study on university students, acquaintance stalkers were almost as persistent as ex-intimate stalkers, with strangers stalking for a distinctly shorter period of time (Björklund *et al.* 2010a).

Consequences of stalking

Victims of stalking often experience a number of negative social, psychological and financial consequences of stalking. These deleterious effects on victims' health and well-being have been well documented in the past two decades (e.g. Dressing *et al.* 2007; Hall 1998; Pathé and Mullen 2002). It is not only the risk of violence and threats that causes considerable harm to the victims, it is also the enduring and unpredictable nature of stalking, which is related to high levels of psychopathology. Consequently, it has been argued that the longer stalking continues, the greater the potential damage to the victim and victims' symptoms are known to endure even after the stalking had ended (Blaauw *et al.* 2002; Purcell *et al.* 2005; McEwan *et al.* 2007).

Thus, stalking victims have reported a broad range of health issues along with other effects of stalking which have been collected into different categories in meta-analysis (Spitzberg 2002; Spitzberg and Cupach 2007). The health concerns drawn from a wealth of studies were categorised into general disturbance referring to emotional or psychological lifestyle changes (e.g. major depression, insomnia, somatic complaints, PTSD), affective symptoms, forms of feelings states (e.g. anger, irritation, fear), cognitive health problems, effects on mental state (e.g. confusion, distrust, loss of self-esteem, helplessness), physical health problems (e.g. loss of appetite, nausea, alcohol/drug problems), social problems (e.g. deterioration in social relationships, changes in lifestyle patterns), and resource problems (disruption of work or school, financial problems). Not very many studies have focused on stalking-related health issues in student populations. A broad range of stalking-related health problems have also been reported by university students. Stalking victims in student samples have reported significantly higher levels of mental health and PTSD symptoms compared to non-victims along with somatisation, depression, and general psychological distress (Amar 2006; Fisher *et al.* 2002). However, more information is needed on how stalking affects young people during their study years, as this topic is still understudied in student samples.

Coping with stalking

Coping can be broadly defined as behavioural and cognitive strategies for managing a stressful situation and associated negative emotions (Lazarus and Folkman 1984). Victims' behavioural attempts to cope with their victimization means taking observable and/or instrumental actions and cognitive means include processing of thoughts, emotions, and perceptions, in order to reduce stress (Frieze *et al.* 1987; Waldrop and Resick 2004). When asked about the victims' needs regarding the help from, for example, the police, the victims usually only want one thing: the stalking to stop (Copson and Marshall 2002). Ending the stalking would naturally be the optimal goal or at least be able to somehow intervene with stalking. Unfortunately, this is not often attainable because of the inherently persistent and enduring nature that characterises stalking. Therefore, instead of assuming that a successful outcome involves mastery or resolution (Folkman and Moskowitz 2004), we might have to search for strategies that might promote coping with prolonged stress or resilience.

Even if there is a growing body of stalking research adding to the nature and scope of stalking, there is still much to be known about the effectiveness of various coping tactics and how to prevent and end stalking. Most studies on coping focused on listing tactics of how behavioural coping strategies work, e.g. moving to a new residence, making one's home safer, or changing the phone number. Taken together, the following coping behaviours have been reported across studies (Spitzberg 2002; Spiztberg and Cupach 2007). Moving inward behaviours represent efforts to hide or overlook the problem (denying, meditating, taking drugs), moving outward (contacting third parties for social support or protection), moving toward or with (negotiating or reasoning with the stalker), moving against tactics represent efforts to deter the pursuer (threatening or harming the stalker), and moving away (attempting to escape the stalker). Most victims use a broad range of behaviours and tactics to cope with stalking. Furthermore, studies show that the frequency of coping methods is positively related to stalking victimization and severity. This could reflect that the more victimized an individual is, the more effort he/she puts in to ending it. On the other hand, it could also mirror a lack of effective coping tactics. All in all, there is still much to be known about what type of coping is effective (Nicastro *et al.* 2000; Spitzberg and Cupach 2003).

One of the most important practical recommendations offered by the police is that it is advisable to request the stalker to stop once only, thereafter all communication should be stopped (Copson and Marshall 2002). All victims do not routinely confront the stalker by asking the stalker to stop, as the stalker is often someone known or close to the victim (De Becker 2002). For example, in one study, the majority of female students (78 per cent) confronted their stalker by specifically requesting the person to stop, whilst only half of the male victims asked their stalker to stop (Bjerregaard 2002). Quite the opposite, victims might at first confront the stalker and try reasoning, which however might encourage the stalker to continue. A classic example of how not to react to a stalker's persistence is the one of persistent calling; if the victim answers the phone after the stalker has called 99 times, the stalker only learns that persistence pays, even if it would take 100 calls. Typically, university students try to deal with stalking by ignoring and avoiding the stalker (Amar 2006; Bjerregaard 2002; Fisher *et al.* 2002). In addition, research shows that the help from friends and family plays an important part in victims' lives, while only a minority of university students seek professional help e.g. health care, counselling services, legal advice (Björklund *et al.* 2010b; Jordan *et al.* 2007; Thompson *et al.* 2007).

Theoretical frames for stalking and violence

The theoretical perspectives on stalking are still in relatively early stages. Much of the current knowledge on stalking is based on empirical studies, which in turn try to distinguish different dimensions and typologies of the stalking phenomenon. A typology can be seen as a pre-theoretical framework including dimensions that are seen as important in explaining the phenomenon in question in a less complex and more manageable and understandable way. Thus, in order to explain the stalking phenomenon, research has identified certain stalking typologies based on, for example, stalker characteristics, underlying motivation, stalking behaviours, and victim-stalker relationship. Also, combinations of these dimensions have been presented in different typologies. Even if typologies have been criticised for not being ultimate explanations or complete theories, they have produced useful information to both theory building and practice (Bartol and Bartol 2008; Mullen *et al.* 2006; Spitzberg and Cupach 2007).

However, some theoretical approaches have been proposed to understand and explain the development of stalking behaviour such as attachment theory, relational goal pursuit theory, and routine activity theory. The attachment theory perspective focuses on attachment styles in relation to stalking behaviour; stalking has been suggested as a behavioural indicator for attachment problems. This line of research is, however, still in its early stages and needs to be further validated. Relational pursuit theory, in turn, sees stalking as originating from the idea that people pursue relationships because they are desired goals (Meloy 2007; Spitzberg and Cupach 2007). The routine activity theory (Mustaine and Tewksburry 1999) focuses on the contextual activities (e.g. daily activities, personal behaviours and characteristics) that may increase the likelihood that people will encounter their pursuers. The idea of routine activity theory is that when people move into the public domain their risk for victimization increases, i.e. certain victim characteristics and actions render them more accessible and vulnerable for potential stalkers. Furthermore, because of certain routine activities typical of the study years, students have been found to be easy targets and therefore more likely to be stalked (Fisher *et al.* 2002; Mustaine and Tewksburry 1999). Also, a neurobiological line of understanding the stalker's behaviour has been introduced (Meloy and Fisher 2005). This line of research has focused on how certain neurotransmitters (dopamine and serotonin) may biologically support the stalker's overly focused interest and attention to the victim with the help of modern fMRI technology.

Clinical and law enforcement implications and public policy

The main causes of health problems and a variety of psychosocial symptoms lie in the nature of stalking, i.e. the lengthy duration and the potential risk of violence, caused by a person whom the victim knows. To intervene in this course of conduct is challenging and calls for multiprofessional co-operation between health care and law-enforcement professionals and many other parties. Even if several European countries have gradually passed anti-stalking laws, countermeasures and information on stalking are still urgently needed at many levels of society, from lay people to professionals. It has recently been argued that due to the lack of knowledge there might not be sufficient professional help, networks or multi-disciplinary interventions available for stalking victims and offenders in continental Europe (Dressing *et al.* 2007). Recognition, treatment and prevention of stalking and violence victimization are demanding tasks both for public policy and for professional practice on working with stalking. How should health care professionals and the law enforcement respond?

As a whole, there is limited information available concerning what coping behaviour, strategies or interventions effectively discourage victimization. It is known that most stalking victims, also in university student populations, turn to family and friends for help and only seldom seek professional help. The positive effect of help and social support depends greatly on how the victims are met by the people they tell about their stalking experiences regardless of whether the person is family, a friend or a professional (Carver *et al.* 1989). Thus, when victims do seek help it is essential that they are taken seriously (Copson and Marshall 2002). Additionally, it is preferable that they can find professionals who are familiar with the dynamics of stalking and related violence (Kilpatrick *et al.* 1997; Roberts and Dziegielewski 1996). However, confronting these issues of violence can be equally difficult for both parties. Thus, there is a need for basic training regarding meeting a victim of violence in a health care setting. At the same time, education and knowledge has been suggested as a way of lowering the obstacles for screening for both health care professionals and victims (Erickson *et al.* 2001; Waalen *et al.* 2000).

As the main concern of stalking is the potential risk of violence, it is only natural that risk assessment has concentrated on violence. However, it has mainly focused on the risk of assault even if serious violence is rare in stalking cases (James and Farnham 2003). It is only recently that the risk assessment and management has started to concentrate also on the lengthy duration of stalking and its potential psychosocial damage to the victim. Altogether, research on risk assessment in stalking cases has led to the acknowledgement of its practical importance not only for the law enforcement but also for clinical practice and management (Dressing *et al.* 2006; McEwan *et al.* 2007; Mullen *et al.* 2006). Currently, the victim-stalker relationship is considered as the most robust predictor for stalking violence and stalking duration (James and Farnham 2003). Thus, along with stalking violence, the significance of persistent stalking has been acknowledged among health care and law enforcement professionals (McEwan *et al.* 2009; Mullen *et al.* 2006).

To conclude, one of the main purposes of working against violence and studying it, is to contribute to its prevention. Violence victimization and youth violence prevention is still at an early stage, especially regarding stalking. Such work should be dealt with on several levels (Carr 2005; Farrell and Flannery 2006; Raden 2001). First, on a public policy level, when national programmes against violence are planned, violence against youth should be taken into account as a major issue in light of the national and international victimization surveys and literature supported by the results of the present study. This issue should also be dealt with when planning education programs for health care professionals. Furthermore, multidisciplinary co-operation between health care and law enforcement should be discussed and enhanced. Second, actions against violence should also be a concern for university administration, teaching staff and student health care settings. Third, on an individual level, the victims of violence and professionals working with the victims should be entitled to information concerning violence; how it might affect health, and how it can be treated. One of the first steps that university authorities can take towards youth-violence prevention is that they acknowledge their role in preventing, reporting and taking action to prevent violence including stalking and related behaviour. Some universities and colleges have policies and procedures on harassment including stalking and bullying. It is important that the universities make a clear statement that no form of harassment is tolerated, and that all members of university have a role in creating a safe learning environment. The second crucial step is to translate the policies into actions along with monitoring the effectiveness of the actions. This can be achieved with a clear action plan, which also commits the authorities and all parties involved to the cause. In the case of stalking the action plan should include baseline information on stalking, raise awareness of stalking, help students to recognize and name stalking, offer ways to report and respond to stalking, refer to appropriate support/help, provide training to the staff and encourage them to partnership working, and all in all, help to create a culture that does not support stalking (e.g. Campus violence white paper by Carr 2005; Harassment policy and procedures at the University of Oxford).

References

Amar, A. F. (2006). College women's experience of stalking: Mental health symptoms and change in routines. *Archives of Psychiatric Nursing,* 20(3): 108–16.

Bartol, C. B. and Bartol, A. B. (2008). *Introduction to forensic psychology: Research and application* (2nd edition.). Los Angeles: Sage.

Bjerregaard, B. (2002). An empirical study on stalking victimization. In: K. E. Davies, I. H. Frieze and R. D. Maiuro (Eds.) *Stalking: Perspectives on Victims and Perpetrators.* New York: Springer. pp. 112–37.

Björklund, K. (2010). *Stalking and Violence Victimization Among Finnish University Students.* University of Helsinki Institute of Behavioural Sciences, Studies in Psychology.

Björklund, K., Häkkänen-Nyholm, H., Roberts, K. and Sheridan, L. (2010a). The prevalence of stalking among Finnish university students. *Journal of Interpersonal Violence,* 25(4): 684–98.

Björklund, K., Häkkänen-Nyholm, H., Sheridan, L. and Roberts, K. (2010b). Coping with stalking among university students. *Violence and Victims,* 25(3): 395–408.

Björklund, K., Häkkänen-Nyholm, H., Sheridan, L., Roberts, K. and Tolvanen, A. (2010). Latent profile approach to duration of stalking. *Journal of Forensic Sciences,* 55(4): 1008–014.

Blaauw, E., Sheridan, L. and Winkel, F. W. (2002a). Designing anti-stalking legislation on the basis of victims' experiences and psychopathology. *Psychiatry, Psychology and Law,* 9(2): 136–45.

Blaauw, E., Winkel, F. W., Arensman, E., Sheridan, L. and Freeve, A. (2002). The toll of stalking: the relationship between features of stalking and psychopathology of victims. *Journal of Interpersonal Violence,* 17(1): 50–63.

Carr, J. L. (2005). *American College Health Association campus violence white paper.* Baltimore, MD: American College Health Association.

Carver, C. S., Scheier, M. F. and Weintraub, J. K. (1989). Assessing coping strategies: a theoretically based approach. *Journal of Personality and Social Psychology,* 56(2): 267–83.

Copson, G. and Marshall, N. (2002). Police care and support for victims of stalking. In J. Boon and L. Sheridan (Eds.), *Stalking and Psychosexual Obsession: Psychological Perspectives for Prevention, Policing and Treatment.* Chichester, UK: Wiley. pp. 49–62.

De Becker, G. (2002). I was trying to let him down easy. In: J. Boon and L. Sheridan (Eds.), 2002. *Stalking and Psychosexual Obsession: Psychological Perspectives for Prevention, Policing and Treatment.* Chichester, UK: Wiley. pp. 35–47.

De Fazio, L. (2009). The legal situation on stalking among the European member states. *European Journal of Criminal Policy and Research,* 15(3): 229–42.

Dovelius, A. M., Oberg, J. and Holmberg, S. (2006). Stalking in Sweden. *Prevalence and Prevention. The Swedish National Council for Crime Prevention.* Stockholm: Brottsförebyggande Rädet.

Dressing, H., Gass, P. and Kuehner, C. (2007). What can we learn from the first community-based epidemiological study on stalking in Germany? *International Journal of Law and Psychiatry,* 30(1): 10–17.

Dressing, H., Kuehner, C. and Gass, P. (2006). The epidemiology and characteristics of stalking. *Current Opinion in Psychiatry,* 19(4): 395–99.

Erickson, M. J., Hill, T. D. and Siegel, R. M. (2001). Barriers to domestic violence screening in the pediatric setting. *Pediatrics,* 108(1): 98–102.

Farrell, A. D. and Flannery, D. J. (2006). Youth violence prevention: are we there yet? *Aggression and Violent Behavior,* 11(2): 138–50.

Fisher, B. S., Cullen, F. T. and Turner, M. G. (2002). Being pursued: Stalking victimization in a national study of college women. *Criminology and Public Policy,* 1(2): 257–08.

Fremouw, W. J., Westrup, D. and Pennypacker, J. (1997). Stalking on campus: The prevalence and strategies for coping. *Journal of Forensic Sciences,* 42(4): 666–69.

Frieze, I. H., Hymer, S. and Greenberg, M. S. (1987). Describing the crime victim: Psychological reactions to victimization. *Professional Psychology: Research and Practice,* 18(4): 299–315.

Folkman, S. and Moskowitz, J. T. (2004). Coping: pitfalls and promise. *Annual Review of Psychology,* 55: 745–74.

Hall, D. M. (1998). The victims of stalking. In J. R. Meloy (Ed.), *The Psychology of Stalking: Clinical and Forensic Perspectives.* San Diego, CA: Academic Press. pp. 113–37.

Haugaard, J. J. and Seri, L. S. (2003). Stalking and other forms of intrusive contact after the dissolution of adolescent dating on romantic relationships. *Violence and Victims,* 18(3): 279–97.

James, D. V. and Farnham, F. R. (2003). Stalking and serious violence. *Journal of the American Academy of Psychiatry and the Law,* 31(4): 432–39.

Jordan, C. E., Wilcox, P. and Pritchard, A. J. (2007). Stalking acknowledgement and reporting among college women experiencing intrusive behaviors: implications for the emergence of a 'classic stalking case'. *Journal of Criminal Justice,* 35(5): 556–69.

Kilpatrick, D. G., Resnick, H. S. and Acierno, R. (1997). Health impact of interpersonal violence 3: implications for clinical public policy. *Behavioral Medicine,* 23(2): 79–85.

Lazarus, R. S. and Folkman, S. (1984). *Stress, appraisal and coping.* New York: Springer.

Logan, T. K., Leukefeld, C. and Walker, B. (2002). Stalking as a variant of intimate violence: implications from a young adult sample. *Violence and Victims,* 15(1): 91–111.

McEwan, T. E., Mullen, P. E., and MacKenzie, R. (2009). A study of the predictors of persistence in stalking situations. *Law and Human Behavior,* 33(2): 149–58.

McEwan, T. E., Mullen, P. E. and Purcell, R. (2007). Identifying risk factors in stalking: a review of current research. *International Journal of Law and Psychiatry,* 30(1): 1–9.

Meloy, J. R. (2007). Stalking: the state of the science. *Criminal Behaviour and Mental Health,* 17(1): 1–7.

Meloy, J. R. and Fisher, H. (2005). Some thoughts on the neurobiology of stalking. *Journal of Forensic Sciences,* 50(6): 1472–480.

Meloy, J. R. and Gothard, S. (1995). Demographic and clinical comparison of obsessional followers and offenders with mental disorders. *The American Journal of Psychiatry,* 152: 258–63.

Mohandie, K., Meloy, R., McGowan, M. G. and Williams, J. (2006). The RECON typology of stalking: reliability and validity based upon a large sample of North American stalkers. *Journal of Forensic Sciences,* 51(1): 147–55.

Mullen, P., MacKenzie, R., Ogloff, J., Pathé, M., McEwan, T. and Purcell, R. (2006). Assessing and managing the risks in stalking situations. *Journal of the American Academy of Psychiatry and the Law,* 34(4): 439–50.

Mullen, P. E. and Pathé, M. (2001). Stalkers and their victims. *Psychiatric Times,* 18(4): 43–6.

Mullen, P. E., Pathé, M. and Purcell, R. (1999). Study of stalkers. *American Journal of Psychiatry,* 156(8): 1244–249.

Mullen, P. E., Pathé, M. and Purcell, R. (2001). Stalking: new constructions of human behaviour. *Australian and New Zealand Journal of Psychiatry,* 35(1): 9–16.

Mustaine, E. E. and Tewksbury, R. (1999). A routine activity theory explanation for women's stalking victimizations. *Violence Against Women,* 5(1): 43–52.

Nadkarni, R. and Grubin, D. (2000). Stalking: why do people do it? The behaviour is newsworthy but complex. *British Medical Journal,* 320(7248): 1486–487.

Nicastro, A. M., Cousins, A. V. and Spitzberg, B. H. (2000). The tactical face of stalking. *Journal of Criminal Justice,* 28(1): 69–82.

Pathé, M. and Mullen, P. E. (1997). The impact of stalkers on their victims. *The British Journal of Psychiatry,* 170(1): 12–17.

Pathé, M. and Mullen, P. E. (2002). The victim of stalking. In J. Boon and L. Sheridan (Eds.), *Stalking and Psychosexual Obsession.* New York: John Wiley and Sons. pp. 1–22.

Purcell, R., Pathé, M. and Mullen, P. E. (2002). The prevalence and nature of stalking in the Australian community. *Australian and New Zealand Journal of Psychiatry,* 36: 114–120.

Purcell, R., Pathé, M. and Mullen, P. (2005). Association between stalking victimization and psychiatric morbidity in a random community sample. *The British Journal of Psychiatry,* 187(5): 420–26.

Raden, A. S. (2001). Youth violence prevention: how does the health care sector respond? Washington, DC: National Health Policy Forum.

Ravensberg, V. and Miller, C. (2004). Stalking among young adults: a review of preliminary research. *Aggression and Violent Behavior,* 8(4): 455–69.

Roberts, A. R. and Dziegielewski, S. F. (1996). Assessment typology and intervention with the survivors of stalking. *Aggression and Violent Behaviour,* 1(4): 359–68.

Rosenfeld, B. (2000). Assessment and treatment of obsessional harassment. *Aggression and Violent Behavior,* 5(6): 529–49.

Rosenfeld, B. (2004). Violence risk factors in stalking and obsessional harassment: A review and preliminary meta-analysis. *Criminal Justice and Behavior,* 31(1): 9–36.

Sheridan, L. P., Blaauw, E. and Davies, G. M. (2003). Stalking: knowns and unknowns. *Trauma, Violence and Abuse,* 4(2): 148–62.

Sheridan, L. P., Davies, G. M. and Boon, J. C. W. (2001). Stalking: perceptions and prevalence. *Journal of Interpersonal Violence,* 16(2): 151–67.

Spitzberg, B. H. (2002). The tactical topography of stalking victimization and management. *Trauma, Violence and Abuse,* 3(4): 261–88.

Spitzberg, B. H. and Cupach, W. R. (2003). What mad pursuit? Obsessive relational intrusion and stalking related phenomena. *Aggression and Violent Behavior,* 8(4): 345–75.

Spitzberg, B.H. and Cupach, W. R. (2007). The state of the art of stalking: taking stock of the emerging literature. *Aggression and Violent Behavior,* 12(1), 64–86.

Spitzberg, B. H., Nicastro, A. M. and Cousins, A. V. (1998). Exploring the interactional phenomenon of stalking and obsessive relational intrusion. *Communication Reports*, 11(1): 33–47.

Spitzberg, B. H. and Rhea, J. (1999). Obsessive relational intrusion and sexual coercion victimization. *Journal of Interpersonal Violence*, 14(1): 3–20.

Tjaden, P., Thoennes, N. and Allison, C. J. (2002). Comparing stalking victimization from legal and victim perspectives. In K. E. Davies, I. H. Frieze and R. D. Maiuro, (Eds.), *Stalking: Perspectives on Victims and Perpetrators*. New York: Springer. pp. 9–30.

Thompson, M., Sitterle, D., Clay, G. and Kingee, J. (2007). Reasons for not reporting victimizations to the police: do they vary for physical and sexual incidents. *Journal of American College Health*, 55(5): 277–82.

Waalen, J., Goodwin, M. M., Spitz, A. M., Petersen, R. and Saltzman, L. E. (2000). Screening for intimate partner violence by health care providers. Barriers and interventions. *American Journal of preventive Medicine*, 19(4): 230–37.

Waldrop, A. E. and Resick, P. A. (2004). Coping among adult female victims of domestic violence. *Journal of Family Violence*, 19(5): 291–302.

Westrup, D., Fremouw, W. J., Thompson, R. N. and Lewis, S. F. (1999). The psychological impact of stalking on female undergraduates. *Journal of Forensic Sciences*, 44(3): 554–57.

7

THE RELATIONSHIP BETWEEN MENTAL HEALTH AND BULLYING

Osman Tolga Arıcak

Introduction

One of the most controversial topics in the bullying and cyberbullying literature is the issue of mental health. Mental health is one of the most important explanatory factors for bullying behaviours. Bullying as a form of aggression and antisocial behaviour (Olweus 1994, 1997) and cyberbullying as an online and electronic form of bullying (Arıcak *et al.* 2008; Dredge *et al.* 2014) attracts our attention to the psychological characteristics of bullies given their intentional and repetitive aspects. Naturally, some questions arise in our minds, such as 'Why does a person hurt another person intentionally and repeatedly? Are there certain discriminative characteristics of bullies from others? Does childhood bullying continue in later stages of life?' At the same time, similar questions emerge for victims: 'What feelings, reactions, and repercussions do victims experience? Does short-term or long-term exposure to bullying affect the mental health of victims?' Currently, these questions are being investigated by researchers. The answers found to these questions are crucial in order to lead policies and develop new prevention and intervention programs for bullying and victimization among university students.

In this chapter, we will briefly define what constitutes mental health, identify factors that influence bullying, and describe the relationship between bullying, victimization, and mental health issues.

Mental health perspective towards bullying

Each human being is a biopsychosocial-spiritual entity (Puchalski *et al.* 2014; Sulmasy 2002). Biological structures, based on genetic components and the environment, interact with each other continuously. Psychological characteristics such as intelligence, personality, and mental health are the results of this interaction

(McClearn 2004; Miller 2002). Because of this interaction, it is impossible to separate mental health from general health. According to the World Health Organization (1946), 'Health is a state of complete physical, mental and social well-being and not merely the absence of disease or infirmity.' Consistent with this definition, mental health is defined as 'A state of well-being in which every individual realizes his or her own potential, can cope with the normal stresses of life, can work productively and fruitfully, and is able to make a contribution to her or his community' (WHO 2013).

Mental health, as a part of general health, affects how we think, feel and act. It also determines how we make decisions, build relationships with other people, and cope with life problems. Some factors can contribute to mental health problems across the lifespan. There are two major contributors to mental health problems: biological factors and life experiences (Mentalhealth.gov 2014).

Biological factors have long been considered as main contributors for mental disorders. According to the biomedical approach, mental illnesses are caused by structural and functional disorders of the nervous system. In particular, many disorders are explained by changes in neurotransmitters, synaptic receptors, and local dysfunctions (Deacon 2013). However, research and treatment processes in mental health applications have shown that biomedical explanations alone are not sufficient to understand the formation of mental disorders. Therefore, a biopsychosocial model that considers life experiences within a holistic approach, has been accepted by mental health professionals as a strong model for elucidating mental disorders (Pilgrim 2002).

Today, the most commonly used tool to diagnose the disorders in clinical psychology and psychiatry is the *Diagnostic and Statistical Manual of Mental Disorders* (DSM-5) (American Psychiatric Association 2013). Although there are more than 150 disorders in DSM-5, bullying is not currently defined as an independent disorder. The major reason is that bullying has been found to be associated with multiple psychiatric problems already defined in DSM such as conduct disorder (Kokkinos and Panayiotou 2004), oppositional defiant disorder (Coolidge *et al.* 2004), antisocial personality disorder (Krastins *et al.* 2014), and attention-deficit hyperactivity disorder (ADHD) (Unnever and Cornell 2003). These disorders are all characterized by problems in emotional and behavioural self-control in DSM-5. The first diagnostic criterion of conduct disorder in DSM-5 (APA 2013, p. 469) states that the afflicted individual 'often bullies, threatens, or intimidates others.' Furthermore, because of its close association with conduct disorder, antisocial personality disorder has dual listing in the chapter on disruptive, impulse-control, and conduct disorders and in the chapter on personality disorders. Olweus (1994, 1997) as the first eminent researcher on bullying also viewed bullying as 'a component of antisocial behaviour.' In his writings, Olweus (1994, p. 1181; 1997, p. 501) notes that, 'from this perspective, it is natural to predict that youngsters who are aggressive and bully others, run an increased risk of later engaging in other problem behaviours such as criminality and alcohol abuse.' Subsequent studies (Luukkonen *et al.* 2011; Renda *et al.* 2011; Sourander *et al.* 2007) have affirmed Olweus' claim.

Which factors influence the bullying?

There is a continuing debate over genetic and environmental influences on aggression and antisocial behaviour (Tuvblad and Beaver 2013; Wang *et al.* 2013). Some research suggests that genetic influences are the primary source of aggression and antisocial behaviour, whereas other research suggests that environmental influences are the primary source of aggression and antisocial behaviour (Jacobson *et al.* 2000). The best approach on this debate is to understand the contributions of each perspective separately.

Genetic influences on bullying

Genetic studies on bullying are relatively new. Ball *et al.* (2008) conducted the first study to investigate bullying with a genetic-informed methodology. They investigated 1,116 twins (N=2232) for bullying and victimization. In the study, the best model demonstrated that genetic factors could explain 61 per cent of the variability in bullying behaviours, while non-shared environmental factors could only explain 39 per cent of the variability. They also discussed how genetic-based characteristics such as impulsivity and sensation seeking could mediate the genetic influences on bullying.

Previous genetic-oriented studies focused primarily on aggressive and antisocial behaviours instead of bullying. However, these studies are informative to understand the genetic influences of bullying as a form of aggressive and antisocial behaviour (Olweus 1997). The first studies on hereditary influence of human aggression, violence and antisocial behaviours appeared four decades ago (Crowe 1974; Rosenthal 1975; Wilson 1975). Although there were some studies on the relationship between heredity and human aggression, most early research focused on behavioural genetics in animals rather than humans (Fuller 1960).

Methodologically there are two different approaches to genetic studies on human subjects: behavioural genetics and molecular genetics. Behavioural genetics studies are based on observation, interview and self-report techniques generally. There are three groups of samples in genetics research on aggression, bullying and antisocial behaviour in the literature: parents and biological children (families), monozygotic (MZ) and dizygotic (DZ) twins, and adopted children. Parents and their biological children are useful subjects as the family members share both the same genes and the same environment. If there is no relationship between parents and children for aggressive or bullying behaviour in the result, it could be concluded that there is no genetic or shared environmental influence for this kind of behaviour. However, if there is a relationship between parents and children, we cannot infer that the relationship is a function of genes or environment. Therefore, research on MZ/DZ twins and adopted children is necessary in order to explore the influences of genes and the environment (Arseneault *et al.* 2003; DiLalla and Gottesman, 1991; Schmidt *et al.* 2002).

There has been considerable research conducted with twins and adopted children reporting genetic influence on aggression and antisocial behaviour (Crowe 1974; DiLalla 2002; Lacourse *et al.* 2014; Moffitt 2005). According to DiLalla (2002, p. 614), 'there is a sufficient evidence of heritable component for aggression in childhood.' The literature reviews of Cadoret (1982) and DiLalla and Gottesman (1991) on early studies demonstrate that genetic factors can explain antisocial behaviour more significantly than environmental factors. Similarly, the results of a meta-analysis on data from 24 genetically informative studies suggest a strong overall genetic effect explaining up to 50 per cent of the variance in aggression (Miles and Carey 1997). Moffitt (2005) reviewed more than 100 quantitative genetic studies on antisocial behaviour and concluded that 'genes influence approximately 50 per cent of the population variation in antisocial behaviours' (p. 58). Moffitt (2005) also showed that while some studies (Lyons *et al.* 1995) suggested that genetic factors could explain 7 per cent of variation in antisocial behaviour, others (Arseneault *et al.* 2003; Hicks *et al.* 2004) suggested that it could explain 80 per cent of the variation.

Beside behavioural genetics research, new emerging molecular studies confirm the effect of genetic components on aggression and antisocial behaviours. Schmidt *et al.* (2002) suggest that there is a significant association between the long allele DRD4 receptor gene and aggression. The genes catechol-O-methyltransferase (COMT) (Rujescu *et al.* 2003) and 5-HT-2A (Giegling *et al.* 2006) are also found to be associated with aggression-related traits. Monoamine oxidase A (MAO-A) function is also related to dopamine, serotonin and epinephrine as the major three neurotransmitters in the brain. These three neurochemicals are associated with mood, impulse control and fight-or-flight reactions. Lower levels of activity in MAO-A alleles have been found to be associated with aggression, violent delinquency and lower inhibitory control (Tuvblad and Beaver 2013).

Environmental influences on bullying

As stated earlier, genetic components explain the variability in aggression and antisocial behaviours between 7 per cent and 80 per cent, with an average rate of influence across the literature of approximately 50 per cent. Therefore, it is clear that some other environmental factors have an effect on bullying and antisocial behaviours. A meta-analysis of 51 twin and adoption studies demonstrate that additive genetic influences can explain 32 per cent, nonadditive genetic influences explain 9 per cent, shared environmental influences explain 16 per cent, and nonshared environmental influences explain 43 per cent of variation in antisocial behaviour (Rhee and Waldman 2002). Based on previous studies, Moffitt (2005) concluded that while shared environmental factors influence 20 per cent of population variation, non-shared environmental factors influence 20 to 30 per cent of variation in antisocial behaviours. The literature suggests that major environmental factors are constellated around dysfunctional familial situations, negative childhood experiences and peer relationships.

Bullying and familial influences

Parenting and parental attitudes play an important role on bullying and antisocial behaviours (Feinberg *et al.* 2007; Krastins *et al.* 2014). According to Nickerson, Mele and Osborne-Oliver (2010), attachment, social support, and family systems form the basis of healthy parent-child relationships. Comparative studies on differences between children who live at home and those who live in institutions also show the importance of parent-child relationships on mental health (Bowlby 1952; Maclean 2003). There is considerable research indicating the relationship between parental attachments and bullying behaviours. In a study conducted with 7,290 adolescents, Marini *et al.* (2006) found that bullies reported higher levels of maternal attachment alienation and attachment problems than non-bully adolescents. In another study conducted with university students from different ethnic backgrounds (Williams and Kennedy 2012), male participants experiencing higher levels of attachment anxiety with their fathers were found to be more likely to enact bullying behaviours than male students with lower levels of attachment anxiety. Female students who demonstrated higher attachment avoidance with their mothers and higher attachment anxiety with their fathers reported higher engagement in physical bullying. In addition, female students were more likely to report engaging in relational aggression when they scored higher on measures of attachment anxiety to their mothers. Williams and Kennedy (2012, p. 332) also stated that 'since paternal uninvolvement and negative family experiences were correlated with victimization, it was predicted that attachment to parents would be linked to victimization.' Schneider, Atkinson, and Tardif (2001) also showed that parental attachment was associated with social competence and intimacy in peer relations.

Social support is another effective and protective variable on bullying behaviours. The literature demonstrates that both parental support and peer support play a pivotal role in bullying (Holt and Espelage 2007). A seven-year longitudinal study by Pettit, Bates, and Dodge (1997) showed that experiencing parental warmth, inductive discipline, and parental support in early years buffer children from externalizing behavioural problems during adolescence. The study of Conners-Burrow *et al.* (2009) also shows the effect of parent and teacher support on bullying. In their study, adolescents who were not engaged in bullying report less depression and more social support than adolescents who bully others.

Family cohesion and functional relationships among family members are other important factors for childhood adjustment (Hill 2002; Nickerson *et al.* 2010). There is substantial evidence that interparental conflict, poor relationship with parents, unstable parental relationship, and having single or divorced parents increase the possibility of bullying behaviours among youngsters (Flouri and Buchanan 2003; Hill 2002; Rutter 2000; Smith *et al.* 1995; Spriggs *et al.* 2007). Studies also show that exposure to domestic violence as a victim or a bystander (Baldry 2003), exposure to physical or sexual abuse (Shields and Cicchetti 2001), harsh discipline (Smith and Myron-Wilson 1998), and a lack of a warm relationship with parents, and both authoritarian and inconsistent parental attitudes (Baldry and

Farrington 2000) are strongly associated with bullying behaviours. All these negative experiences facilitate engagement in bullying behaviours in all levels of education including university. As might be expected, students who are bullied by parents or siblings often bully others without guilt. We can predict that this might also influence the behaviour of students who bully or are bullied.

Bullying and peer influences

Friends at university also have an influence on the development of bullying and antisocial behaviours. Typically, people show a negative attitude towards bullying. However, social milieu and group norms shape the relationship among peers. Peer context and group dynamics are very important determinants of bullying behaviour (Pozzoli and Gini 2010). According to Myers and Cowie (2013) and Sutton and Smith (1999), bullying is a group process and, as a result, many young people can become involved in bullying if the group creates suitable conditions. Salmivalli *et al.* (1996) also indicate that bullying occurs in a group generally. Bullies are usually supported by their group assistants or reinforcers. Thus, group cooperation facilitates perpetration. Hamarus and Kaikkonen (2008) claim that peer pressure is a very important creator of bullying behaviours. There are some common peer experiences and behaviours that lead to bullying including having fun, amusement, teasing, misleading, misrepresentation and some group rituals.

Another contributor to the occurrence of bullying is being victimized by peers. Exposure to bullying, such as physical or sexual abuse, humiliation, intimidation and rejection by peers, incite some people to bully others in the same way. Frequent exposure to these kinds of behaviours may also maintain and reinforce bullying behaviours. Thus, 'cycles of bullying between youngsters and their peers could support the development of chronic bullying behaviours' (Lacourse *et al.* 2014, p. 8). Kim and Leventhal (2008) report that both exposure to bullying and engagement in bullying are associated with antisocial behaviour and severe suicidal ideation.

Finally, the literature demonstrates the effect of environmental and contextual factors on the formation of bullying as they interact with genetic components. Interaction between genetic components and environmental factors (GxE) determines the complex relationship between bullying and mental health problems. Unlike the classic chicken-egg discussion, we will consider this issue in the context of the bidirectional relationship model.

Personality characteristics of bullies

The literature related to personality characteristics of bullies mostly focuses on externalizing disorders. According to Olweus (1997, p. 500), 'one of the distinctive characteristics of the bullies is their aggression toward others.' As mentioned before, bullying is defined as a form of aggression (Olweus 1994). However, some externalizing characteristics make bullying more complicated. For example, one of these characteristics is impulsivity, which is related to poor self-control and deviant behaviour (Unnever and Cornell 2003). Low self-control and high impulsivity make engaging in bullying easy. The extended meta-analytic study of Ruiz, Pincus and Schinka (2008) shows the relationship between antisocial personality and impulsivity. They also demonstrate that low levels of agreeableness and conscientiousness, high excitement seeking, low deliberation and low self-discipline are predictive and associated characteristics of an antisocial personality. A longitudinal study covering from age eight to early adulthood demonstrates that people engaging in bullying in childhood are more likely to exhibit antisocial personality traits than other groups (Sourander *et al.* 2007). Another study examining the personality traits of bullies shows that pure bullies have higher extraversion, psychoticism, and neuroticism scores than non-bully peers. Bullies also exhibit greater emotional inhibition than non-bullies (Connolly and O'Moore 2003). Research based on DSM-IV-TR (*Diagnostic and Statistical Manual of Mental Disorders-IV-Text Revision*) by Coolidge, DenBoer, and Segal (2004) revealed that bullies had significantly higher passive aggression (in Axis II), aggression, dangerousness, emotional liability, and disinhibition scores (in other clinical scales) than the non-bully group.

Cowie and Jennifer (2008) identify a relationship between narcissism and bullying. They make a connection between narcissistic personality and bullying, stating that 'narcissistic individuals tend to be self-focused, highly competitive, exhibitionistic and aggressive people who have lack of empathy and who tend to be manipulative and self-seeking in their interpersonal relationships' (Raskin and Novacek 1989, cited in Cowie and Jennifer 2008, p.57). Daly (2006) also reports that high personal self-esteem and narcissism are associated with bullying, and there is a predicted interaction between personal self-esteem, narcissism, and bullying. Additionally, Olweus (1997) describes other characteristics of bullies such as a positive attitude toward violence, hostility, and a strong need to dominate others.

Psychiatric symptomatology as predictor of bullying

'Most lifetime mental disorders have first onset during or shortly before the typical university age and these problems can be precipitated or exacerbated by the variety of stressors in university life' (Eizenberg *et al.* 2007, p. 534), including bullying and victimization. A large body of literature shows the relationship between bullying and psychiatric symptoms. Different studies (Luukkonen *et al.* 2010; Rønning *et al.* 2009; Sourander *et al.* 2007) show that psychiatric symptoms appear in frequent bullies at a higher rate as compared to infrequent bullies. The most notable symptoms related to bullying are psychotic symptoms. Kelleher *et al.* (2008) investigated psychiatric symptoms in 211 adolescents in Ireland and reported that bullies showed significantly higher psychotic symptoms than victims and non-bullies. They also showed that 'adolescents reporting psychotic symptoms were six times more likely to have experienced child physical abuse, four times more likely to have experienced child sexual abuse, and ten times more likely to have witnessed domestic violence than adolescents who did not report such symptoms' (2008, p. 379). This finding is also important for identifying a relationship between familial influences and mental health. In another study, Arıcak (2009) proposed a path model explaining cyberbullying and cyber victimization. Somatization, obsessive-compulsive symptoms, interpersonal sensitivity, depression, anxiety, hostility, phobic anxiety, paranoid ideation and psychotic symptoms were taken as predictors in the model. Data revealed that the best predictors of cyberbullying were hostility and psychotic symptoms. Similarly, Palmer and Thakordas (2005) reported that all types of bullying such as physical, verbal, direct and indirect were significantly correlated with a high level of hostility. Hostility and psychotic symptoms, occurring alongside a lack of empathy, evoke the antisocial personality disorder related to psychopathy (Kiehl 2006).

The relationship between anxiety, depression, and bullying is a controversial issue. While some studies (Kaltiala-Heino *et al.* 2010; Roland 2002; Yang *et al.* 2013) claim that engaging in bullying is associated with anxiety and depression, others suggests no association (Arıcak 2009; Fekkes *et al.* 2004). In the light of literature, it is hard to say whether anxiety or depression causes bullying, or whether bullying itself causes these kinds of mood problems. Instead of the causal relationship, anxiety and depression can be considered as comorbid conditions for bullying (see APA 2013, p. 475).

Effects of bullying on victims

Victimization is another face of bullying. There is also a significantly growing body of literature on victimization. Victimization may occur at any point in the lifespan. However, research shows that some people tend to be a victim or even are more likely to be continuously victimized than others (see chapter 4 by Pörhölä in the present book) (Smith *et al.* 2004). Ball *et al.* (2008) report that genetic endowments have a major effect (73 per cent) on victimization compared to the environment (27 per cent), whereas the behavioural-genetic study of Brendgen *et al.* (2008) shows that peer victimization is influenced by environmental factors and not associated with the genetic disposition of children. Arseneault, Bowes, and Shakoor (2010, p. 721) claim that 'being bullied is not a situational event and can last for several years.' The reasons for victimization are beyond the scope of this paper. Regardless of the reasons, it is clear that short-term or long-term bullying has detrimental effects on victims (Cowie 2013). The literature on victimization shows that the seriousness of these detrimental effects depends on type, frequency, intensity, severity of bullying, and the personal characteristics of the victim. However, the most severe effects of bullying described in the literature indicate that mental health problems result from victimization (Turner *et al.* 2013).

Mental health problems in victims

Literature related to mental health problems in victims mostly focuses on internalizing disorders. Both cross-sectional and longitudinal studies show that anxiety and depression are the most common psychological outcomes of bullying

(Arseneault *et al.* 2010; Hawker and Boulton 2000; Reijntjes *et al.* 2010). In particular, a higher level of victimization is associated with generalized anxiety, agoraphobia, panic disorder (Copeland *et al.* 2013), social isolation, low self-esteem, increased self-harm behaviour (Arseneault *et al.* 2010; Cowie 2013), suicidality (Klomek *et al.* 2007), and psychosomatic symptoms (Gini and Pozzoli 2009).

Schreier *et al.* (2009) report that there is a significant association between childhood victimization and psychotic symptoms in adolescence if victimization is chronic and severe. Similarly, another longitudinal study of Wolke *et al.* (2013) shows that exposure to bullying in childhood increases the risk of developing psychotic experiences in adolescence. Moreover, Wolke *et al.* (2012) report that chronic victims who are bullied by peers show borderline personality symptoms at a significantly higher rate than non-victimized people.

In a remarkable case study conducted by Cowie and Myers (2014), university students were divided into three groups as bully, victim and bystander. Students were given a role-play scenario and invited to assume their assigned roles within their groups. The result of the study showed that while all victims described the nature of the relationship depicted in the scenario as bullying and exclusion, bullies and bystanders identifed the scenario as joking or fun. Content analysis also revealed that all students in the victim group were unhappy and felt sad. Although this was based on a fictional case study, the finding suggests that exposure to bullying creates negative emotions such as unhappiness, anxiety or depression.

When one considers these findings, it should be addressed that there is not enough evidence showing a direct cause-effect relationship between victimization and mental health problems in the literature. As Reijntjes *et al.* (2010, p. 250) state, 'the findings suggest a symmetrical bi-directional association between peer victimization and mental health problems.' In this light, we should read the findings as cautious and inconclusive.

Conclusion

Although there is a growing body of literature on the relationship between bullying, cyberbullying and mental health, the existing literature has generally focused on the child and adolescent population (Cowie *et al.* 2013), and almost all studies state the long-term effect and future directions of bullying and victimization in terms of mental health problems.

Though only a few researchers such as Arıcak (2009), Cowie and Myers (2014), Schenk, Fremouw and Keelan (2013) have studied the relationship between bullying, cyberbullying, and mental health problems in university students, their findings are consistent with other bullying studies conducted on children and adolescents.

Under the light of meta-analytic studies, both cross-sectional and longitudinal research has revealed that there is a strong relationship between bullying, cyberbullying, victimization, and mental health problems (Cowie 2013; Doane *et al.* 2014; Reijntjes *et al.* 2010; Wolke *et al.* 2013). Although there are some inconsistent results in terms of variables such as sex, age, and social context in the literature, the general finding that a relationship exists between bullying and mental health problems is consistent. The only issue, as stated before, is that existing literature does not give us any directional or causal relationship between bullying and mental health problems. It seems that this ambiguity would continue for a long time because of the nature of the problem and the ethical considerations related to experimental studies on bullying.

Finally, there is a dearth of research into bullying among university students. Further research is needed to perform meta-analytic studies on relationships between bullying, victimization, and mental health problems in university students. Although some individuals come to university with a predisposition to bully or be bullied, there is evidence that interventions at individual, group and policy levels can alleviate the problem. Studying university students would enable a better understanding of the longitudinal outcomes of bullying behaviours, which would in turn inform policies and future research with children, adolescents and young adults. These studies would also provide valuable information to develop prevention and intervention programs to cope with bullying and victimization at university and how successful coping strategies might work.

References

American Psychiatric Association (2013). *Diagnostic and Statistical Manual of Mental Disorders.* (5th ed.) Arlington, VA: American Psychiatric Publishing.

Arıcak, O. T. (2009). Psychiatric symptomatology as a predictor of cyberbullying among university students. *Eurasian Journal of Educational Research,* 9(34): 167–84.

Arıcak, T., Siyahhan, S., Uzunhasanoğlu, A., Sarıbeyoglu, S., Cıplak, S., Yılmaz, N. and Memmedov, C. (2008). Cyberbullying among Turkish adolescents. *CyberPsychology and Behavior,* 11(3): 253–61.

Arseneault, L., Bowes, L. and Shakoor, S. (2010). Bullying victimization in youths and mental health problems: 'much ado about nothing'? *Psychological Medicine,* 40(5): 717–29.

Arseneault, L., Moffitt, T. E., Caspi, A., Taylor, A., Rijsdijk, F. V., Jaffee, S., Ablow, J. C. and Measelle, J. R. (2003). Strong genetic effects on cross-situational antisocial behavior among 5-year-old children according to mothers, teachers, examiner-observers, and twins' self-reports. *Journal of Child Psychology and Psychiatry,* 44(6): 832–48.

Baldry, A. C. (2003). Bullying in schools and exposure to domestic violence. *Child Abuse and Neglect,* 27(7): 713–32.

Baldry, A. C. and Farrington, D. P. (2000). Bullies and delinquents: personal characteristics and parental styles. *Journal of Community and Applied Social Psychology,* 10(1): 17–31.

Ball, H. A., Arseneault, L., Taylor, A., Maughan, B., Caspi, A. and Moffitt, T. E. (2008). Genetic and environmental influences on victims, bullies and bully-victims in childhood. *The Journal of Child Psychology and Psychiatry,* 49(1): 104–12.

Bowlby, J. (1952). *Maternal Care and Mental Health* (2nd ed.). Geneva: World Health Organization.

Brendgen, M., Boivin, M., Vitaro, F., Girard, A., Dionne, G. and Perusse, D. (2008). Gene-environment interaction between peer victimization and child aggression. *Development and Psychopathology,* 20(2): 455–71.

Cadoret, R. J. (1982). Genotype-environment interaction in antisocial behavior. *Psychological Medicine,* 12(2): 235–39.

Conners-Burrow, N. A., Johnson, D. L., Whiteside-Mansell, L., McKelvey, L. and Gargus, R. A. (2009). Adults matter: protecting children from the negative impacts of bullying. *Psychology in the Schools,* 46(7): 593–604.

Connolly, I. and O'Moore, M. (2003). Personality and family relations of children who bully. *Personality and Individual Differences,* 35(3): 559–67.

Coolidge, F. L., DenBoer, J. W. and Segal, D. L. (2004). Personality and neuropsychological correlates of bullying behavior. *Personality and Individual Differences,* 36(7): 1559–69.

Copeland, W. E., Wolke, D., Angold, A. and Costello, E. J. (2013). Adult psychiatric outcomes of bullying and being bullied by peers in childhood and adolescence. *JAMA Psychiatry,* 70(4): 419–26.

Cowie, H. (2013). The immediate and long-term effects of bullying. In I. Rivers and N. Duncan (Eds.) *Bullying: Experiences and Discourses of Sexuality and Gender.* New York: Routledge. pp. 10–18.

Cowie, H., Bauman, S., Coyne, I., Myers, C., Pörhöla, M. and Almeida, A. (2013). Cyberbullying amongst university students: an emergent cause for concern? In P. K. Smith and G. Steffgen (Eds.), *Cyberbullying Through the New Media: Findings from an International Network.* New York: Psychology Press. pp. 165–77.

Cowie, H. and Jennifer, D. (2008). *New Perspectives on Bullying.* New York: McGraw Hill Open University Press.

Cowie, H. and Myers, C. A. (2014). Bullying amongst university students in the UK. *The International Journal of Emotional Education,* 6(1): 66–75.

Crowe, R. R. (1974). An adoption study of antisocial personality. *Archives of General Psychiatry,* 31(6): 785–91.

Daly, A. L. (2006). *Bullying, Victimization, Self-esteem, and Narcissism in Adolescents.* Online Published Doctoral Dissertation. Adelaide: Flinders University.

Deacon, B. J. (2013). The biomedical model of mental disorder: a critical analysis of its validity, utility, and effects on psychotherapy research. *Clinical Psychology Review,* 33(7): 846–61.

DiLalla, L. F. (2002). Behavior genetics of aggression in children: review and future directions. *Developmental Review,* 22(4): 593–622.

DiLalla, L. F. and Gottesman, I. I. (1991). Biological and genetic contributors to violence: Widom's untold tale. *Psychological Bulletin,* 109(1): 125–29.

Doane, A. N., Pearson, M. R. and Kelley, M. L. (2014). Predictors of cyberbullying perpetration among college students: an application of the Theory of Reasoned Action. *Computers in Human Behavior,* 36: 154–62.

Dredge, R., Gleeson, J. and Garcia, X. P. (2014). Cyberbullying in social networking sites: an adolescent victim's perspective. *Computers in Human Behavior,* 36: 13–20.

Dsm5.org, 2013. *Highlights of Changes from DSM-IV-TR to DSM-5.* Available at http://www.dsm5.org/Documents/changes%20from%20dsm-iv-tr%20to%20dsm-5.pdf, pp. 1–19. [Accessed on 7 May 2014].

Eizenberg, D., Gollust, S. E., Golberstein, E. and Hefner, J. L. (2007). Prevalence and correlates of depression, anxiety, and suicidality among university students. *American Journal of Orthopsychiatry,* 7(4): 534–42.

Feinberg, M. E., Button, T. M., Neiderhizer, J. M., Reiss, D. and Hetherington, E. M. (2007). Parenting and adolescent antisocial behavior and depression: evidence of genotype x parenting environment interaction. *Archives of General Psychiatry,* 64(4): 457–65.

Fekkes, M., Pijpers, F. I. M. and Verloove-Vanhorick, S. P. (2004). Bullying behavior and associations with psychosomatic complaints and depression in victims. *The Journal of Pediatrics*, 144(1): 17–22.

Flouri, E. and Buchanan, A. (2003). The role of mother involvement and father involvement in adolescent bullying behavior. *Journal of Interpersonal Violence*, 18(6): 634–44.

Fuller, J. L. (1960). Behavior genetics. *Annual Review of Psychology*, 11(1): 41–70.

Giegling, I., Hartmann, A. M., Möller, H. J. and Rujescu, D. (2006). Anger- and aggression-related traits are associated with polymorphisms in the 5-HT-2A gene. *Journal of Affective Disorders*, 96(1): 75–81.

Gini, G. and Pozzoli, T. (2009). Association between bullying and psychosomatic problems: a meta-analysis. *Pediatrics*, 123(3): 1059–65.

Hamarus, P. and Kaikkonen, P. (2008). School bullying as a creator of pupil peer pressure. *Educational Research*, 50(4): 333–45.

Hawker, D. S. J. and Boulton, M. J. (2000). Twenty years' research on peer victimization and psychosocial maladjustment: a meta-analytic review of cross-sectional studies. *Journal of Child Psychology and Psychiatry*, 41(4): 441–55.

Hicks, B. M., Krueger, R. F., Iacono, W. G., McGue, M. and Patrick, C. J. (2004). Family transmission and heritability of externalizing disorders. *Archives of General Psychiatry*, 61(9): 922–28.

Hill, J. (2002). Biological, psychological and social processes in the conduct disorders. *Journal of Child Psychology and Psychiatry*, 43(1): 133–64.

Holt, M. K. and Espelage, D. L. (2007). Perceived social support among bullies, victims, and bully-victims. *Journal of Youth and Adolescence*, 36(8): 984–94.

Jacobson, K. C., Prescott, C. A. and Kendler, K. S. (2000). Genetic and environmental influences on juvenile antisocial behaviour assessed on two occasions. *Psychological Medicine*, 30(6): 1315–325.

Kaltiala-Heino, R., Fröjd, S. and Marttunen, M. (2010). Involvement in bullying and depression in a 2-year follow-up in middle adolescence. *European Child and Adolescent Psychiatry*, 19(1): 45–55.

Kelleher, I., Harley, M., Lynch, F., Arseneault, L., Fitzpatrick, C. and Cannon, M. (2008). Associations between childhood trauma, bullying and psychotic symptoms among a school-based adolescent sample. *The British Journal of Psychiatry*, 193(5): 378–82.

Kiehl, K. A. (2006). A cognitive neuroscience perspective on psychopathy: evidence for paralimbic system dysfunction. *Psychiatry Research*, 142:(2–3): 107–128.

Kim, Y. S. and Leventhal, B. (2008). Bullying and suicide. A review. *International Journal of Adolescent Medicine and Health*, 20(2): 133–54.

Klomek, A. B., Marrocco, F., Kleinman, M., Schonfeld, I. S. and Gould, M. S. (2007). Bullying, depression, and suicidality in adolescents. *Journal of the American Academy of Child and Adolescent Psychiatry*, 46(1): 40–9.

Kokkinos, C. M. and Panayiotou, G. (2004). Predicting bullying and victimization among early adolescents: Associations with disruptive behavior disorders. *Aggressive Behavior*, 30(6): 520–33.

Krastins, A., Francis, A. J. P., Field, A. M. and Carr, S. N. (2014). Childhood predictors of adulthood antisocial personality disorder symptomatology. *Australian Psychologist*, 49(3): 142–50.

Lacourse, E., Boivin, M., Brendgen, M., Petitclerc, A., Girard, A., Vitaro, F., Paquin, S., Ouellet-Morin, I., Dionne, G. and Tremblay, R. E. (2014). A longitudinal twin study of physical aggression during early childhood: evidence for a developmentally dynamic genome. *Psychological Medicine*: 1–11. Available at http://dx.doi.org/10.1017/S0033291713003218.

Luukkonen, A. H., Rasanen, P., Hakko, H., Riala, K. and The STUDY-70 Workgroup (2010). Bullying behavior in relation to psychiatric disorders and physical health among adolescents: a clinical cohort of 508 underage inpatient adolescents in Northern Finland. *Psychiatry Research,* 178(1): 166–70.

Luukkonen, A. H., Riala, K., Hakko, H. and Rasanen, P. (2011). Bullying behaviour and criminality: a population-based follow-up study of adolescent psychiatric inpatients in Northern Finland. *Forensic Science International,* 207(1–3): 106–10.

Lyons, M. J., True, W. R., Eizen, S. A., Goldberg, J., Meyer, J. M., Faraone, S. V., Eaves, L. J. and Tsuang, M. T. (1995). Differential heritability of adult and juvenile antisocial traits. *Archives of General Psychiatry,* 52(11): 906–15.

Maclean, K. (2003). The impact of institutionalization on child development. *Development and Psychopathology,* 15(4): 853–84.

Marini, Z. A., Dane, A. V., Bosacki, S. L. and YLC-CURA (2006). Direct and indirect bully-victims: differential psychosocial risk factors associated with adolescents involved in bullying and victimization. *Aggressive Behavior,* 32(6): 551–69.

McClearn, G. E. (2004). Nature and nurture: interaction and coaction. *American Journal of Medical Genetics Part B (Neuropsychiatric Genetics),* 124B(1): 124–30.

Mentalhealth.gov (2014). *What is mental health?* Available at http://www.mentalhealth.gov/basics/what-is-mental-health/index.html. [Accessed 10 April 2014].

Miles, D. R. and Carey, G. (1997). Genetic and environmental architecture of human aggression. *Journal of Personality and Social Psychology,* 72(1): 207–17.

Miller, P. H. (2002). *Theories of Developmental Psychology* (4th edition). NY: Worth Publishers.

Moffitt, T. E. (2005). Genetic and environmental influences on antisocial behaviors: Evidence from behavioral–genetic research. *Advances in Genetics,* 55: 41–104.

Myers, C. A. and Cowie, H. (2013). University students' views on bullying from the perspective of different participant roles. *Pastoral Care in Education,* 31(3): 251–67.

Nickerson, A. B., Mele, D. and Osborne-Oliver, K. M. (2010). Parent-child relationships and bullying. In S. R. Jimerson, S. M. Swearer and D. L. Espelage (Eds.) *Handbook of Bullying in Schools: an International Perspective.* New York: Routledge. pp. 187–97.

Olweus, D. (1994). Annotation: bullying at school: basic facts and effects of a school-based intervention program. *Journal of Child Psychology and Psychiatry,* 35(7): 1171–90.

Olweus, D. (1997). Bully/victim problems in school: facts and intervention. *European Journal of Psychology of Education,* 11(4): 495–510.

Palmer, E. J. and Thakordas, V. (2005). Relationship between bullying and scores on the Buss-Perry aggression questionnaire among imprisoned male offenders. *Aggressive Behavior,* 31(1): 56–66.

Pettit, G. S., Bates, J. E. and Dodge, K. A. (1997). Supportive parenting, ecological context, and children's adjustment: a seven-year longitudinal study. *Child Development,* 68(5): 908–23.

Pilgrim, D. (2002). The biopsychosocial model in Anglo-American psychiatry: past, present and future? *Journal of Mental Health,* 11(6): 585–94.

Pozzoli, T. and Gini, G. (2010). Active defending and passive bystanding behavior in bullying: the role of personal characteristics and perceived peer pressure. *Journal of Abnormal Child Psychology,* 38(6): 815–27.

Puchalski, C. M., Vitillo, R., Hull, S. K. and Reller, N. (2014). Improving the spiritual dimension of whole person care: reaching national and international consensus. *Journal of Palliative Medicine*, 17(6): 642–56.

Reijntjes, A., Kamphuis, J. H., Prinzie, P. and Telch, M. J. (2010). Peer victimization and internalizing problems in children: a meta-analysis of longitudinal studies. *Child Abuse and Neglect*, 34(4): 244–52.

Renda, J., Vassallo, S. and Edwards, B. (2011). Bullying in early adolescence and its association with anti-social behaviour, criminality and violence 6 and 10 years later. *Criminal Behaviour and Mental Health*, 21(2): 117–27.

Rhee, S. H. and Waldman, I. D. (2002). Genetic and environmental influences on antisocial behavior: a meta-analysis of twin and adoption studies. *Psychological Bulletin*, 128(3): 490–529.

Roland, E. (2002). Aggression, depression, and bullying others. *Aggressive Behavior*, 28(3): 198–206.

Rønning, J. A., Sourander, A., Kumpulainen, K., Tamminen, T., Niemela, S., Moilanen, I., Helenius, H., Piha, J. and Almqvist, F. (2009). Cross-informant agreement about bullying and victimization among eight-year-olds: whose information best predicts psychiatric caseness 10-15 years later? *Social Psychiatry and Psychiatric Epidemiology*, 44(1): 15–22.

Rosenthal, D. (1975). Heredity in criminality. *Criminal Justice and Behavior*, 2: 3–21.

Rujescu, D., Giegling, I., Gietl, A., Hartmann, A. M. and Möller, H. J. (2003). A functional single nucleotide polymorphism (V158M) in the COMT gene is associated with aggressive personality traits. *Biological Psychiatry*, 54(1): 34–9.

Ruiz, M. A., Pincus, A. L. and Schinka, J. A. (2008). Externalizing pathology and the five-factor model: a meta-analysis of personality traits associated with antisocial personality disorder, substance use disorder, and their co-occurrence. *Journal of Personality Disorders*, 22(4): 365–88.

Rutter, M. (2000). Psychosocial influences: critiques, findings, and research needs. *Development and Psychopathology*, 12(3): 375–405.

Salmivalli, C., Lagerspetz, K., Björkqvist, K., Österman, K. and Kaukiainen, A. (1996). Bullying as a group process: participant roles and their relations to social status within the group. *Aggressive Behavior*, 22(1): 1–15.

Schenk, A. M., Fremouw, W. J. and Keelan, C. M. (2013). Characteristics of college cyberbullies. *Computers in Human Behavior*, 29(6): 2320–27.

Schmidt, L. A., Fox, N. A., Rubin, K. H., Hu, S. and Hamer, D. H. (2002). Molecular genetics of shyness and aggression in preschoolers. *Personality and Individual Differences*, 33(2): 227–38.

Schneider, B. H., Atkinson, L. and Tardif, C. (2001). Child-parent attachment and children's peer relations: a quantitative review. *Developmental Psychology*, 37(1): 86–100.

Schreier, A., Wolke, D., Thomas, K., Horwood, J., Hollis, C., Gunnell, D., Lewis, G., Thompson, A., Zammit, S., Duffy, L., Salvi, G. and Harrison, G. (2009). Prospective study of peer victimization in childhood and psychotic symptoms in a nonclinical population at age 12 years. *Archives of General Psychiatry*, 66(5): 527–36.

Shields, A. and Cicchetti, D. (2001). Parental maltreatment and emotion dysregulation as risk factors for bullying and victimization in middle childhood. *Journal of Clinical Child Psychology*, 30(3): 349–63.

Smith, J., Twemlow, S. W. and Hoover, D. W. (1995). Bullies, victims and bystanders: a method of in-school intervention and possible parental contributions. *Child Psychiatry and Human Development*, 30(1): 29–37.

Smith, P. K. and Myron-Wilson, R. (1998). Parenting and school bullying. *Clinical Child Psychology and Psychiatry,* 3(3): 405–17.

Smith, P. K., Talamelli, L., Cowie, H., Naylor, P. and Chauhan, P. (2004). Profiles of non-victims, escaped victims, continuing victims and new victims of school bullying. *British Journal of Educational Psychology,* 74(4): 565–81.

Sourander, A., Jensen, P., Ronning, J. A., Niemela, S., Helenius, H., Sillanmaki, L., Kumpulainen, K., Piha, J., Tamminen, T., Moilanen, I. and Almqvist, F. (2007). What is the early adulthood outcome of boys who bully or are bullied in childhood? The Finnish 'from a boy to a man' study. *Pediatrics,* 120(2): 397–404.

Spriggs, A. L., Iannotti, R. J., Nansel, T. R. and Haynie, D. L. (2007). Adolescent bullying involvement and perceived family, peer and school relations: commonalities and differences across race/ethnicity. *Journal of Adolescent Health,* 41(3): 283–93.

Sulmasy, D. P. (2002). A biopsychosocial-spiritual model for the care of patients at the end of life. *The Gerontologist,* 42(3): 24–33.

Sutton, J. and Smith, P. K. (1999). Bullying as a group process: an adaptation of the participant role approach. *Aggressive Behavior,* 25(2): 97–111.

Turner, M. G., Exum, M. L., Brame, R. and Holt, T. J. (2013). Bullying victimization and adolescent mental health: general and typological effects across sex. *Journal of Criminal Justice,* 41(1): 53–9.

Tuvblad, C. and Beaver, K. M., 2013. Genetic and environmental influences on antisocial behavior. *Journal of Criminal Justice,* 41(5): 273–76.

Unnever, J. D. and Cornell, D. G., 2003. Bullying, self-control, and ADHD. *Journal of Interpersonal Violence,* 18(2): 129–47.

Wang, P., Niv, S., Tuvblad, C., Raine, A. and Baker, L. A. (2013). The genetic and environmental overlap between aggressive and non-aggressive antisocial behavior in children and adolescents using the self-report delinquency interview (SR-DI). *Journal of Criminal Justice,* 41(5): 277–84.

Williams, K. and Kennedy, J. H. (2012). Bullying behaviors and attachment styles. *North American Journal of Psychology,* 14(2): 321–38.

Wilson, H. (1975). Juvenile delinquency, parental criminality and social handicap. *British Journal of Criminology,* 15(3): 241–50.

Wolke, D., Lereya, S. T., Fisher, H. L., Lewis, G. and Zammit, S. (2013). Bullying in elementary school and psychotic experiences at 18 years: a longitudinal, population-based cohort study. *Psychological Medicine:* 1–13. Available at http://dx.doi.org/10.1017/S0033291713002912.

Wolke, D., Schreier, A., Zanarini, M. C. and Winsper, C. (2012). Bullied by peers in childhood and borderline personality symptoms at 11 years of age: a prospective study. *Journal of Child Psychology and Psychiatry,* 53(8): 846–55.

World Health Organization (1946). Preamble to the constitution of the World Health Organization as adopted by the international health conference, New York, 19–22 June 1946. Available at http://www.who.int/about/definition/en/print.html. [Accessed on 10 April 2014].

World Health Organization (2013). Mental health: a state of well-being. Available at http://www.who.int/features/factfiles/mental_health/en. [Accessed on 10 April 2014].

Yang, S. J., Stewart, R., Kim, J. M., Kim, S. W., Shin, I. S., Dewey, M. E., Maskey, S. and Yoon, J. S. (2013). Differences in predictors of traditional and cyber-bullying: a 2-year longitudinal study in Korean school children. *European Child and Adolescent Psychiatry,* 22(5): 309–18.

PART IV

The social context of bullying at university

8

CYBER-AGGRESSION AMONG MEMBERS OF COLLEGE FRATERNITIES AND SORORITIES IN THE UNITED STATES

Jessica Simmons, Sheri Bauman, and Johanne Ives

Introduction

Today's college students are digital natives for whom digital technology is not a novelty but rather a part of the fabric of their lives. The availability and increasing affordability of smartphones, tablets and laptop computers makes it commonplace for college students to live digitally. As of January 2014, 98 percent of American adults age 18 to 29 owned a cell phone and 83 percent had a smart phone. In addition, 81 percent use their phones to send and receive text messages, and 60 percent use them to access the Internet (Pew Research Internet Project 2014 http://www.pewinternet.org/fact-sheets/mobile-technology-fact-sheet/). Ninety percent of that age group use social networking sites, 67 percent of them access those sites from their phones.

The term *cyberbullying* is widely used to describe online aggressive behavior, but our earlier focus groups with college students (Baldasare *et al.* 2012) showed that they find the term juvenile and inappropriate for the kinds of negative behavior they observe and experience. Therefore, we will use the term *cyber-aggression* to refer to hurtful actions perpetrated using digital technology. Students also felt strongly that whether or not a given communication was hurtful should be determined by the recipient rather than the sender. Thus, we will retain that perspective in this chapter.

While most digital communications are positive or neutral in tone, aggressive behavior online is not unknown. In fact, it is the few tragic incidents of cyber-aggression that are sometimes sensationalized by the media, that give the impression that cyberbullying is a major problem. The few empirical investigations revealed that the prevalence of victimization in colleges and universities ranged from 9 percent to 34 percent, with variations attributed to measurement differences. It was the suicide of Tyler Clementi in 2010, a college freshman who was humiliated online, which prompted the authors to investigate the presence of cyberbullying at their large public university in the southwestern United States.

In our survey of 1,078 students at the university, although overall rates of cyberbullying and victimization were quite low, we found that members of sororities and fraternities (known as Greek organizations) were more frequent victims of cyber-aggression than their non-member peers, and more specifically, more often reported being humiliated via technology (Bauman and Baldasare, in press). Facebook was the most frequently reported vehicle for such activities, but others were also used. The focus groups that are the subject of this chapter were conducted to gain a deeper understanding of these findings.

Greek life: sororities and fraternities

In the United States, fraternities and sororities are gender-specific organizations that were originally established to meet cultural and academic needs of students (Whipple and Sullivan 1998). The very first collegiate fraternity, Phi Beta Kappa, was founded in 1776 at the College of William and Mary during the American Revolution. Phi Beta Kappa was the first organization to identify itself using Greek letters, establish secret rituals to commemorate their beliefs and values, and design symbols that only members of that fraternity wore (Whipple and Sullivan, 1998). Later, in 1870, when women were allowed to enroll in college, Kappa Alpha Theta was founded as the first Greek fraternity for women. In 1906, the first Black Greek Letter Organization (BGLO), Alpha Phi Alpha Fraternity Inc., was founded at Cornell University (Ross 2000). Cultural-based fraternities and sororities emerged on college campuses when founding members realized the value of these tight-knit communities. Their national presence has been growing as more students of color are attending college. In the 1970s there were a few Latino Greek Letter Organizations (LGOs) founded on college campuses, but it was not until the mid to late 1990s that LGOs became more prominent on campuses across the country (Muñoz and Guardia 2009). These groups, among others, expanded throughout colleges and universities around the country.

Originally, some of these organizations were designed for students of specific religions, ethnicities, and academic interests, but most are now predominantly social in focus. Many students join these groups in their first or second year of college, as a way to make friends, partake in social and community events, and form lifelong friendships and support systems. While the prevalence and popularity of Greek life membership varies by university and region of the United States, it has been a fixture in American universities for hundreds of years. At the university at which this study was conducted, there are 47 sororities and fraternities, with about 5,200 students in the community, making up 16 percent of the undergraduate population. In 2012, students of color composed 37 percent of the undergraduate population at this institution; slightly fewer than 24 percent of Greek students were non-white. Seventeen of the 47 chapters are BGLOs or cultural-based sororities and fraternities. Members pay fees ranging from $115 to $1,402 annually. Some chapters have housing available at additional cost; about 700 women live in sorority houses. Potential members go through a recruitment process known colloquially as 'rush,' and must be selected by current members for admission to the group.

The current study

The theoretical framework that guided our exploration is that of social identity theory (Tajfel and Turner 1979). From this perspective, it is natural to categorize objects and people into groups in order to sort out the social environment. It would be too overwhelming, for example, to have to figure out each animal individually, so we might mentally categorize them as predators (i.e. dangerous) or companions (pets). With humans, we may categorize them by gender, race, socioeconomic class, and many other characteristics. We also identify with some of those groups, and incorporate them into our social identity. For example, one may think of herself as an African-American female professional. Once she has identified with a given social group, she tends to compare that group with others, and seeks to maintain the belief that one's own group compares well with other groups. This process of social comparison increases our individual self-esteem. However, this also generates rivalries between groups, as each group seeks to maintain its elevated status and as members act to preserve that status which is tied to their self-esteem.

To gain an understanding of the higher rates of involvement in cyber-aggression among students in Greek life, we conducted focus groups with students who are members of sororities and fraternities on campus. The semi-structured discussions allowed participants to hear others' comments and engage in interactions that provide depth and breadth to the discussion, and provided an opportunity for the researchers to probe responses (Taylor and Bogdan 1998). The study was approved by the university's IRB.

Method

Participants

The focus group included seven students (five female). Due to cancellations by participants scheduled for the second focus group, a face-to-face interview was conducted with one male student. Of the eight participants, six were from 'multicultural' or National Panhellenic Council (NPHC) sororities, which they differentiated from the 'mainstream' (National Panhellenic Conference or North American Interfraternity Council) chapters in several ways. First, the multicultural sororities' (and fraternities that also have such organizations) membership was comprised of women from racial/ethnic minorities. Second, these chapters did not have houses in which members could live or host social events. Third, the dues for these chapters were much lower than those of mainstream sororities. Finally, the women in the multicultural sororities and fraternities identified much more strongly with their organizations, seeing it as a highly salient aspect of their self-concept and identity and an essential support system for their college success. In order to protect the privacy of participants, names of participants used in this chapter are pseudonyms.

Procedure

The researchers worked with the third author, the Assistant Dean of Students for Fraternity and Sorority Programs, to arrange the groups. At the beginning of the fall semester, the first author attended a meeting with presidents of all Greek Life organizations and presented the focus group information and opportunity. Students were offered pizza in appreciation of their participation. Additional efforts to recruit participants were via emails sent to subscribers of a Greek life listserv maintained by the university. When students emailed regarding their interest, a Doodle poll was created and emailed to students to find the best time for the focus group(s).

A protocol for the focus groups was developed and used to guide the discussion. During the 90-minute session, verbatim notes were taken by the first author while the second author led the group. With students' consent, the sessions were also audio recorded. Following the meetings, the written notes were transcribed and compared to the audio recordings to ensure accuracy and completeness. The same procedure was used for the interview.

Data analysis

Because this was a follow-up study, our theoretical sensitivity (Glaser and Strauss 1967) and presence on the campus enhanced the process by which we gave meaning to the data and detected salient remarks by participants. Because the quantity of data was manageable, open coding was done collaboratively by the first two authors. First, the authors read and re-read the transcripts to immerse themselves in the data. Then, each participant's utterance was coded with a keyword or phrase that captured the essential meaning. Then the codes were reviewed and combined into general categories (Miles and Huberman 1994). Categories were then combined into broader themes, described below.

Prevalence

Students in both the focus group and interview reported that they did not believe cyber-aggression was a major issue within the university Greek life community. However, they described how inter-chapter rivalries, recruitment competition, and poor behavior at social events generated online exchanges that were sometimes disrespectful and aggressive.

Social media use

Facebook

Participants endorsed Facebook above all other social media for their fraternity and sorority connections. Students in Greek life use Facebook's ability to create organization pages and private groups to communicate within their own social circles. Participants reported using Facebook to host individual sorority and fraternity 'pages' where their members could communicate privately or publicly to raise awareness or advertise events. One fraternity member explained, 'Each sorority has a Facebook page, and when we have philanthropic events, we post a link to our event on their page. [For example,] who wants a t-shirt, who wants tickets to our events ...'

Facebook was also used for aggressive purposes. Emma described the use of memes (i.e. Internet images, sometimes with sayings attached to them) to discriminate against or make fun of a specific fraternity or sorority. In addition to memes, students reported the existence of Facebook pages made for the sole purpose of targeting other groups. Participants stated that these pages are nearly always anonymous, meaning that the pages are created without revealing the identity of the page's creator. Anonymity was viewed by participants as a way to protect their personal and organization's reputation. If the author of a page were unknown, it would be difficult to hold an individual or organization accountable for the inappropriate content.

Participants talked about positive uses of Facebook as well. One female student who is part of a multicultural group, explained,

> As recently as last year, two brothers passed away in a car accident in Texas. In a matter of 24 hours there were already people raising money to pay for funeral expenses. A huge part of Greek life is community and networking. You have this network of people from around the country, who are from both the brothers' fraternity and other fraternity and sororities from around the country, who heard about this story. Their particular organization got support from the whole Greek community.

Yik Yak

In addition to Facebook, another social media tool that was frequently mentioned by participants is the smartphone app, Yik Yak. Yik Yak's popularity has gained momentum in the past few years, particularly on college campuses. On this app, users post brief anonymous messages that are distributed to the 500 Yik Yak users who are geographically closest to the sender. Then recipients of the posts are able to rate those posts 'up' or 'down.' According to our participants, Yik Yak was most often utilized during *rush* (formal recruitment), which is typically a week-long event used for North American Interfraternity Council (NIC), or National Panhellenic Conference (NPC) organization recruitment either before, or at the beginning of the semester, in which undergraduate students visit a number of Greek organizations to meet with current members and express their interest in joining. Participants explained that recruitment is a competition, in which hopeful students are competing for a 'bid' or invitation of acceptance into their organization of choice and the chapters are trying to look as appealing as possible to attract the 'best' students, who will continue their Greek legacy. Sometimes, in order to appear better than other organizations, members take action on apps like Yik Yak, to talk negatively about their competition. During the first focus group, a male student from a NIC fraternity explained, 'We seek out Yik Yaks about our organization and others. I think the use of Yik Yak is more common among the mainstream groups, as we use it to fix our reputations.' Emma continued, 'Doing this [using Yik Yak] is kind of like saving face.'

In the interview session, the male student who represented a NIC fraternity also referenced Yik Yak while discussing recruitment. He explained,

'We use technology because then we don't need to say something to someone's face. During rush, we use Yik Yak to say crap about one another. I've posted things because I thought they were funny, people did that everywhere. You might be trying to make yourself look better… if we see one girl saying that her sorority is going to one frat's event, we might say, 'Oh they suck, come to ours instead.' It's about being better.'

He also explained his fraternity's lack of favor for Facebook as a way to make themselves outwardly look better than other organizations, 'People want to do everything anonymously. That's why Yik Yak is so popular.'

Twitter

Only one participant reported witnessing cyberbullying on Twitter:

I've seen so many crazy things on Instagram and Twitter. Mostly Twitter. There is a Twitter page only for the Divine Nine [the less formal name also used to refer to the historically Black Greek letter organizations that comprise the National Pan-Hellenic Council NPHC chapters]. Four or five of these groups feel they're more powerful. [The page] is only for them, and its purpose is only to trash talk about one another. And only members of the Divine 9 can follow the page on Twitter. Even if you request to follow their page, you're going to get denied. They talk about the other five organizations (referencing five of the Divine Nine that do not currently have chapters on the campus where the focus groups were conducted. I was caught in-between all of this on campus because I was friends with so many people in different organizations.'

This participant went on to explain that she has also witnessed sorority women using Twitter to make fun of one another, particularly after big social events.

Instagram

Instagram is a website that is usually accessed via smartphone apps. Individuals use Instagram to share their photos. These photos can have short captions included with them, and users have the ability to 'like' a photo. Then, users have the ability to share these images on Facebook, so potentially, they can reach a wide audience. This platform was mentioned by a number of students throughout the focus group. They described how memes (i.e. pictures meant to be funny or provocative in nature with or without accompanying sayings or phrases) can often be used to make fun of other organizations and their endeavors. More specifically, students might use Instagram to share photos or memes that put down other Greek organizations on campus.

Diversity

In the discussion of cyber victimization and the use of technology as a means of communication, the theme of the division of social/mainstream NPX and NIC organizations and multicultural groups was frequently expressed. Emma explained that this divide begins with sorority recruitment. She explained,

> 'From a recruitment standpoint there is just so much competition to get people. [For us,] there are fewer minority groups, and the number of students interested in joining us is even smaller. The mainstream groups begin recruiting earlier in the school year for rush. So then there are less people, and therefore, more competition, for minority groups.'

While some minorities join the mainstream groups, historically, white students have made up the majority. One ethnic minority student who was a member of a NIC fraternity noted, 'Caucasians are way more common in the mainstream groups. Just looking at the history of Greek life, sororities and fraternities have been based on Christian values, so mainstream groups are the better place to represent those values.' He continued, 'Other groups are more about the idea of diversity and embracing that.' Another male student agreed, 'Yeah, they have different points of view.'

Sometimes, minority students who join traditionally white sororities or fraternities are subject to the scrutiny by members of the multicultural chapters. Emma explained,

> I know a black female in a mainstream sorority and she is not loving it because the majority of individuals in that sorority don't identify the way she does. If you don't join one of the multicultural chapters, you can get

scrutinized because you don't fit in, and then you're not part of their community. Does it play out outline? Yes, definitely, via memes, Facebook pages… People always want a justification. Black girl in a white sorority – why? And vice versa. The thought people have is, 'What's your ulterior motive?

This idea of joining the 'right' group can also be a problem for individuals who are mixed race. Emma, who is mixed, explained,

'My mom wanted me to be in a mainstream group like she was, but that wasn't my goal at all. I didn't feel like I belonged or was welcomed. I didn't understand why I felt that way. For mixed people, it's not really about how you identify yourself, it's more how other people identify you.'

With regard to diversity, one participant spoke about the public image of Greek life being a white activity. She said,

'I think that now, with technology being so popular, it's sometimes difficult because the image we see, as minorities, [are similar to what] we see in the images online. That is that the majority of [Greek life people] are white. Even on Facebook and around campus, everything you see [related to Greek life] is of white traditional Greek life individuals wearing their colors and letters. You don't see us. … If you walk around campus, you're going to see the mainstream students more easily – so, it's like, kind of what happens in our everyday lives is translated online.'

Another participant added,

'In our world of Greek life, we have so much pride for our principles, how we were founded, where we came from, the fact that we are minority groups, so if anyone has anything negative to say, it automatically turns into a competition.'

We also asked about students who identify as lesbian, gay, bisexual, transgender, and queer (LGBTQ), and whether those students were welcomed by their Greek life peers. 'There are lots of organizations that cater to that community [LGBTQ]. Organizations pride themselves on diversity. I know individuals who target other individuals, but not necessarily organizations as a whole.' A different student continued,

In our council [governing bodies of several sororities and fraternities], we're not supportive, and fraternities are especially not supportive. Frats are all about being macho men, so if a guy isn't like that, he's likely to become a target. Not one organization is accepting. Some of them even get heat for accepting gay guys. It's like, you knew they were like that [identified as LGBTQ] and you accepted them – what does that say about your organization? It was a big deal. There was one college student in Maryland who was denied induction into a fraternity, and people speculated it was because he was gay – and that's probably true.'

However, a NIC fraternity member disagreed. He said,

'No, they aren't targeted. There are actually a couple of students in my frat who are openly gay and no one cares. Really, they're an asset because a lot of gay guys know a lot of girls and they'll bring them around. I mean, I don't mind it because it's the twenty-first century and it's not a big deal anymore. Maybe back in the 1980s when fraternities were becoming a big thing it might have been a big deal because it was less accepted to be LGBTQ, but nowadays I don't think people care too much.'

While this fraternity appeared to be open-minded and relatively accepting, there were stipulations around how individuals represented themselves. This interview participant explained,

'We're a Jewish fraternity [mainstream], so we try not to judge others if they're cool people, and we try to hang out with them. I know there are other fraternities who have taken in others who are gay, but for the most part, though, you might get made fun of if you accept someone who is – not to be like close-minded or anything – but like a 'flaming' [flamboyant] gay. Someone who walks around with tight Capri pants, you know, have the interesting haircuts… those are the ones who might make your group kind of bad. I don't want to sound closed-minded, but it's harder to get along with the ones whose whole life is around being gay. Like the ones in our group, it's a part of their life, but they do other things. They're really involved in school activities, they have lots of friends who they hang out with… They're just normal people, it's just their sexual preference. But I don't really ever hear of anyone say bad things, like, 'Oh that girl is a lesbian.''

It seems important to note here that a male participant in the focus group, who was also a member of a mainstream fraternity, lingered after others left and told the researchers that he is gay and had not divulged that to his fraternity brothers. He felt certain they would no longer accept him if they knew.

Reputation

Participants expressed how important building and maintaining group reputation, popularity, and prestige are to Greek life groups. As one student pointed out, Greek groups are run as a business, and just like with businesses, networking, reputation, and namesake are imperative for maintaining stability, student interest, finances, and longevity. Interestingly, however, unlike for the majority of businesses, the reputations of Greek groups are built on the backs of undergraduate college students and their quality is geared towards their same-aged peers.

The importance of reputation of the sorority or fraternity was of paramount importance to the participants. The need to have a positive reputation was threatened by negative actions such as Yik Yak comments, and online smear campaigns that were designed to enhance the stature of one organization at the expense of other Greek groups. Their competitiveness with one another was framed as the desire to appear favorably and to be well-respected in the larger community. Participants stressed that in order to get ahead, you must put one another down. The participants in multicultural groups, who described themselves as closer and more supportive of one another, were quick to put mainstream groups down for behavior that they admitted to engaging in themselves.

Within this theme, we identified several different perspectives or audiences for whom the reputation is pitched. For example, to appear desirable to the student body, having the most physically attractive members, fun parties, and best houses are the preferred strategies. Reputation for the public audience may include hosting philanthropic events and fundraising. One participant provided described her view of how this unfolds: 'Mainstream groups do community service – they raise funds and donate thousands of dollars. So, they raise a lot of money for causes, but they also do a lot of bad things.' Such feelings can inflame animosities between the groups. One participant described a time when a fight broke out between two fraternities at a public philanthropic event hosted by a sorority. He reported that the girls were upset because this event, designed to enhance their reputation, was disrupted by this conflict.

Public persona is also important given that Greek life is often associated in the press with raucous parties and excessive alcohol consumption. This is especially noteworthy because nearly half of undergraduate students at these events are likely underage. One participant observed that

> Groups are careful about what they put online – in terms of the public. You're not allowed to post pictures of parties or drinking because it makes your group look bad. That's PR [public relations]. People might take pictures at someone else's party, but you don't have to say everyone was drunk. You might just take a picture in front of someone's letter, which says enough. That's why we like hanging out with sororities; they have these rules too.

Acknowledging that it is difficult to ensure that photos are not taken given the ubiquity of cell phones, he said, 'Well it's only a problem if there is alcohol in the picture. If not, you can't tell there is anything illegal going on. You could just say it was a sober party.'

The multicultural Greek students had a slightly different take on the idea of NPC sorority and NIC fraternity parties and reputation. One student expressed frustration,

> 'The mainstream groups, at least historically, have not and are not reprimanded for having these huge blow-out events. Some events are okay, but the thing to do there is drink underage and then get on the bus [campus shuttle] drunk. It happens at their group houses and no one gets in trouble. With the minority groups, we do this too, but we don't post about it. We're miles away from campus, at our own houses. They're not even afraid to associate their organizations with what they're doing.'

Another student explained, 'You're not even supposed to be drinking with your letters on.'

Pride

While the mainstream and multicultural groups differed in their views on maintaining a positive reputation, they agreed that a positive reputation of the organization must be preserved. Members took great pride in their organization, and cared deeply that outsiders viewed them as admirable groups. To explore this idea, we inquired about the motivation for online attacks.

> In Greek life, it's more that you're sometimes taught to get on the bandwagon with other people. There is a lot of groupthink – more and more people join in. When it comes to Greek organizations, if someone is older and has been around others who don't agree with how they think, it's like, 'Why don't you agree with me? Why don't you have loyalty to me? Why are you taking someone else's side? You're not motivated to self-think in Greek life. Loyalty is to your [Greek] brother or sister and you can't cross that line. It's about pride.'

Another student continued,

> No one wants to feel like your organization is second best. No one wants another one to make them feel like you made a bad decision in joining [that particular group]. It's all about maintaining your pride, which is refreshing because you're in a group and you get closer [with the other members].

Finally, a member summarized this theme:

> Mainstream organizations aren't the same as us, which is why a lot of the minority groups were founded. We don't pride ourselves on just being Latino. When I talk to other groups, they don't have the same love for their organizations as I have for mine.'

Aggression within and between groups

Although the differences between the mainstream organizations and the multicultural ones appear in the descriptions of several of the themes above, it was such a prominent concept that we discuss it here as an additional theme. In the focus group, minority students frequently took pains to distinguish themselves from the predominantly white Greek organizations. When the facilitator reported the findings from the survey noted above, and requested participants' thoughts about them, Casey responded,

> '[In Greek life], there is a wide network of students you interact with. It's all about power and influence, honestly. Everyone wants to be better than everyone else and the best way to do that is to put down others. In my council, National Pan-Hellenic Council, they downplay [cyberbullying] a lot because they don't call it what it is. I feel like the bigger organizations or chapters will undercut others. I feel we have a better reputation than more popular councils (i.e. governing boards), the ones with the fancy houses on campus. They have bad reputations.'

She went on to say,

> 'There are thousands of [Greek life students], and they have the most negative reputations on campus. At [another local university], for example, the Greek population is large as well. [The university's] reputation is downplayed because of the number of Greek organizations.'

The NIC group member knew very little of the multicultural groups, and said about them,

> 'I have no idea what they do. They just do stuff with each other. I know they do a lot of the same things that social ones do, but they only hang out with one another. ... [Unlike the social groups], it's a way to get to know people of the same ethnicity.'

What can be done?

Participants reflected on whether any approach might reduce the quantity of cyber-aggression among Greek life students. One student explained,

> Things come down from 20 years ago. It's how you're brought up – if you teach your kid to be a bully, they're going to be a bully. If you're taught to hate or dislike other organizations, that's how you're going to feel. How you treat those who come after you – that starts with us. We influence the other people coming after.

Another participant added:

> It's an important point. I think there is some hesitance in that because [if you treat other organizations well], people will start to think you're watered down. If you're brought in to care about others, that doesn't work. You're supposed to be the best organization, so you can't care about other people. You get respect from boasting that you're the best. In my organization, we're going to give you your brownie points if you have pride in your organization. There is pressure [to be the best], but you do give props to other passionate people.

Cyberbullying prevention video

In an effort to combat cyberbullying, the Office of the Dean of Students created a video, *Cyber Bullying – Bully in the Room*. It begins with a young woman lying in bed after a night of partying. As she is looking at her phone, a male student enters and begins reading her several cruel comments that were left on her Facebook pictures from the previous night. He reads such comments, 'Cute duck face…Is it hunting season already? Hmm, not something a friend of mine would say but whatever…', 'Do you even REMEMBER doing any of this? What were you doing?' and 'Desperate for attention.' As he reads the comments, laughing, the young woman becomes increasingly and visibly upset. The end of the video has a message encouraging students to seek help from the Office of the Dean of Students if they are facing similar experiences.

Participants in the focus group shared their reactions to the video. Although they laughed during the viewing, they concluded the video was unrealistic. One student said:

> I've never seen anything like that [happen]. Friends stick up for one another and it makes you look bad when you post something mean.
>
> It's not like only one girl will go out and get super drunk – they're always with friends. And, there are thousands of people who do this every night. I don't know. Cyberbullying doesn't really seem like an issue to me. I've never heard or seen anyone saying, 'This really affected me…'. You might hear a few situations here and there in the media, but it's not common.

One woman said that she understood the message the video was trying to give, but that she would have preferred something more realistic. Other focus group members agreed.

While the video was a thoughtful initiative to target the issue of cyberbullying on campus, our students found it hard to take seriously. Nevertheless, the video got their attention and generated lively discussion, which is perhaps an admirable accomplishment of prevention messaging.

Discussion

The focus group and interview took a different direction from the one the researchers anticipated. That difference was largely due to the composition of the group, with the majority of members being from multicultural groups. It is important to note that all members of Greek organizations should have received invitations to participate, yet 75 percent of those who participated were in the multicultural organizations. They clearly felt so strongly about the positive attributes of their organizations (as distinct from what they saw as the frivolous value of mainstream organizations) that perhaps they wanted to ensure that they were not excluded from this opportunity to clarify how their organizations use digital technology in the collegiate context.

One of the findings was that although the students were clear that cyberbullying was not a big problem among Greek life students, they described many incidents of aggressive behavior perpetrated using technology, which was directed primarily towards members of competing organizations. That suggests that using the term 'cyberbullying' with college students is likely to underestimate the prevalence of aggressive digital behavior.

Our findings also suggest that cyber-aggression among Greek life students serves to protect the reputations of the organizations, and by extension, the individuals in those organizations. Our observation of the 'rush week' activities (our building is in close proximity to many of the Greek houses) supports the participants' comments about the competitive nature of the chapters.

Our theoretical framework, social identity theory, was clearly supported by the data. The university in which the study was conducted has more than 30,000 students. For an incoming freshman, finding a social niche is an essential and perhaps daunting task. Many bring the idea that joining a sorority or fraternity is a way to establish a social identity. In some cases, they may be continuing a family tradition, as parents often encourage students to seek membership in the sorority or fraternity to which they belonged in their own college days. Once they have adopted this identity, it becomes important to believe that their own group is superior to others, as Tajfel and Turner (1979) theorized.

Our data also support the related concept of stereotyping. It was obvious that the multicultural groups and the mainstream members had stereotypical images of the other, and that these images fueled the competitiveness they felt.

Limitations

As with any study, there are limitations that must be acknowledged. In this case, the small number of participants is a significant disadvantage. Not only was the number small, but also the lack of representation of NPC and NIC Greek life students adds to the difficulty in generalizing these findings. However, we think the fact that the few students who did participate were largely from multicultural organizations, which are smaller, less expensive, and with fewer resources, is revealing about who felt it was important to talk about the issue.

Conclusion

Greek life is a prevalent American college phenomenon. Such groups are appealing to new students at a large university because they appear to provide a vehicle to establish a social identity at a time when developmentally, this is a salient task. Participants in our study were clear that while negative behavior can occur online, cyberbullying and personal attacks were not really a problem. Instead, the real issue was described as competitiveness and segregation across groups, which can play out online through social media.

The separation between mainstream (NPC/NIC) and multicultural groups was evident and unexpected. Many focus group participants from multicultural groups did not feel welcome in the mainstream sororities and fraternities. In a diverse university as in a diverse society, such a perception is counter-productive. One of the functions of a university experience is to prepare for the adult workplace. To achieve in the current globalized world, and in the workplace of a country that is soon to have a 'minority majority' population, young adults need to celebrate diversity rather than fear it. Seeing people of different ethnicities and of different sexual orientations as 'other' will not stand the graduates, or society at large, in good stead.

In addition, prejudice and stereotypical views applied to sexual minorities as well, with participants emphasizing that in most Greek organizations, LGBTQ students would be unwelcome because they would, by their very presence, taint the reputation of the organization. Note that one of our participants had not revealed his sexual orientation to his fraternity brothers for fear of ostracism. One must wonder how damaging this must be to the self-esteem of the young man, who seeks 'brotherhood,' but believes he can have it only at the expense of his true identity. However, these exclusionary themes may not be unique to fraternity and sorority life. We speculate that most clubs or organizations would not want to have the reputation for being 'the gay club' if that was not their mission. Our study uncovered the marginalization that students of color and LGBTQ students experience both in person and online. Many LGBTQ individuals do not come out at work or to their families for the same reason. These populations continue to be 'othered' regardless of the social context and this manifests itself in person and digitally.

Although participants understood that these organizations ideally should mirror the diversity of campus, the minority students stressed that they felt more comfortable in their multicultural sororities. We speculate that many of those students may be first generation college students, who find navigating the large campus daunting. If they determine that a way to develop a support system is via participation in Greek life, and begin to explore options, they would quickly notice that the mainstream organizations are costly, attract members with more financial resources and social capital, and who are more acculturated to the Greek world (e.g. via parental participation). They may then choose a multicultural organization where they perceive members are more like them, both ethnically and socially.

The problem with this decision is that it perpetuates the stereotypes, discourages interaction with diverse populations, and does not reflect the demographics of the national or international population. If the students are to become leaders and change-makers in society, they must have opportunities that enrich their understanding of, and valuing of, those who are different from themselves. Perhaps the councils that govern Greek life on campus should make it a priority to provide a bridge between the predominately white Greek letter organizations and multicultural organizations. Greek letter organizations that can provide students of color with positive and healthy learning environments that create affinity and connection to the university are also important. In considering the implications of this study, it will be important to reflect on the non-white student's experiences to assist in recommending practices that may help to teach white students about whiteness, white privilege, and multiculturalism. Boschini and Thompson (1998) offered several suggestions to support diversity and address issues of racial segregation within the Greek community. Their suggestions included making a commitment to diversity as a Greek community and institution, assessment of the institution and Greek community, which should be complemented by a plan to address the areas identified by the assessment as needing attention, and the allocation of resources (time and money) to build strong and impactful educational and support mechanisms. Developing Greek organizations into positive learning communities that are a safe and comfortable place for non-white students will be critical for remaining relevant as college students are becoming more diverse. Greek life is founded on friendship, bonding, and connections. It often requires students to be leaders of their communities and engage in positive initiatives for the greater good. The best way to do that would be to model acceptance and inclusion in their sororities and fraternities for the rest of campus and beyond.

Finally, as this study illuminated, as more initiatives and prevention programs are designed to target the issue of cyberbullying, they need to intentionally address issues of race, gender, and sexual orientation. Prevention programs cannot ignore that racism is a theme that undergirds much of the online aggression or competition among students and student groups. The students are eager to broaden the topic to racism, segregation, and marginalization because these realities cannot be removed even in the digital world.

References

Baldasare, A., Bauman, S., Goldman, L. and Robie, A. (2012). Cyberbullying? Voices of college students. In L. A. Wankel and C. Wankel (Eds.) 2012. *Misbehavior Online in Higher Education: Cutting-edge Technologies in Higher Education*, (5). UK: Emerald Group Publishing Limited. pp. 127–55.

Bauman, S. and Baldasare, A. (in press). Cyber aggression among college students: Demographic differences, predictors of distress, and the role of the university. *Journal of College Student Development*.

Boschini, V. and Thompson, C. (1998). The future of the Greek experience: Greeks and diversity. *New Directions for Student Services,* no. 80. San Francisco, CA: Jossey-Bass. pp. 19–27.

Glaser, B. and Strauss, A. (1967). *The Discovery of Grounded Theory.* Hawthorne, NY: Aldine Publishing Company.

Miles, M. B. and Huberman, A. M. (1994). *Qualitative Data Analysis* (2nd ed.). Thousand Oaks, CA: Sage Publications.

Muñoz, S. M. and Guardia, J. R. (2009). Nuestra historia y futuro (our history and future): Latino/a fraternities and sororities. In C. L. Torbenson and G. Parks (Eds.), *Brothers and Sisters: Diversity in College Fraternities and Sororities.* Madison, N.J.: Fairleigh Dickinson University Press. pp. 104–32.

Pew Research Internet Project (2014). *Mobile Technology Fact Sheet.* Available at http:// www.pewinternet.org/fact-sheets/mobile-technology-fact-sheet. [Accessed on 20 November 2014].

Ross, L. (2000). Alpha Phi Alpha Fraternity Inc. *The Divine Nine: The History of African American Sororities and Fraternities.* New York: Kensington Publishing Corp. pp. 3–44.

Tajfel, H. and Turner, J. C. (1979). An integrative theory of intergroup conflict. In W. G. Austin and S. Worchel (Eds.), *The Social Psychology of Intergroup Relations.* Monterey, CA: Brooks/Cole. pp. 33-47.

Taylor, S. J. and Bogdan, R. (1998). *Introduction to Qualitative Research Methods: A Guidebook and Resources* (3rd ed.). New York: John Wiley and Sons.

Whipple, E. G. and Sullivan, E. G. (1998). Greeks as communities of learners. In E. G. Whipple (Ed.), *New Challenges for Greek Letter Organizations: Transforming Fraternities and Sororities into Learning Communities* (New Directions for Student Services, 81). San Francisco, CA: Jossey-Bass. pp. 87–94.

9

BULLYING AT GREEK UNIVERSITIES

An empirical study

Theodoros Giovazolias and Maria Malikiosi-Loizos

Bullying is a constantly growing phenomenon encountered in most countries and at different educational levels. Although bullying has been studied extensively in the school context over the last decades, much less is known about the phenomenon in the university environment. However, the experience from the relevant research on students' well-being often reveals links with their exposure to some forms of peer rejection and victimization. The absence of systematic research of bullying in the university context impedes the effort to better capturing the students' experience during this transformative age phase.

Over the last decade, several research studies have been conducted and published, relevant to bullying and victimization in the Greek schools. However, no attention has yet been drawn to the study of this phenomenon in the Greek higher education institutions. Many research studies report the relationship between bullying and several academic, social and mental health issues. This empirical paper aims to investigate the occurrence of bullying in a sample of Greek undergraduate students from different institutions. To the authors' knowledge, this is the first attempt of examining the phenomenon in the Greek university context. The present study will examine variables including the nature of bullying (traditional and cyberbullying), the profile of the perpetrators and the victims, as well as the relationship with students' remembered parenting, self-esteem, loneliness and well-being. The implications of the findings are discussed both within the current socio-political situation in Greece and the need for tailored counselling interventions.

Introduction

Research on bullying in the higher education context seems to be scarce. Although some attention has been drawn to bullying among faculty members (Lewis 2004; Lipsett 2005) as well as between students and faculty members (Lee and

Hopkins-Burke 2007, as cited in Coleyshaw (2010), there seems to be a gap in relevant research concerning student aggressive relationships at college (Coleyshaw 2010). Relevant British studies show 7 per cent of students have been victims during their studies, 79 per cent of them victimized by other students and 21 per cent by a staff member (Cowie *et al.* 2013). Similar results have been reported in the USA (Bauman and Newman 2013), with 3.7 per cent of students having been bullied some time during their studies. In another American study exploring bullying in college, Chapell *et al.* (2004) found 33.4 per cent of students have seen bullying episodes on campus; 18.5 per cent reported having been bullied; 29.4 per cent had witnessed a faculty member bully a student, while 14.5 per cent were victims of bully college teachers.

It is extraordinary that so far no one has become interested in studying bullying in Greek higher education, although discussions held on TV and in newspapers often refer to incidents of bullying in the context of the university. To the present researchers' knowledge, this is one of the first attempts to look into the different forms bullying takes in higher education. The focus of this first research attempt is to investigate the profile of the perpetrators and the victims involved.

Bullying in Greek schools

A plethora of Greek studies have been conducted to examine the constantly rising phenomenon of bullying in Greek schools. In a recent international study on bullying, Greece was ranked fourth and sixth highest for boys and girls respectively, among 40 other countries (Craig *et al.* 2009). Another similar cross-national study found that bullying in Greece had increased by 28.7 per cent between 1994 and 2006 (Molcho *et al.* 2009). Researchers and academics from all over Greece have been trying not only to explore but also to identify the different internal and external factors leading to aggressive behaviour in young children and adolescents. In recent years, we noticed an interest in studying bullying also at the kindergarten level, as increasingly small children engage in aggressive behaviour (Vlachou *et al.* 2013a, 2013b).

We find the first research attempts to study bullying in the Greek schools as early as the 1980s. However, the explosion of relevant research came with the dawn of the twenty-first century. One of the first reports on bullying in Greek schools appeared in Smith's collective volume *Violence in Schools: The Response in Europe* by Houndoumadi *et al.* (2003). In studying bullying in primary education they reported 14.7 per cent of pupils identified as victims and 6.3 per cent as bullies, with 4.8 per cent being identified as both victims and bullies. Similar results were found about ten years later by Giovazolias *et al.* (2010). Their research in Greek primary education schools showed 15 to 16.2 per cent of the pupils being victims of bullying, with 2.7 per cent of them being bullies, and 7.8 per cent being both victims and bullies. Research in Greek high schools was first conducted in the 1990s by Fakiolas and Armenakis (1995). More recently, Artinopoulou, (2010) reported the percentage of bullying in high school ranged from between 10 to 25 per cent. In terms of their roles in the bullying episodes, 5.7 per cent are identified as perpetrators, 13.3 per cent as victims and 5 per cent as bully/victims (Makri-Botsari 2010).

Looking into the types of bullies and bullying as well as into the stressful effects they have on children's well-being, a cross-national retrospective study conducted in early 2000 with college students, focused on students' recall of their worst school experiences. Greece was one of the ten participating countries, and the preliminary results were presented at the 2004 APA Convention (Hyman *et al.* 2004). Strong similarities were found between countries, the most frequently reported type of school victimization being verbal and relational bullying. For Greek males, perpetrators of the worst experience in school were other students and peers (52.6 per cent). For Greek females, the perpetrators were approximately equal numbers of student and school personnel (48.7 per cent) (Hyman *et al.* 2004)

Cyberbullying seems to be mounting as well, as it has received serious research attention by academics, national authorities, and European Commission funded programs. In the 2011 European Kids Online Final Report (Livingstone *et al.* 2011), Greece is placed in fourth place from the bottom of the list of European countries regarding the prevalence of online bullying in children aged 9 to 16. More specifically, across Europe, 6 per cent of nine to 16-year-old Internet users report having been bullied online, whereas in Greece the respective percentage is 4 per cent. In a Greek study of 528 high school students, it was found that 17 per cent had received obscene or offensive messages, 9 per cent threatening messages, 7.7 per cent had received fearful messages, 14 per cent sexually abusive messages, 6.8 per cent had been blackmailed, and 12 per cent were victims of nasty rumours (Artinopoulou 2010). At college level, Kokkinos *et al.* (2014) found similarly offensive and sexually abusive messages to be most frequently reported. Similar studies have been conducted by academics in other parts of Greece coming to similar conclusions. A thorough review article of research on cyberbullying in Greece covering studies conducted up to 2012, has been recently published by Antoniadou and Kokkinos (2013).

Contrary to a large portion of research conducted at the primary and secondary school level, similar research in Greek higher education institutions is scarce. Bullying and cyberbullying has infused higher education but serious study attempts are only now starting to appear.

Characteristics of bullies and victims

A good understanding of bully and victim profiles is very important for prevention and intervention programs. The profiles of bullying participants have been extensively studied over the years, looking for anticipatory and risk factors involved. One first general finding is that bullies and victims encountered in elementary school continue to some extent this type of behavior through all educational levels (Chapell *et al.* 2006; Curwen *et al.* 2011).

Bullying has been found to have a negative impact on the emotional health and well-being of children and young people. As far as bullies are concerned, individual factors have been found to be related to self-confidence and power (Bushman and Baumeister 1998) but also to emotional immaturity, inferiority, loneliness, feelings of depression (Piotrowski and Hoot 2008), as well as low self-esteem, fear and anxiety (Cowie 2014). Regarding children, victims of bullying incidents are characterized by low self-esteem, introversion, and low assertiveness (Rigby 2007). Young people involved in bullying episodes have been found to experience depressive symptoms, loneliness, and poor self-worth, among other negative mental health problems (Houbre *et al.* 2006; Murray-Harvey and Slee 2007). Cyberbullies and especially cyber victims have been similarly reported to have a low self-esteem and high depression (Hinduja and Patchin 2010).

A study on the relation between cyberbullying and psychiatric symptoms concluded that some psychiatric symptoms can be significant predictors of cyberbullying (Arıcak 2009). More specifically, hostility and psychoticism as well as phobic anxiety significantly predicted cyberbullying. On the other hand, interpersonally sensitive people seem to protect themselves from cyberbullying by avoiding suspicious relationships through the Internet (Arıcak 2009).

Several Greek studies have attempted to identify predictive factors of victims and bullies in Greek schools. Looking into the factors related to bullying behaviour, research reflects on individual, family and other group variables (Andreou 2004; Smith *et al.* 2004). In studying the psychosocial profile of Greek university students participating in cyberbullying, Kokkinos *et al.* (2014) came to similar conclusions; more specifically, victims of cyberbullying scored significantly higher in (social) anxiety, hostility and depression than the rest of the group. They also concluded that cyberbullying is associated with low affective empathy and narcissism.

Self-esteem

The relationship of bullying with self-esteem has long been studied. It seems that high scores on bully/victim scales are often associated with low scores in self-worth and low self-concepts (Houbre *et al.* 2006). Also, levels of self-esteem may differ depending on the role children assume in bullying episodes (Boulton and Underwood 1992; Andreou 2000). In another Greek study, Andreou (2001) looked at the relationship between bully/victim problems and the coping strategies children use when confronted with a peer argument. Results suggested that both bullying and victimization are associated with self-evaluation in diverse domains, and emotional coping strategies in adverse peer interactions.

Regarding cyberbullying, results on self-esteem vary greatly. Since cyberbullying is a form of invisible bullying, which can occur without disclosure of one's identity, perpetrators gain a sense of extra power and may act even more aggressively since there are no bystanders in the bullying episodes. It has been suggested that this type of behaviour characterizes narcissistic personalities who are often reported as having high self-esteem (Miller and Campbell 2008).

Gender differences

Research findings are conclusive in that boys are more likely to become involved in bullying incidents both as victims and bullies than girls. Similarly, it has been found that more male university students get involved in bullying than female ones (Chapell *et al.* 2006). Similar findings are reported in relation to cyberbullying (Arıcak 2009). Greek studies similarly conclude that bullying behaviour is more permanent among boys compared to girls (Kokkinos *et al.* 2014).

Family role

The role of family on children's involvement in bullying has been evidenced by numerous studies. Most of them seem to agree that the family factors contributing to bullying behaviour have to do with lack of emotional support and poor bonding (Perren and Hornung 2005; Lodge 2014). Similarly, it has been stressed that warm parental relationships contribute to children's emotional well-being.

Parental acceptance or rejection has been found to be a major predictive factor of the child's development and adjustment. As Rohner *et al.* (2012) assert, parental acceptance and rejection form the warmth dimension of parenting. Research findings seem to agree that children coming from loving families feel good about themselves, have emotional stability and a positive worldview (Rohner 2004; Giovazolias 2014). The seeds of self-worth and self-adequacy are planted in the accepting and warm family environment early in life. On the other hand, in studying the correlates of bullying, research indicates a relevance of bullying to parental over control (Gladstone *et al.* 2006) and discipline (Kuppens *et al.* 2009, as mentioned in Williams and Kennedy 2012).

Although initial research using the Parent Acceptance–Rejection Questionnaire (PARQ) looked into parental acceptance or rejection treating parents as a group, recent research has shed light into the different roles and the effect each parent has on children. It seems that the father's emotional involvement and expression of love is specifically associated to the child's well-being. Similarly, Harper and Fine (2006) found the positive father-child relationship and parental warmth to be related to the child's well-being.

Parenting has been found to be closely related to bullying in Greek studies as well, in that children with good parental relationships seem to become much less involved in bullying episodes than children with bad relationships with their parents (Georgiou 2008). Flouri and Buchanan (2002) claimed that fathers' involvement in family life may act as a protective factor against a child's victimization.

The present study examines some of the variables related to bullying and cyberbullying in higher education, including personality, emotional well-being, self-esteem and their relationship to students' remembered parenting. We also test the interplay of these variables, namely the mediational effect of loneliness in the relationship between the experience of victimization and well-being.

Methodology

Participants

The sample consisted of 464 undergraduate students from six different universities across the Greek region (Athens 45.1 per cent, Piraeus 10.6 per cent, Thessaloniki 11.7 per cent, Crete 13.6 per cent, Ioannina 8.9 per cent, Thrace 10.1 per cent). The gender distribution was 52 male students (11.2 per cent), and 412 female students (88.8 per cent). The mean age of the sample was 21.27 (SD = 3.85) years of age. 17.9 per cent of the participants were in their first year of study, 31.9 per cent in their second year, 32.8 per cent in their third year and 17.2 per cent in their fourth year or higher.

Measures

Demographics

Participants completed a demographic questionnaire, where they reported their age, gender, ethnicity, and other relevant information.

Cyberbullying – traditional bullying

In order to assess the incident of cyberbullying and traditional bullying we used the questionnaire developed by Campbell *et al.* (2011). In the first section, after reading a definition of cyberbullying, respondents were asked 12 questions about the incidence, frequency, and severity of cyberbullying experienced in the previous 12 months. Sample items included 'How often have you been cyberbullied in the last 12 months?' 'What sort of things have you been cyberbullied about?' The second section repeated the same 12 items as section one, but inquired about traditional forms of bullying.

Parental acceptance–rejection

Perceived parental acceptance and rejection was measured using the Parental Acceptance-Rejection Questionnaire – Adult version (PARQ Adult, Rohner 2005). Participants responded to two versions of the child PARQ, assessing their perceptions of remembered maternal (PARQ Mother) and paternal (PARQ Father) acceptance-rejection, respectively. These are self-report questionnaires consisting of 24 items each, including identical items for the mother and for the father, e.g. 'My mother/my father makes me feel wanted and needed', and 'My mother/my father goes out of her/his way to hurt my feelings'. Participants indicated how well each statement described their perceived parents' behavior on a four-point Likert-like scale (from 'almost always true' to 'almost never true'). High scores denote higher perceived rejection. Both scales had high reliability with a = .94 (mother and father versions).

Self-esteem

Self-esteem was measured using the Greek version of the Rosenberg Self-Esteem Scale (Rosenberg 1965), which was shown to have good validity and reliability (Hagborg 1993). The scale contains ten items scored on a four-point Likert scale, ranging from one (does not apply to me at all) to four (applies to me very well). A sample item includes 'I feel that I have a number of good qualities'. Cronbach's alpha for this study was a = .86.

Loneliness

Loneliness was measured with the University of California Los Angeles Loneliness Scale (UCLA; Russell *et al.* 1980). The scale has 20 items with responses on a four-point Likert scale ranging from *never* to *often*. It consists of ten positively worded and ten negatively worded statements reflecting satisfaction with social relationships. Higher scores indicate greater loneliness. The reliability of the scale was high (a = .89).

Well-being

We measured subjective well-being using the Flourishing Scale (FS; Diener and Biswas-Diener 2008). The Flourishing Scale consists of eight items describing important aspects of human functioning ranging from positive relationships, to feelings of competence, to having meaning and purpose in life. The scale was called 'Psychological Wellbeing' in an earlier publication, but the name was changed to more accurately reflect the content because the scale includes content that goes beyond psychological well-being narrowly defined. Each item of the FS is answered on a 1 to 7 scale that ranges from 'strong disagreement' to 'strong agreement'. High scores indicate a positive view of one's self in important areas of functioning. Cronbach's alpha was a = .85.

Procedure

Participants filled out the questionnaires during an ordinary lecture. The average time of completion was 20 minutes. There was no payment or other incentive to complete the questionnaires. This study has full approval from the Institutional Review Board (IRB) of the University of Crete. The data were collected during the 2013 spring semester. Eventually, they were encoded, transferred, and analyzed with SPSS 21, at the University of Crete.

Data analysis

The collected data were analyzed using descriptive statistics, whereas gender differences in the variables under consideration were studied using non-parametric tests such as chi-square tests and independent-samples t test. Correlations among the study variables were tested using the Spearman rank correlation method, as the variables were not normally distributed. The proposed mediation model was tested using PROCESS, a versatile modelling tool for observed variable mediation and moderation. This approach, based on bootstrapping, is considered an advancement over previous methods of assessing mediation, because of the increased reliability of findings (Hayes 2013). The analyses were based on 5,000 bootstrapped samples, using bias-corrected 95 per cent confidence intervals.

Results

Descriptive statistics

Traditional bullying

Of the 464 participants, 6.3 per cent reported being a victim of traditional bullying in the preceding 12 months. Across all participants, a χ^2 test indicated that being a victim of traditional bullying was not independent of gender [χ^2 (1, N=464) = 12.22, $p<$ .01, Fisher's p = .002].

Analysis of the standardized residuals revealed that a significantly higher than expected number of male participants had been traditionally bullied (standardized residual = 5.8). The majority of victims reported that they had been victimized by a male (51.7 per cent). 27.6 per cent of the victims reported that they had been victimized because of their appearance whereas 17.2 per cent because of their grades or intelligence (e.g. calling them a geek etc.). The most common form of bullying (65.5 per cent) was social exclusion (e.g. being excluded and rumour spreading), followed (with 55.2 per cent) by the verbal form (e.g. teasing or hurtful name calling).

Regarding the reaction of victimized participants to this experience, a large proportion (28 per cent) chose to do nothing about it, mainly because they did not know what to do or who to talk to (37.5 per cent) or because they did not want to get involved (25 per cent). Of those participants who decided to report their experience, 25.1 per cent talked to their friends and 20.7 per cent discussed it with their parents.

Interestingly, 44.8 per cent of the victimized participants reported that this experience had a big impact on their lives. Independent samples t test revealed that participants who reported being bullied perceived their mothers to be more rejecting compared to participants who did not report such experience [t (464) = 2.11, $p<.05$]. This group (victims) also reported higher levels of loneliness [t (464) = -2.17, $p<05$] and lower levels of well-being [t (464) = 2.41, $p<.05$] than the non-victim group. Regarding the perpetrators of bullying behaviour, 1.7 per cent of the total sample reported that they had bullied someone in the past 12 months (25 per cent once a week).

Cyberbullying

Concerning the experience of cyberbullying, 3.2 per cent of the total sample reported being a victim of this form of bullying in the preceding 12 months. Across all participants, a χ^2 test indicated that being a victim of cyberbullying depended again on the gender of participants [χ^2 (1, N=464) = 7.63, $p< .01$, Fisher's $p = .018$]. Analysis of the standardized residuals revealed that a significantly higher than expected number of male participants had been cyberbullied (standardized residual = 3.3). The majority of victims reported that they had been victimized by a male (73.3 per cent). 60 per cent of the victims reported that they had been victimized because of their appearance, whereas 26.7 per cent because of their sexuality (e.g. being called gay, fag, or dyke).

Regarding the reaction of victimized participants to this experience 40 per cent chose to do nothing about it, mainly because they thought that it wouldn't have made a difference (33.3 per cent) did not know what to do, or who to talk to (37.5 per cent). Of those participants who decided to report their experience, 26.7 per cent talked to their friends and 20 per cent discussed it with their parents.

Further, 40 per cent of the victimized participants reported that this experience had a big impact on their lives. Independent samples t-test revealed no differences in the victimized and non-victimized participants regarding perceived parental rejection, self-esteem, loneliness and well-being. Regarding the perpetrators of cyberbullying behaviour, 1.3 per cent of the total sample reported that they had cyberbullied someone less than once a week in the past 12 months.

Correlations

We found significant associations between victimization and loneliness ($rho = .10$, $p<.05$), victimization and well-being ($rho = -.10$, $p<.05$) and victimization and perceived maternal rejection ($rho = .11$, $p<.01$). Perceived paternal rejection was also associated to a large extent ($rho = .41$, $p<.05$) with the frequency of being a victim. Further, perceived maternal rejection was significantly associated with bullying behaviours ($rho = .13$, $p<.01$). The frequency of bullying others was significantly and negatively associated with perceived well-being ($rho = -.71$, $p<.05$).

The correlations regarding cyberbullying revealed significant associations between cyber-victimization and loneliness ($rho = .10$, $p =.05$) and the frequency of being cyberbullied and self-esteem ($rho = -.56$, $p<05$). Being a cyberbully was also significantly associated with paternal rejection ($rho = .11$, $p<05$).

Mediation analysis

We then tested the mediation model (see Figure 1), where the experience of victimization was entered as the independent variable, perceived well-being as the dependent variable, and perceived loneliness as the mediating variable.

The analysis showed that although the experience of being a victim has a significant total effect on well being (c: B=-3.087, SE=1.282, BCa CI [-5.605, -.568]), after controlling for the effect of perceived loneliness as the mediator (a: B=3.962, SE=1.794, BCa CI [.436, 7.488]; b: B=-.440, SE=.026, BCa CI [-.492, -.389]) the direct effect of victimization on well-being has disappeared (c': B=-1.340, SE=1.015, BCa CI [-3.334, .654]). The indirect effect of victimization on well-being scores through perceived loneliness (B=-1.746, BCa CI [-3.551, -.218]) and indicates full mediation by perceived loneliness, and represents a small effect size (κ^2=.075, BCa CI [.011, .148]) (Preacher and Kelley 2011). This means that in our sample the experience of being victimized by fellow students leads first to the development of feelings of loneliness, which (feelings of loneliness) in turn result in lower levels of perceived well-being.

Discussion

The present study aimed to explore the prevalence of both traditional bullying and cyberbullying in the Greek university context. It also attempted to shed light on the relationship of this phenomenon with students' remembered parental acceptance and rejection, and its impact on variables such as self-esteem, loneliness and well-being. To our knowledge, this is the first study that explores the traditional forms of bullying behaviours among Greek students (there is one recent study investigating cyberbullying in this population, see Kokkinos *et al.* 2014), as well as its relationship with the impact of both forms (traditional and cyberbullying) on their psychological adjustment as measured by the levels of perceived self-esteem, loneliness and well-being.

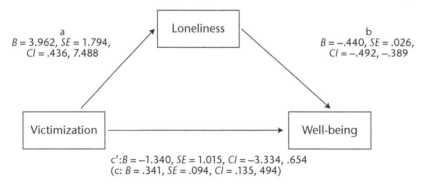

FIGURE 9.1 The indirect effect of victimization on well-being through loneliness scores (direct total effect of victimization to well-being scores in parentheses).

Our first finding suggested that more males than females are involved in bullying and cyberbullying, both as perpetrators and victims. This result is in line with previous research, which has shown that males assume these roles more often than females (Hong *et al.* 2007; Kokkinos *et al.* 2014), especially with regards to cyberbullying. However, it should be noted here that the prevalence rates of both forms are lower in our study compared to results from other studies. For example, Wensley and Campbell (2012) in a study using the same measure of bullying, found that 20.8 per cent of their sample reported being a victim of traditional bullying (ours was 6.3 per cent) and 11.6 per cent of cyberbullying (ours was 3.2 per cent) in the preceding 12 months. These differences may be partly explained due to participants' year of study (the Wensley and Campbell study involved only first year students, whereas our study included students from subsequent years as well); with regards to this, relevant research has shown that bullying behaviours tend to decline with age (Nansel *et al.* 2001). On the other hand, 5.1 per cent reported being a perpetrator in traditional bullying (ours was 1.7 per cent) and 3.8 per cent were perpetrators in cyberbullying (ours was 1.3 per cent).

An interesting finding concerns the reaction of victims, both of bullying and cyberbullying, as it was found that a large proportion decided not to report their experience to anyone, mainly because they felt that they did not know where to turn to in order to get useful help. Similar studies on victims' passive reactions to bullying report fear of retaliation, feelings of fear, shame, powerlessness and embarrassment (Myers and Cowie 2013). Although such kinds of response were included in the questionnaire to be checked, it is interesting that our participants did not tick them. In turn, many of those who decided to report their harmful experience discussed it with friends or parents. This is not surprising considering that close relationships continue to characterize Greek family life (Kalogeraki 2009) and friendships (Malikiosi-Loizos and Anderson 1999). But still, this result points to the need for raising awareness regarding the management of bullying incidents (in any form) within the university context.

The most frequent bullying behaviours were indirect (being excluded, rumour spreading, name calling), which is similar to other studies (Arıcak 2009). Another finding was that the experience of victimization (mainly in its traditional form) had a negative effect on victims' lives, impacting on their sense of loneliness and their perceived well-being (Cowie 2014). This finding is in line with other studies that have found that the exposure to bullying behaviours has serious consequences on the psychological and physical health of both youths and students (Nansel *et al.* 2001; Chapell *et al.* 2004; Houbre *et al.* 2006). Similar results have been reported in another Greek study as well; both bullies and victims were characterized by low self-esteem and low self-worth (Andreou 2000).

The mediation analysis provided further insight to these relationships, as it was shown that traditional (but not cyberbullying) victimization led to feelings of loneliness that in turn resulted in lower levels of perceived well-being by students. It is likely then that the victims of bullying isolate themselves from social interactions within the university context (i.e. course attendance, student groups, etc.), and that this isolation gradually affects their overall sense of happiness. Given the fact that the attendance in most courses in Greek universities are not mandatory, we could assume that most of these 'cases' would remain 'undetected' possibly for a long period of time either from the teaching staff or from the university counselling services.

Another finding concerned the association of remembered paternal and maternal rejection with the involvement in bullying behaviours, either as a bully or as a victim. Our results indicated that both perceived paternal and maternal rejection was largely associated with the frequency of being a victim of traditional bullying, whereas paternal rejection was also significantly associated with being a cyberbully. These results confirm previous studies that have suggested that parenting (Lodge 2014) and especially paternal rejection (Flouri and Buchanan 2002; Kokkinos 2013; Papadaki and Giovazolias, in press) contributes significantly to the prevalence of bullying behaviour. Although most of these studies have focused on the parental role on bullying during childhood and adolescence, our results provide preliminary indication that these relationships may partly explain the phenomenon in university students as well.

Limitations

This study has a number of limitations; although the sample came from six different institutions (from almost every geographical region of Greece), the gender distribution (females in the vast majority) limits the possibility for any conclusive suggestions.

Another limitation of our study was the statistical procedures applied, which did not allow for the simultaneous control of two-way relationships between variables. Furthermore, the cross-sectional design limits the possibility of determining causal relationships among the variables examined. Further studies might employ a longitudinal design in order to control for these interactions. For example, further research is needed with regards to the mediational effect of loneliness in the relationship of victimization with well-being, as we know of no previous study examining this model, especially in university students.

Implications

Although bullying and cyberbullying seem to be less advanced in Greece than in other countries, preventive as well as intervention measures need to be taken by the higher education institutions in order to help students become more resilient in facing stressful situations. Such measures need to focus primarily on student involvement in different activities in order to increase their self-worth, sociability, and problem-solving skills.

Training in empathy should be seriously considered, since the research literature indicates that self-conscious emotions and empathy seem to increase with age, and young adults seem to become more sensitive and considerate of the impact of their behaviour on others (Curwen *et al.* 2011).

The Greek authorities have been asked to provide student-counselling centres on campuses. However, even today, very few counselling centres exist at Greek universities. Most if not all of them, are understaffed with no funds and, therefore, unable to address effectively students' psychological needs. As is frequently mentioned, Greece faces the most serious economic crisis of its modern history (Efthimiou *et al.* 2013). Research data suggest that health conditions have deteriorated especially in vulnerable groups (students are a group that has been affected to a great extent) (Kentikelenis *et al.* 2011). However, serious reductions in universities' budgets impede the adequate provision of such services.

An alternative resource that universities can provide students with is peer support. The research literature proves consistently the beneficial role of social support systems on students' well-being and alleviation of stress (Rigby 2000; Davidson and Demaray 2007; Cowie and Myers 2014). Such systems have become very popular in schools and universities, based on the assumption that students have altruistic feelings and want to offer help spontaneously to their peers when in difficult situations. They prove to be efficient in encountering problems related to bullying and cyberbullying as well (Cowie 2011; Houlston *et al.* 2011). Peer supporters share similar values and experiences and can take different supportive roles in bullying episodes, including being a friend, a student advocate, an active bystander, a peer counsellor, and many more. The basic aim of peer-helping programmes is to educate the students involved to offer their friendship and emotional support, as well as to help their peers become more resilient and acquire problem-solving and conflict resolution skills.

No peer-support programs addressing issues of bullying have been developed so far in Greek higher education institutions, contrary to the other two educational levels (i.e. primary and secondary). In the Greek higher education institutions, the only peer-counselling centre exists at the University of Athens, which operates on a voluntary basis, supervised by relevant faculty members. Students involved are trained in empathy, active listening, as well as in basic communication and counselling skills. Issues addressed include, among others, adjustment to college life, separation from family, loneliness and relationships. They are approached mainly through emotional support, providing information when applicable and friendly discussions where needed. The primary focus of peer support services is prevention and effective resolution of dysfunctions that will lead to self-fulfillment and well-being; it may then be suggested that prevention programmes should be developed in order to educate students on how to defend themselves, or how to be proactive in bullying episodes if involved as victims or bystanders (Malikiosi-Loizos 2014).

In conclusion, this exploratory study confirmed the existence of both traditional forms of bullying and cyberbullying among Greek university students. Although the existence of relatively small percentages of both victims and bullies in both forms (i.e. traditional and cyberbullying), it was found that the experience of such behaviours is related to participants' perceived parenting and has both direct and indirect effects on their self-esteem, feelings of loneliness and eventually their overall well-being. To our knowledge, this is the first study in Greece that investigates both forms of bullying in relation to the variables mentioned. We hope that future studies will expand the knowledge regarding these under-examined phenomena within the university context.

References

Andreou, E. (2000). Bully/victim problems and their associations with psychological constructs in 8- to 12-year-old Greek schoolchildren. *Aggressive Behavior*, 26: 49–56.

Andreou, E. (2001). Bully/victim problems and their association with coping behavior in conflictual peer interactions among school-age children. *Educational Psychology*, 21(2): 59–66

Andreou, E. (2004). Bully/victim problems and their association with Machiavellianism and self-efficacy in Greek primary school children. *British Journal of Educational Psychology*, 74: 297–309.

Antoniadou, N. and Kokkinos, C. M. (2013) A review of research on cyber-bullying in Greece. *International Journal of Adolescence and Youth*, 18: 1–17.

Arıcak, O. T. (2009). Psychiatric symptomatology as a predictor of cyberbullying among university students. *Eurasian Journal of Educational Research*, 34: 167–84.

Artinopoulou, V.(2010). *Σχολική Διαμεσολάβηση*. (School Mediation) [in Greek]. Athens. Nomiki Vivliothiki.

Bauman, S. and Newman, M. L. (2013). Testing assumptions about cyberbullying. Perceived distress associated with acts of conventional and cyberbullying. *Psychology of Violence*, 3: 27–38.

Boulton, M. J. and Underwood, K. (1992). Bully/victim problems among middle school children. *British Journal of Educational Psychology*, 62: 73–87.

Bushman, B. and Baumeister, R. (1998). Threatened egotism, narcissism, self-esteem, and direct and displaced aggression: Does self-love or self-hate lead to violence? *Journal of Personality and Social Psychology*, 75: 219–29.

Campbell, M. A., Spears, B., Slee, P., Kift, S. and Butler, D. (2011). The prevalence of cyberbullying in Australia. *Paper presented at the 5th World Conference and IV Iberoamerican Congress on Violence in School*. Investigations, Interventions, Evaluations and Public Policies Mendoza. Argentina.

Chapell, M., Casey, D., De la Cruz, C., Ferrell, J., Forman, J., Lipkin, R., Newsham, M., Sterling, M. and Whittaker, S. (2004). Bullying in college by students and teachers. *Adolescence*, 39: 53–64.

Chapell, M. S., Hasselman, S. L., Kitchin, T., Lomon, S. N., MacIver, K. W. and Sarullo, P. L. (2006). Bullying elementary school, high school, college. *Adolescence*, 41(164): 633–48.

Coleyshaw, L. (2010). The power of paradigms: a discussion of the absence of bullying research in the context of the university student experience. *Research in Post-Compulsory Education*, 15(34): 377–86.

Cowie, H. (2011). Peer support as an intervention to counteract school bullying: Listen to the children. *Children and Society*, 25: 287–92.

Cowie, H. (2014) Peer support in secondary schools: How young people themselves can make schools safer [Στήριξη ομηλίκων στη δευτεροβάθμια εκπαίδευση: πώς μπορούν οι ίδιοι οι νέοι να κάνουν τα σχολεία πιο ασφαλή]. In M.Malikiosi-Loizos (Ed.) *Peer Counseling in Education [Συμβουλευτική ομηλίκων στην εκπαίδευση]*. Athens: Pedio. pp. 165–87.

Cowie, H. and Myers, C. A. (2014) Bullying amongst university students in the UK. *The International Journal of Emotional Education*, 6(10): 66–75.

Cowie, H., Bauman, S., Coyne, I., Myers, C., Pörhölä, M. and Almeida, A. (2013). Cyberbullying amongst university students: an emergent cause for concern? In P. K. Smith and G. Steffgen (Eds). *Cyberbullying Through the New Media*. London: Routledge. pp. 165–77.

Craig, W., Harel-Fisch, Y., Fogel-Grinvald, H., Dostaler, S., Hetland, J., Simons-Morton, B., Molcho, M., Gaspar de Mato, M., Overpeck, M., Due, P. and Pickett, W. (2009). The HBSC Violence and Injuries Prevention Focus Group, and the HBSC Bullying Writing Group. A cross-national profile of bullying and victimization among adolescents in 40 countries. *International Journal of Public Health*, 54: 216–24.

Curwen, T., McNichol, J. S. and Sharpe, G. W. (2011). The progression of bullying from elementary school to university. *Journal of Humanities and Social Science*, 1(13): 47– 54.

Davidov, M. and Grusec, J. E. (2006). Untangling the links of parental responsiveness to distress and warmth to child outcomes. *Child Development*, 77: 44–58.

Davidson, L. M. and Demaray, M. K. (2007). Social support as a moderator between victimization and internalizing-externalizing distress from bullying. *School Psychology Review*, 36: 383–405.

Diener, E. and Biswas-Diener, R. (2008). *Happiness: Unlocking the Mysteries of Psychological Wealth*. Malden: Blackwell Publishing.

Efthimiou, K., Argalia, E., Kaskaba, E. and Makri, A. (2013). Economic crisis and mental health. What do we know about the current situation in Greece? *Encephalos*, 50: 22–30.

Fakiolas, N. and Armenakis, A. (1995). Εμπλοκή μαθητών και χρηστών τοξικών ουσιών σε βιαιότητες. [in Greek] (The involvement of students and illegal substance users in violent incidents). *Sygxroni Ekpaidefsi*, 81: 42–50.

Flouri, E. and Buchanan, A. (2002). Life satisfaction in teenage boys: The moderating role of father involvement and bullying. *Aggressive Behavior*, 28: 126–33.

Georgiou, S. N. (2008). Bullying and victimization at school: The role of mothers. *British Journal of Educational Psychology*, 78: 109–25.

Giovazolias, T., Kourkoutas, E., Mitsopoulou, E. and Georgiadi, M. (2010). The relationship between perceived school climate and the prevalence of bullying behavior in Greek schools: Implications for preventive inclusive strategies. *Procedia- Social and Behavioral Sciences*, 5: 2208–215.

Giovazolias, T. (2014). The moderating role of parental power/prestige on the relationship between parental rejection and psychological maladjustment in a Greek student sample. *Cross-Cultural Research*, 48(3): 240–49.

Gladstone, G. L., Parker, G. B. and Malhi, G. S. (2006) Do bullied children become anxious and depressed adults? A cross-sectional investigation of the correlates of bullying and anxious depression. *Journal of Nervous and Mental Disease*, 194(3): 201–08.

Hagborg, W. J. (1993). The Rosenberg self-esteem scale and Harter self-perception profile for adolescents: a concurrent validity study. *Psychology in the Schools*, 30: 132–36.

Harper, S. E., and Fine, M. A. (2006) The effects of involved nonresidential father's distress, parenting behaviors, inter-parental conflict, and the quality of father-child relationships on children's well-being. *Fathering: A Journal of Theory, Research, and Practice about Men as Fathers*, 4(3): 285–311.

Hayes, A. F. (2013). *Introduction to Mediation, Moderation and Conditional Process Analysis: A Regression-Based Approach*. New York: The Guildford Press.

Hinduja, S. and Patchin, J. W. (2010). Cyberbullying and self-esteem. *The Journal of School Health*, 80: 614–62.

Hong, Y., Li, X., Mao, R. and Stanton, B. (2007). Internet use among Chinese college students: implications for sex education and HIV prevention. *CyberPsychology and Behavior*, 10: 161–69.

10

CROSS-CULTURAL COMPARISONS OF BULLYING AMONG UNIVERSITY STUDENTS

Perspectives from Argentina, Estonia, Finland and the United States

Maili Pörhölä, Kristen Cvancara, Esta Kaal, Kaja Tampere and Beatriz Torres

Introduction

This chapter compares bullying experiences among university students between four countries and aims to provide an understanding of the cultural features that might affect these experiences. We start by providing a summary of the results from a cross-cultural survey conducted among undergraduate students in Argentina, Estonia, Finland and the United States. We continue discussing the ways in which the current cultural, political, historical and economic status and challenges in each country might explain the cross-cultural differences and similarities detected in students' bullying experiences in higher education.

Previous cross-cultural research involving over 40 countries indicates that health patterns vary significantly across countries, suggesting that cultural characteristics may influence young people's well-being and health behaviors by creating health inequalities between countries and regions (Craig *et al.* 2009; Currie *et al.* 2012). Important to this research is the distinction that a country may encompass many cultures (due to varied ethnic, race, gender, sexual orientation, ability and/or socioeconomic status differences, etc.). Thus, cultural differences may exist within and across various countries. Currie *et al.* (2012) emphasize two implications from their cross-cultural work that prompted the current study. First, that the prevalence of detrimental health patterns among young persons documented across countries calls for international and national policies and actions to address the determinants of observed health inequalities. And second, that professionals working to improve young persons' well-being should consider how social environments support and/ or deter the development of health-promoting behaviors. Educational contexts from kindergarten to university are among the most important social environments people experience that impact on psychosocial development and well-being. In these contexts, young people meet with their peers and are engaged in social relationships that can have a significant impact on their short- and long-term well-being.

For example, negative associations between well-being and experiences of victimization by peers in educational contexts have been clearly demonstrated in a number of studies (for reviews, see Hawker and Boulton 2000; Pörhölä 2009; Reijntjes *et al.* 2010) that indicate peer bullying is an important determinant of well-being in an individual's social environment. For victims, studies indicate that the negative impacts of being bullied on psychosocial and physical well-being are both short-term (Due *et al.* 2005; Houbre *et al.* 2006) and long-term (Jantzer *et al.* 2006; Newman *et al.* 2005; Schäfer *et al.* 2004). A bully's well-being and health behaviour is also negatively affected over time (Glew *et al.* 2005; Nansel *et al.* 2001). Furthermore, individuals who have been victims and/or bullies in childhood and adolescence have a tendency to be engaged in abusive relationships in the same roles later in life (Chapell *et al.* 2006; Curwen *et al.* 2011; De Souza and Ribeiro 2005; Pörhölä 2011). As roles are carried forward throughout adulthood, an increased number of issues are likely to impact on individual well-being. The means of providing health services and social support for these individuals varies across countries, which is speculated to contribute to the cultural inequalities noted.

Studying bullying phenomena within higher educational contexts across countries is especially relevant due to the variation of reported incidence rates that indicate cultural factors may affect the acceptance of bullying behaviors. Findings from international collaborative research projects, such as the Health Behaviour in School-aged Children (HBSC) surveys (cf. Craig *et al.* 2009; Currie *et al.* 2012), indicate the number of students involved in bullying (i.e. bullying others, being bullied, or acting in dual roles as both a bully and a victim) at least two or three times a month ranges from 8.6 percent to 45.2 percent among boys, and from 4.8 percent to 35.8 percent among girls aged 11 to 15 years (Craig *et al.* 2009). While research on bullying at school has substantially increased since the 1970s all around the world, this research has mainly focused on bullying in elementary and middle schools. However, a small number of surveys conducted in colleges, universities, and vocational higher education institutions indicate that bullying exists in higher education too, and suggest that its occurrence rates vary greatly between countries (Ahmer *et al.* 2008; BMA 2006; Chapell *et al.* 2004; Curtis *et al.* 2007; Mukhtar *et al.* 2010; NUS 2008; Pörhölä 2011; Sinkkonen *et al.* 2012; see also Cowie *et al.* 2013, for a review). Since the measures, samples and analyses used to research higher education contexts have varied significantly between the individual studies, more research is needed to examine whether cultural factors within countries influence young adults' bullying experiences, and consequently contribute to inequalities in individuals' health and well-being between countries and regions that may transfer into adulthood. This chapter reviews findings from a cross-cultural study that demonstrates that bullying is a prevalent phenomenon among young adults at universities, and discusses significant similarities and differences across countries regarding its prevalence and nature.

Cultural variation and gender differences in bullying and victimization experiences among university students

In the following, we provide a review based on the main results from a cross-cultural study by Pörhölä *et al.* (in submission). For this study, data were collected by survey methods from undergraduate university students in four countries: Argentina (N = 969), Estonia (N = 1,053), Finland (N = 4,403) and the United States (N = 2,082). While convenience samples were used in Argentina and the USA; in Estonia and Finland, the respondents represented the target population well for the background variables (i.e. educational sector [academic university versus university of applied sciences], age group, duration of studies, study region, and field of studies), except for gender (males were slightly underrepresented). Therefore, caution must be taken when generalizing the results across the different countries. The study used similar measures and analyses, to examine university students' experiences of bullying.

Pörhölä *et al.* (in submission) found the number of students who reported having been bullied by their fellow students varied notably between the four countries compared. The highest rates of victimization were reported in Argentina (roughly 25 percent of Argentinean respondents indicated they had been bullied by other student(s) at least occasionally; USA, 11 percent; Finland, 5 percent; Estonia, 2 percent). The highest rates of bullying other students at least occasionally were also reported in Argentina, followed by the USA, Finland, and finally Estonia, with the differences between countries being relatively small. In each country, victimization was reported more frequently than bullying, suggesting that either a relatively small number of students bully a greater number of fellow students, or bullying behaviors remain unidentified by many of those who are perceived as bullies.

TABLE 10.1 Country comparisons of the rates of victimization and bullying and gender differences

Country	Rates of Victimization and Bullying		Gender Differences	
	Victimization	Bullying	Victimization	Bullying
Argentina	Highest	Highest	No	Males report more than females
Estonia	Lowest	Lowest	No	Males report more than females
Finland	Moderate	Moderate	Females report more than males	No
United States	Moderate	Moderate	No	Males report more than females

In the samples collected from university students by Pörhölä *et al.* (in submission), gender differences in bullying roles varied between the countries compared. Statistically significant gender differences among victims were detected only in Finland where female students reported being bullied by fellow student(s) more than males. The non-significant findings in the Argentina, Estonia and USA data sets may indicate that females start to become less vulnerable to bullying and succeed to develop better skills to defend themselves against bullying in young adulthood. In contrast, gender differences among bullies suggest there may be continuity in the aggressive and abusive behavior of the masculine gender. For example, male university students reported having bullied their fellow students more frequently than female students did in Argentina, Estonia, and the USA; gender differences in bullying behavior were found to be non-significant only in Finland. Previous findings from elementary and middle school levels indicate clear gender differences in both bullying behavior and victimization in most countries, with male students being more often engaged in bullying behaviors and female students being more likely in the role of victim (Craig *et al.* 2009; Currie *et al.* 2012; Nansel *et al.* 2001).

The Health Behaviour in School-aged Children (HBSC) surveys among elementary and middle school students indicate some differences in the rates of bullying between some of the countries that were compared in the study by Pörhölä *et al.* (2009). While the rates of bullying victimization reported by students in the HBSC from age 11 to 15 years were on the average level in Finland and the USA, Estonia differed from these countries in that, at age 11 and 13 years, the rates of victimization were among the highest, but then gradually decreased, being close to the average level at age 15 years. The rates of bullying others were also on the average level in Finland and the USA, whereas students in Estonia reported higher than average levels of bullying behavior in all age groups (Currie *et al.* 2012). However, Argentina was not among the countries examined in the HBSC surveys. According to Lavena (n.d.), there are no formal reporting of school violence statistics in Argentina as most information comes indirectly through varied sources. For example, Roman and Murillo (2011) found Argentina has the largest number of reported insults and threats, robberies, physical mistreatment and episodes of violence in sixth grade compared to other countries in Latin America. Physical violence affects more than 40 percent of primary school children in Argentina. Similarly to other Latin American countries, in Argentina more than half of primary school students report having been bullied by peers. Roman and Murillo also found that in Argentina, and other Latin American countries, boys suffered more insults and threats, robberies and physical and verbal violence than girls. In another study in secondary schools, D'Angelo and Fernández (2011) found in Buenos Aires that 66.1 percent of students in 2009 reported being subject to bullying, including experiences of mistreatment or humiliation by peers, being mocked, being excluded from activities by peers, and being told hurtful things.

Comparing the findings of Pörhölä *et al.* (in submission) to previous studies indicates that differential gender effects are associated with bullying behavior across countries and cultures, as well as different prevalence rates. Previous studies among university students also suggest that there may be cultural variance regarding gender differences in bullying. In the study by Chapell *et al.* (2004) in the USA, male students reported that they had bullied other students in college significantly more than female students did, but both genders were equally victimized. However, in the *NUS Student Experience Report* (2008) in the UK, it was found that female students were more likely than male students to say that they had experienced bullying in the university. On the contrary, in the study by Bennett *et al.* (2011), male college students reported more electronic victimization than female students.

To conclude, the findings from the cross-cultural comparisons conducted by Pörhölä *et al.* (in submission) suggest some culture-specific trends in bullying continue from childhood to young adulthood in the four countries compared. While the reporting of bullying victimization seems to remain high from elementary school to university in Argentina and moderate in the USA, the results suggest a slightly decreasing trend in Finland, and a notable decreasing trend from elementary school to university in Estonia. Due to the differences in measurement across existing studies and the lack of extensive cross-cultural research, direct comparisons between the results from primary and secondary school and university cannot be made.

The nature of bullying reported by university students in Argentina, Estonia, Finland and the United States

Differences among university students' bullying experiences do not only vary across countries by rate and by gender, they have also been found to differ according to the nature of the bullying behavior experienced. In the cross-cultural study on university students' experiences of bullying in four countries (Pörhölä *et al.* in submission), the most often experienced form of bullying reported by females across the four countries was found to be unjustified criticism, belittling, or humiliation related to studies (varying from approximately 13 percent to 15 percent, between countries). Male students in Finland and Estonia also reported this as the most frequent form of bullying they experienced (although males reported it to occur less frequently than females reported). In contrast, males in the Argentina sample reported verbal attacks (e.g. abuse, name-calling and threats) and males in the USA sample reported mocking or criticism related to personal qualities (e.g. appearance, age, gender, religion and background) to be the most frequent form of bullying experienced.

An interesting shift from bullying others because they are successful in elementary and middle school to bullying others because they are less successful in college is a noteworthy trend reflected in the current study. The fact that study-related criticism occurred so frequently in the university samples may be explained due to the cognitive development of individuals who are able to criticize others' study performance because they have developed the intellectual capacity and understanding of learning demands and goals relevant in educational contexts, which is not yet developed at a very young age. Linking this finding to an implication beyond the educational setting, research on workplace bullying shows that persistent unjustified criticism, belittling and humiliation related to the target person's professional skills and work performance are among the most frequently reported forms of bullying at work (Einarsen *et al.* 2003; Keashly and Jagatic 2003; Salin 2001). We speculate that the nature of bullying experienced in young adulthood (e.g. in the university setting) is likely to shift to reflect the forms typically reported in the workplace.

Beyond the most frequent forms reported, university students in the four countries disclosed (Pörhölä *et al.* in submission) other forms of bullying as well. Experiences of verbal attacks and mocking or criticism related to personal qualities were experienced to almost the same extent across the countries involved in the study. Damage to peer relationships or social discrimination was reported more often by female than male students in each of the countries except for Argentina, where the rates were higher for males than females. The experiences of technologically mediated insulting or harassment (e.g. via the Internet or phone) varied from less than 1 percent in Estonia to 4 to 5 percent in Argentina and the USA. The least often experienced form of bullying in university was physical damage to the person or his or her belongings, the number of students reporting these experiences varying from 0 percent among female students in Estonia, to approximately 3 percent among male students in Argentina.

Interpretations of the cultural characteristics in university students' experiences of bullying

To summarize, findings from elementary and middle schools (Craig *et al.* 2009; Currie *et al.* 2012), and university contexts (Pörhölä *et al.* in submission) suggest that significant cross-cultural differences exist in the ways in which various forms of bullying are identified and interpreted, tolerated, encouraged or discouraged, and sometimes even generated within a particular culture. By sharing our cultural experiences and theoretical understanding from different disciplines, we discuss in the following how some cultural differences and similarities might explain the variation in university students' experiences of bullying in the four countries examined. These countries (Argentina, Estonia, Finland and the United States) differ not only geographically and in size, but also culturally, politically, historically, and economically. In addition to impacting on the societal decisions in important matters affecting individuals' lives (e.g. provision of education, care for children and the elderly, healthcare, work, and social services), these cultural differences may have resulted in such developments in higher education contexts in these countries, which can be reflected in university students' well-being and relationships with their fellow students. These factors cover many areas and include equal accessibility to higher education and the availability and costs of health services and student counseling. The adaptation of students to socioeconomic considerations as well as ethnic, cultural, political and religious diversity, and the manifestation of status hierarchies between students and teachers, may prompt different levels of psychosocial well-being. Tensions and solidarity, competition and collaboration, and feelings and perceptions of inclusion and exclusion, among students and student groups, in different countries are also factors that affect well-being. Following is a brief summary of each country's characteristics to create a richer understanding of the potential elements embedded in culture that may impact bullying phenomena across the four countries studied by Pörhölä and colleagues. We begin with Argentina where the respondents reported the highest frequency of bullying, and continue with the USA, Finland, and finally Estonia where the lowest rates were reported. (Statistical facts are primarily based on the information provided on the websites of Central Intelligence Agency, Estonia.eu, Instituto Nacional de Estadisticas y Censos (2010), Official Statistics of Finland, and the United States Census Bureau).

Argentina

Argentina is the second largest country in South America, with approximately 43 million inhabitants. It is situated between the Andes and the Atlantic Ocean and features a variety of climates and topographical regions, including rich plains to rugged mountainous regions. Argentina is a diverse country made up of varied European immigrants (predominantly from Spain and Italy), which settled after its independence from Spain in 1816. Ninety-seven percent of Argentinians are white (Spanish or Italian descent), whereas 3 percent is mestizo and/or have Amerindian ancestry. Further, 95.5 percent of the population are native Argentinians, whereas 4.5 percent are foreign born, primarily from border countries. Throughout its history, Argentina underwent varied internal political conflicts, military dictatorships and several economic crises, in some cases leading to violent public protests. Although Argentina is a republic, it has experienced many years of military dictatorships returning to democracy in 1983. The Gross Domestic Product (GDP) per capita of Argentina is 14,760.20 USD (2013). The most common religion is Roman Catholic, however, other religions are openly practiced and recognized. A big gap between rich and poor, and rural versus urban communities adds to the diversity of the population in Argentina. While almost 64 percent of the population has some form of health insurance, the rest (36 percent) lacks health insurance. Primary and middle school education is universal and free, and by law children aged 6 to 14 are required to attend school. However, retention rates vary due to geographical location and the socioeconomic status of individuals. Although free attendance to public universities enables a variety of students access to higher education, only 3.2 percent of the population completes a university degree.

The Argentinian sample was collected from university students in Cordoba, the second largest city in Argentina with 1.3 million inhabitants. Of the respondents, 94.5 percent identified themselves as Argentinians and 5.5 percent Peruvians. In addition to several federal initiatives that encourage respect for diversity and multiculturalism, the National University of Cordoba has a specific program destined to promote the inclusion of diverse students in university life. While a majority of students at the university have health insurance coverage through their parents, marriage, work, or university system, over a fifth does not have any health coverage. Nevertheless, the university offers primary care services as well as prescription medication for free to students (Secretaria de Asuntos Estudiantiles 2014).

Regarding the awareness of school bullying, in the Spanish language there is no term that refers to bullying, even though people can understand and identify the phenomenon. Even though the national congress recently passed anti-bullying legislation in schools in Argentina and the English term 'bullying' has begun to be used more frequently by the media, the term bullying was not widely used in 2012 when the data was collected. The fact of not having one term to refer to this phenomenon may have brought different interpretations in respondents' minds when they were asked to respond to it in the questionnaire, as more students chose to report general experiences of bullying than the more detailed bullying behaviors that were listed.

There are several possible explanations for why Argentina data showed a higher frequency of bullying and violent behaviour. Noel *et al.* (2009) believe that the increase of certain forms of violence (particularly in schools) is a result of 'the process of deterioration, decline in living standards, precarious economic conditions, and social fragmentation' (p. 48). Another explanation emerges from the country's experiences of political and economic instability. Noel *et al.* (2009) argue that one possible contributing factor may be the fact that Argentinian society is experiencing what the authors labelled as 'a virulent egalitarianism' (p. 48) as authority symbols, currently under critique, are looked at with the suspicion of being 'authoritarian.' This reaction to authority has its roots in previous experiences with dictatorship regimes where freedom of speech was censored.

United States

The USA is a large, diverse country comprised of many different cultures and geographic regions. Approximately 318.9 million people live in the USA; however, 5.4 million inhabitants live in Minnesota where the sample was collected. Minnesota is a state located in the northern Midwest region of the country and shares a border with Canada. Compared to the USA, Minnesota's population is more homogeneous in that 86.2 percent of individuals report white/caucasian ethnicity (compared to 77.7 percent in the USA), and fewer black/African American (5.7 percent in Minnesota, 13.2 percent in the USA) and Hispanic/Latino (5.0 percent in Minnesota, 17.1 percent in the USA) reside in the state. The USA is a federal constitutional republic, governed by a democracy since the inception of the country in 1776. Both federal and state systems of power function to govern citizens, which results in some variation in services and laws across states (e.g. education systems, family law and contract law). The GDP per capita of the USA is 53,142.89 USD (2013). Although Christianity is the most common reported religious affiliation (75.9 percent), many religions are practised. Social security and public assisted healthcare are services provided in the USA, but these are reserved for the elderly and the poor.

Compared to Finland and Estonia, higher education opportunities are available across the USA at private and public colleges and universities, but attendance requires acceptance and the personal funds to pay for tuition and living expenses. Financial assistance is available through state and federal agencies, but most students must incur large loans to obtain their university degree. Regarding cultural homogeneity, the USA differs from Finland and Estonia in that there is greater diversity in the USA population in general, which contributes to an even greater diversity of socioeconomic status and intellectual preparedness among students. This feature is accentuated through discourse involving diversity as a common topic on campuses, usually resulting in some controversy and at times open conflict. Although low cost healthcare is provided to students on most university campuses, the services provided are limited. As a result, it is typical that families bear the responsibility of covering healthcare costs for students in higher education, which complicates availability and access to services. While the USA has actively focused on building public awareness of bullying in both primary and secondary education settings, there is little awareness of bullying or specific programs to diminish it in higher education.

Even though social knowledge of bullying is high in the USA, the existence of bullying behaviors in schools is reported at some of the highest rates among the developed world. Why? It may be due in part to the cultural and economic diversity that exists across the country and throughout various regions, which is expressed via tensions among students, the inconsistency of social practices with constitutional tenants identifying free speech and equality for all despite race, creed, or color, and the presence of mediated messages that are increasingly displaying violent messages on television and in advertising to youth (Anderson *et al.* 2003; Capella *et al.* 2010; Glascock 2008). Embedded within the culture are themes of individualism, which when combined with a variety of negative family communication practices, may desensitize student notions regarding appropriate and acceptable behavior when interacting with others in educational settings.

Finland

Finland is a small country with 5.5 million inhabitants, located in North Europe. It has been an independent country since 1917, after having been a grand duchy in the Russian empire for 108 years, and a part of Sweden for 600 years before that. Finnish and Swedish are the official languages. Finland's population (2013) is homogenous in that the native language of 89.3 percent of citizens is Finnish; 5.3 percent are Swedish speakers, and a small minority (0.04 percent) of indigenous people are Sami speakers. The number of people with foreign ancestry (e.g. Russian or Estonian) is 5.3 percent. Finland is a republic with a parliamentary democracy, and has been a member of the European Union since 1995. The GDP per capita of Finland is 47,218.77 USD (2013). Although Christianity is the main religion (75.3 percent), the increasing number of those who do not have the membership of any religious community is over 20 percent. Characteristics of the country include a high standard of public education, social security and healthcare, all financed by the state. There are only public universities in Finland.

Since higher education in Finland is free of charge, and financial aid is provided for all university studies by the state, all young people have equal access to higher education, regardless of their family background or financial situation. Students are selected through entrance examination, and usually enter university in a specific major or program of study. Once admitted, students do not need to compete with each other to maintain their student status, to finance their studies, or to earn an academic degree. This kind of security may decrease students' stress level and prevent competition between them, and partly explain the relatively low rates of bullying in Finland. A second point is that university students in Finland are socioeconomically, intellectually, and culturally homogeneous, which may prevent tensions between students and student groups. Intellectual differences between students within study programs are usually relatively small due to precisely determined student selection criteria and practices. Ethnic/cultural diversity is low: international students and staff members represent a small minority. Although international students attending Finnish universities have reported more bullying and victimization (social exclusion, in particular) than Finnish students (Lavikainen 2010), tensions between Finnish and international students are not seen on campuses. Political and religious diversity is also relatively small, and issues related to this diversity are rarely discussed on campuses. A third point is that health services are available for all university students at a very low cost, which can be helpful for students who have issues with their well-being, and may further decrease the level of bullying. And the fourth point is the increased number of studies on school bullying, the national-level intervention programs developed to prevent it, and media attention directed to the phenomenon have increased general awareness of school bullying. Some universities and student unions have taken initial steps to increase awareness of bullying also in higher education.

Estonia

Estonia is a small country with approximately 1.3 million inhabitants, located in the Baltic region of Europe next to Latvia and Russia. The Republic of Estonia declared its independence in 1918; this was followed by the Soviet occupation from 1940–91. It has been fully independent again since 1991, and joined the European Union in 2004. The GDP per capita of Estonia is 18,478.27 USD (2013). The majority of the population consists of Estonian nationals (69 percent), with the next largest ethnic group identifying as Russian (26 percent); the rest consists of small minorities of Ukrainian, Belarusian, Finns, and other nationals. The official language is Estonian. The country does not adhere to a common religion. Similar to the other countries in the current study, Estonia provides free public education to children until the age of 16. Both public and private universities exist in the country.

Unlike in Finland, university studies have not been free of charge for the majority of students in Estonia, which may have some influence on the socioeconomic situation of students. Although very recent changes in Estonia have provided tuition benefits to students, those sampled in the current study did not have this benefit. Estonia is quite similar to Finland in that university students in Estonia are also socioeconomically, intellectually, and culturally homogenous and that health services are provided for students at a very low cost. Even though the lowest rates of bullying among university students were detected in Estonia, cultural differences may indicate a different explanation from the low rates reported in Finland due to the political history of Estonia. Being occupied by the Soviet Union for almost 50 years, the families in Estonia may have experienced such forms of cultural discrimination through which they could have learned to categorize some forms of abuse (e.g. verbal hurting, criticizing) as 'softer' forms, resulting in a desensitization to bullying. Through family communication practices, young adults might also have been socialized to understand that admitting to victimization may indicate weakness and vulnerability, which could be a risk for their personal safety. Therefore, even as anonymous respondents, Estonian students might avoid revealing their personal experiences of being bullied.

Conclusions

The research on bullying in higher education is still scarce and little is known about its cultural variation. In this chapter, we reviewed findings from four countries to demonstrate that bullying occurs also among higher education students, with significant cultural variation in its prevalence.

We indicated some cultural factors that might have an impact on university students' lives, thus explaining the cultural variation in bullying experiences. These include factors such as cultural and socioeconomic diversity among university students, education policies that can either encourage or discourage competition or collaboration, as well as the availability of support for well-being issues. Further, we suggest that the political and historical developments of a country could explain the ways in which individuals perceive and interpret different forms of bullying in their peer relationships, and how they react to them. Also, social awareness of bullying in educational contexts and intervention programs developed to reduce it, vary between the countries we compared. This might have an effect on the ways in which university students and personnel identify bullying and how acceptable they perceive different forms of it. However, a general notion in all four countries is that bullying in university is still under-examined, not identified, and rarely discussed in public.

The cultural features we discussed can have long-term effects on individuals' lives and well-being, thus explaining the cultural trends detected in the bullying experiences from elementary school to university. While these society-level cultural factors appear important determinants to be considered to explain the variation in students' bullying experiences across countries, further research is needed to fully understand the roots of such differences. Future studies might also benefit from paying attention to differences in cultural norms and expectations related to individual's communication behavior (cf. Hofstede 2001), particularly among peers in educational contexts. What kinds of communication norms and expectations are embedded in each culture and expressed and learned through the family and school systems in which children are socialized? For example, to what extent do these cultural norms encourage direct versus indirect expression of an individual's thoughts and feelings? Do cultural norms affect the perception and presentation of oneself as a unique individual with unique goals, versus a member of a group, similar to others and with shared goals? Particular for families, investigations of parenting practices (Georgiou 2008) and family interactions may also indicate relationships between communication patterns established in the home and the development of norms and expectations that may relate to the experiences and expressions of bullying reported in different cultures. Furthermore, media can also have an influential cultural role affecting general attitudes towards particular groups of individuals, identifying marginalized groups, and, consequently, affecting who bullies, who is victimized, and what forms of bullying are expressed and experienced in a particular culture.

To conclude, cultural variations in university students' bullying experiences call for international collaboration in research and theory development, as well as international and national policies and actions. These need to address bullying as a significant determinant of health inequalities in young adulthood, and advise professionals working with young adults to consider how learning environments could be developed to support pro-social behaviors and discourage bullying.

References

Ahmer, S., Yousafzai, A. W., Bhutto, N., Alam, S., Sarangzai, A. K. and Iqbal, A. (2008). Bullying of medical students in Pakistan: A cross-sectional questionnaire survey. *PLoS ONE*, 3(12): e3889. doi:10.1371/journal.pone.0003889

Anderson, C. A., Berkowitz, L., Donnerstein, E., Huesmann, L. R., Johnson, J. D., Linz, D. and Wartela, E. (2003). The influence of media violence on youth. *Psychological Science in the Public Interest*, 4(3): 81–110.

Bennett, D. C., Guran, E. L., Ramos, M. C. and Margolin, G. (2011). College students' electronic victimization in friendships and dating relationships: Anticipated distress and associations with risky behaviors. *Violence and Victims* 26(4): 410–29.

British Medical Association (BMA) (2006). *Medical students' welfare survey report*. Available at http://www.bma.org/ap.nsf/content/WELFARE2006. [Accessed on 28 August 2011].

Capella, M. L., Hill, R. P., Kees, J. and Rapp, J. M. (2010). The impact of violence against women in advertisements. *Journal of Advertising*, 39(4): 37–51.

Central Intelligence Agency. The world factbook. Available at http://www.cia.gov/library/publications/the-world-factbook/geos/xx.html. [Accessed on 19 December 2014].

Chapell, M., Casey, D., De la Cruz, C., Ferrell, J., Forman, J., Lipkin, R., and Whitaker, S. (2004). Bullying in college by students and teachers. *Adolescence*, 39: 53–64.

Chapell, M. S., Hasselman, S. L., Kitchin, T., Lomon, S. N., MacIver, K. W. and Sarullo, P. L. (2006). Bullying in elementary school, high school, and college, *Adolescence*, 41: 633–48.

Cowie, H., Bauman, S., Coyne, I., Myers, C-A, Pörhölä, M. and Almeida, A. (2013). Cyberbullying amongst university students: an emergent cause for concern? In P. K. Smith and G. Steffgen (Eds.), *Cyberbullying Through the New Media*. London: Psychology Press. pp. 165–77.

Craig, W., Harel-Fisch, Y., Fogel-Grinvald, H., Dostaler, S., Hetland, J., Simons-Morton, B. and the HBSC Bullying Writing Group (2009). A cross-national profile of bullying and victimization among adolescents in 40 countries. *International Journal of Public Health*, 54: 216–24.

Currie, C., Zanotti, C., Morgan, A., Currie, D., de Looze, M., Roberts, C. and Barnekow, V. (Eds.) (2012). *Social Determinants of Health and Well-being Among Young People. Key Findings from the Health Behaviour in School-aged Children (HBSC) Study: International Report from the 2009/2010 Survey*. Copenhagen, Denmark: WHO Regional Office for Europe. Available at http://www.euro.who.int/HBSC. [Accessed on 24 June 2012].

Curtis, J., Bowen, I. and Reid, A. (2007). You have no credibility: Nursing students' experiences of horizontal violence. *Nurse Education in Practice*, 7: 156–63.

Curwen, T., McNichol, J. S. and Sharpe, G. W. (2011). The progression of bullying from elementary school to university. *International Journal of Humanities and Social Science*, 1(13): 47–54. (doi:10.1007/s00038-009-5413-9).

D'Angelo, L. A., and Fernández, D. R. (2011). Clima, conflictos y violencia en la escuela. Fondo de las Naciones Unidas para la Infancia (UNICEF) – Facultad Latinoamericana de Ciencias Sociales (FLACSO). Buenos Aires, Argentina.

De Souza, E. R., and Ribeiro, J. (2005). Bullying and sexual harassment among Brazilian high school students. *Journal of Interpersonal Violence*, 20(9): 1018–38.

Due, P., Holstein, B. E., Lynch, J., Diderichsen, F., Gabhain, S. N., Scheidt, P. and the Health Behaviour in School-Aged Children Bullying Working Group (2005). Bullying and symptoms among school-aged children: International comparative cross-sectional study in 28 countries. *European Journal of Public Health*, 15(2): 128–32.

Einarsen, S., Hoel, H., Zapf, D., and Cooper, C. L. (2003). The concept of bullying at work. The European tradition. In S. Einarsen, H. Hoel, D. Zapf, and C. L. Cooper (Eds.), *Bullying and Emotional Abuse in the Workplace: International Perspectives in Research and Practice*. London: Taylor and Francis. pp. 3–30.

Estonia.eu. (2015). Official gateway to Estonia. Available at http://estonia.eu/about-estonia/country/estonia-at-a-glance.html. [Accessed on 12 January 2015].

Georgiou, S. N. (2008). Parental style and child bullying and victimization experiences at school. *Social Psychology of Education*, 11: 213–27.

Glascock, J. (2008). Direct and indirect aggression on prime-time network television. *Journal of Broadcasting and Electronic Media*, 52(2): 268–81.

Glew, G. M., Fan, M.-Y., Katon, W., Rivara, F. P. and Kernic, M. A. (2005). Bullying, psychosocial adjustment, and academic performance in elementary school. *Archives of Pediatrics and Adolescent Medicine*, 159(11): 1026–031.

Hawker, D. S. J., and Boulton, M. J. (2000). Twenty years' research on peer victimization and psychosocial maladjustment: A meta-analytic review of cross-sectional studies. *Journal of Child Psychology and Psychiatry and Allied Disciplines*, (41): 441–55.

Hofstede, G. (2001). Culture's consequences: Comparing values, behaviors, institutions, and organizations across nations. Thousand Oaks, CA: Sage.

Houbre, B., Tarquinio, C., Thuillier, I. and Hergott, E. (2006). Bullying among students and its consequences on health. *European Journal of Psychology of Education*, (21): 183–208.

Instituto Nacional de Estadisticas y Censos (INDEC) (2010). Censo Nacional de Poblacion, Hogares y Viviendas 2010. Censo del Bicentenario. Serie B, Nro. 2, tomo 1. Available at http://www.censo2010.indec.gov.ar/archivos/censo2010_tomo1.pdf. [Accessed on 19 December 2014].

Jantzer, A. M., Hoover, J. H. and Narloch, R. (2006). The relationship between school-aged bullying and trust, shyness and quality of friendships in young adulthood: A preliminary research note. *School Psychology International*, 27: 146–56.

Keashly, L. and Jagatic, K. (2003). By any other name: American perspectives on workplace bullying. In S. Einarsen, H. Hoel, D. Zapf and C. L. Cooper (Eds.), *Bullying and Emotional Abuse in the Workplace: International Perspectives in Research and Practice*. London: Taylor and Francis. pp. 31–61.

Lavena, C. (n.d.). Primera Aproximacion a la Violencia Escolar en Argentina. Universidad de San Andres, Argentina. pp. 1–13. Available at http://www.udesa.edu.ar/files/EscEdu/Resumen%20Ma/Lavena.pdf. [Accessed on 28 September 2014].

Lavikainen, E. (2010). *Opiskelijan ammattikorkeakoulu 2010. Tutkimus ammattikorkeak-ouluopiskelijoiden koulutuspoluista, koulutuksen laadusta ja opiskelukyvystä* [Student's university of applied sciences 2010. Research on the study tracks, views on the quality of education, and own ability to study of students in the universities of applied sciences]. Helsinki, Finland: Opiskelijajärjestöjen tutkimussäätiö Otus.

Mukhtar, F., Daud, S., Manzoor, I., Amjad, I., Saeed, K., Naeem, M. and Javed, M. (2010). Bullying of medical students, *Journal of the College of Physicians and Surgeons Pakistan*, 20(12): 814–18.

Nansel, T. R., Overpeck, M., Pilla, R. S., Ruan, W. J., Simons-Morton, B. G., and Scheidt, P. (2001). Bullying behaviors among U.S. youth: Prevalence and association with psychosocial adjustment. *Journal of the American Medical Association*, 285: 2094–100.

National Union of Students (NUS) Student Experience Report (2008). Available at http://www.nus.org.uk/PageFiles/4017/US_StudentExperienceReport.pdf. [Accessed on 3 March 2011].

Newman, M. L., Holden, G. W. and Delville, Y. (2005). Isolation and the stress of being bullied. *Journal of Adolescence*, 28(3): 343–57.

Noel, G., Miguez, D., Gallo, P., Bianchi, M., Lionetti, L., Pomes, A. L. and Varela, P. (2009). *Violencia en las escuelas desde una perspectiva cualitativa*. 1a ed. Ministerio de Educación de la Nación. Buenos Aires, Argentina.

Official Statistics of Finland (OSF). Helsinki, Finland: Advisory Board of OSF. Available at http://tilastokeskus.fi/meta/svt/index_en.html. [Accessed on 29 December 2014].

Pörhölä, M. (2009). Psychosocial well-being of victimized students. In T. A. Kinney and M. Pörhölä (Eds.), *Anti and Pro-Social Communication: Theories, Methods, and Applications* (Language as Social Action, Vol. 6.). New York: Peter Lang. pp. 83–93.

Pörhölä, M. (2011). Kiusaaminen opiskeluyhteisössä [Bullying in university community]. In K. Kunttu, A. Komulainen, K. Makkonen and P. Pynnönen (Eds.), *Opiskeluterveys*. Helsinki, Finland: Duodecim. pp. 166–68.

Pörhölä, M., Cowie, H., Cvancara, K., Kaal, E., Kunttu, K., Myers, C.-A., Tampere, K. and Torres, B. (in submission). *Cultural Variation and Gender Differences in University Students' Experiences of Bullying and Victimization in Five Countries*.

Reijntjes A., Kamphuis, J. H., Prinzie, P. and Telch, M. J. (2010). Peer victimization and internalizing problems in children: A meta-analysis of longitudinal studies. *Child Abuse and Neglect,* 34(4): 244–52.

Roman, M. and Murillo, F. Javier (2011). America Latina: Violencia entre estudiantes y desempeño escolar. *Revista Cecopal* 104: 37–54.

Salin, D. (2001). Prevalence and forms of bullying among business professionals: A comparison of two different strategies for measuring bullying. *European Journal of Work and Organizational Psychology,* 10: 425–41.

Schäfer, M., Korn, S., Smith, P. K., Hunter, S. C., Mora-Merchán, J. A., Singer, M. M. and van der Meulen, K. (2004). Lonely in the crowd: Recollections of bullying. *British Journal of Developmental Psychology,* 22: 379–94.

Secretaria de Asuntos Estudiantiles (2014). Subsecretaria de Inclusion y Ciudadania Estudiantil. Available at http://www.unc.edu.ar/vidaestudiantil/gestion/secretaria-de-asuntos-estudiantiles. [Accessed on 19 December 2014].

Sinkkonen, H.-M., Puhakka, H. and Meriläinen, M. (2012). Bullying at a university: students' experiences of bullying. *Studies in Higher Education.* Available at DOI:10.1080/03075079.2011.649726.

United States Census Bureau website. Available at http://www.census.gov/population/international/data/idb. [Accessed on 4 October 2014].

PART V

Interventions and policies

11

THE ROLE OF THE THERAPIST IN HELPING UNIVERSITY STUDENTS WHO HAVE BEEN BULLIED

A case study of sexual bullying

Maria Luca

Introduction

The extreme manifestation of what appears to be harmless sexual innuendo among university students (but is in fact malign) is presented to student counselling services, though often those who are sexually bullied are unable to seek help. This chapter will explore sexual bullying among university students, especially where trust is betrayed, and discusses the impact of betrayal on the mental health of the person. A vignette of a sexually bullied individual highlights the lived experience in being sexually bullied and explores appropriate psychological interventions. The chapter concludes with a discussion on how universities could play a part in supporting victims of sexual bullying and implications for student counselling services.

There are times when sexual bullying among university students remains undetected, unreported or even romanticized as part of a normal and growing sexualized culture. This creates a climate of fear of exposure, with the implication that the person bullied suffers in silence. Such a climate may also induce guilt and shame, both compromising the individual's self-esteem and sense of relational belonging to the peer group, and perpetuating feelings of being an 'outsider', as well as self-blame. The trauma associated with sexual bullying often remains elusive until the habitual coping mechanisms in the individual break down with negative consequences and an adverse impact on psychological health, compromising the individual's studies.

Bullying among university students is becoming a major concern in academic settings. Research has found high percentages (32 per cent boys, 22 per cent girls) of young people engaging in this form of aggression (Espelage *et al.* 2011), a statistic that cannot be ignored. Bullying can take the form of direct, face-to-face harassment, including belittlement, derogatory remarks, exclusion and sexual innuendo, and increasingly cyberbullying, which is conducted anonymously by perpetrators through social media and mobile phones. The consequences of being bullied on the mental health of young people are far ranging and include depression, post-traumatic stress, decreased self-esteem, suicidal ideation and withdrawal from studies. A sense of betrayal of trust pervades the self-esteem of the bullied person with huge consequences for the sense of self, psychological and academic functioning.

Recognition of the widespread nature of problems associated with bullying, particularly the consequences for mental health, is fundamental if universities are to develop appropriate prevention and treatment strategies to help victims. Ideas on what drives young people to bully others are well documented in the literature and in this book, and are not reviewed in this chapter.

Types of sexual bullying among university students

There are various forms of sexual harassment. For a typology of sexual harassment on the Internet, see Barak (2005). According to Barak, harassment in cyberspace is common and manifests in such forms as sexually offensive messages, gender-humiliating remarks and can be active or passive. Sexting is also a medium of sexual harassment among university students. It involves sending and receiving sexually explicit materials, including images through mobile phones (Walker *et al.* 2011). Sexting is a punishable offence in the US. For instance, a girl may consent to taking explicit photos of herself with a boyfriend. When they break up, he shares these photos with friends and other students. As a consequence, she becomes the target of sexual bullying. For the purposes of this chapter three core types of sexual bullying are created: aggressive overt; aggressive covert; resentful sexual bullying.

Aggressive overt sexual bullying

Domination and control of a person is often the motivation of this type of sexual bullying. It is conducted openly and occurs mostly in intimate relationships where the perpetrator uses strategies to frighten, cause anxiety, harm the self-esteem and ultimately triumph over the victim. A common characteristic in sadomasochistic relationships, if persistent, this behaviour can damage the confidence of the victim. How the perpetrator's actions are experienced by the victim would determine whether this type of bullying could be adopted. One example from my clinical work is of an intelligent 30-year-old woman who willingly took photos of her genitalia (sometimes urinating), breasts and backside in public places, texting these to her boyfriend to demonstrate her love. She resented having to use these means; however, her self-esteem and sense of self-worth were so low, she felt that if she failed to comply with the perpetrator's demands she would be rejected. On the face of it, she appeared to be a fellow enthusiast in sexual games of domination and control (she being the submissive one). Nevertheless, she was also aware that the perpetrator enjoyed humiliating and degrading her, using threats that he would end their relationship if she failed to comply. She resented having to perform these humiliating acts, but also believed she had no other option. She sought therapy to help her break free from what she considered destructive and ultimately damaging behaviour.

Aggressive covert sexual bullying

In contrast to aggressive overt sexual bullying, aggressive covert sexual bullying is subtle and often goes undetected by others. Perpetrators use social media sites to spread gossip and rumours intended to sexually humiliate. Cyberbullying becomes a form of aggressive covert sexual bullying when it involves demeaning a person because of that person's gender or that person's sexual activity. Perpetrators use mobile phones or the Internet, disseminate sexually explicit photographs and spread rumours intended to harm the victim and compromize their sense of self-worth.

Resentful sexual bullying

This type of bullying is intended to distress and humiliate the victim either because the bully has a grievance against the victim or desires social status among the peer group. Scorned lovers who find it difficult to accept the end of a relationship sometimes resort to spreading rumours intended to hurt the victim's reputation and status. Individuals whose amorous desires are rejected can and do resort to stalking behaviours as well as language such as name calling e.g. 'slut', or 'whore', or use sexual images and comments to vent their anger and harass the victim. Factors contributing to resentful sexual bullying are jealousy and possessive behaviour. At the root of persistent resentful stalking is a self-centred personality, harbouring the belief of self-entitlement and an inability to cope with rejection. An inability to cope with rejection from a partner can develop into stalking behaviours as the media reports. Portrayals of individuals who developed murderous resentment towards an ex-girlfriend who rejected them are testament to the dangers of resentful sexual bullying. Bindel (2005) begins her reporting of a tragic case by saying:

> 'Moments before Rana Faruqui was killed in August 2003, a 999 operator heard her pleading with her ex-boyfriend, Stephen Griffiths: "You are not allowed to come anywhere near me, Steve, Steve, leave me alone, leave me alone." She had been cleaning the stables on her Berkshire farm when Griffiths stabbed her to death with a hunting knife'.

The article highlights that stalking is not just a problem for celebrities and that one in five women in Britain and one in 20 men will be victims of a stalker at some time in their lives.

A common form of sexual bullying is through sexting. The following clinical vignette illustrates how sexting reinforced a young woman's low self-esteem, caused shame and humiliation, became a catalyst of early childhood trauma, led to the development of obsessive compulsive disorder (OCD) with compulsive washing and to self-destructive behaviours such as cutting.

A case study of a double betrayal

Some years ago, Counselling Services at a university referred Violetta, a 21-year-old beautiful, intelligent and sensitive young woman, who moved to the UK from a European country to study. This was towards the end of her first year BA course and she was depressed and anxious with the pending examinations. It was a humid summer day and the consulting room window was open. Violetta looked at the open window, paused, then looked at me and asked whether I could close the window. I had no idea at this point what her request had meant, but I closed the window and settled into my chair ready to conduct the initial assessment. She went on to describe how her mother worked long hours to finance her education and aspired for her to break free of the family's working-class struggle, an aspiration that weighed heavily on Violetta. To fail had been associated with disappointing her mother and appearing ungrateful of her hard labour and sacrifice to make this dream real. The following exchange is an excerpt from this initial assessment session:

Therapist: What brings you here?

Violetta: I haven't been to class for the last two weeks and my attendance in the last four months has been sporadic. I have exams coming up and I'm anxious I will fail (cries); (pause). I just cannot get out of bed in the mornings. My flatmate is worried about me and suggested I talk to student services. They thought it might help if I talk to a professional.

Therapist: What do you think has caused this problem?

Violetta: I don't know… I just feel upset and cry a lot, then my sleep is affected, I keep thinking about…well, I'm thinking about what happened to me last year and get upset…I haven't told anyone about it.

Therapist: Take your time. It is obvious that what happened last year is pretty upsetting for you.

Violetta: Yeah… (looks away, her eyes filled with tears. I watch Violetta's distress expressed in silence, with teardrops falling as the witnesses to an unspoken trauma. Eventually she began to sob and reached for the tissues). Sorry (pause). I worry that I will not be able to sit my exams if I continue to feel this way. Why am I like this?

Therapist: Well, we are here to try to understand why you feel this way. It seems that you have been feeling upset for some time now. Have you spoken to anyone? Do you have friends you can talk to?

Violetta: I have friends from college, but can't talk to them about it. My mum and I speak regularly on the phone but I haven't told her what happened. I don't want to upset her. Her relationship with my stepfather is getting worse. They are talking about divorce and my sister Stephanie has been caught shop lifting recently, so my mum is going through a hard time. When my dad left when I was seven she worked day and night to support us and is now paying for my studies. Her father died two years ago and I think she is not over that yet. My stepfather drinks a lot and gets aggressive with mum and my sister.

Therapist: So the situation at home worries you and makes it difficult for you to focus on your own problems?

Violetta: The thing is…I don't know how to say it…the thing is, well, I was in a relationship for 3 months with J. We met at college. We fell for each other and sex was great! But then we started fighting… he flirted with other girls and began telling me I was not attractive and that he didn't fancy me anymore. We split up around Christmas. It was a very upsetting time for me and I spent a lot of time alone trying to study but couldn't.

Initial assessment and formulation

At initial assessment, Violetta complained of a one-year history of depressive symptoms. These included poor sleep pattern, impaired concentration affecting her studies and feelings of guilt and shame. She also reported anxiety and panic that she would fail in her studies, obsessive washing and cleaning, delusional thoughts such as seeing scissors and other sharp objects flying around in her bathroom and toilet, anxiety in wearing dresses or skirts and the occasional self-harm. For the last six months these had become progressively debilitating. I asked if she had any suicidal thoughts and she said, regularly, but never acted on them. Her self-esteem appeared to have also deteriorated in the last six months.

When Violetta started therapy, she said her expectation was to rebuild her low self-esteem and feel better about herself so she could successfully complete her studies. She said that she never had therapy before, felt anxious about it, and there were too many issues she wants to sort out, and that she sometimes feels dizzy thinking about them. She hoped to understand why she feels this way.

Judging from Violetta's distraught demeanour, I was careful to regulate the exploration pace, so not to push her into disclosing and re-experiencing traumatic information that at this stage she might not be able to handle. It would be premature, especially in the absence of a clear formulation and knowledge of how resilient the client is and what coping mechanisms she adopts to manage powerful feelings and the impact of these on her daily functioning, to focus her on the core conflict. I used the assessment to enable me to obtain a general view of Violetta's place in the world, identify core conflicts and early traumas, evaluate current functioning and impact of her symptoms on her daily life, evaluate her suicidal ideation, whether active or passive, as well as discuss her expectations of how therapy could help. I listened with respect and empathy, trying to understand Violetta's experiences, at times sharing my understandings. This is an important approach in helping clients to develop trust, which fosters a working alliance and opens the door for more in-depth work.

I approach initial sessions with an open mind and use non-judgemental, empathic questioning, to encourage clients to open up. Violetta was able to describe lucidly during this initial session her family's problematic situation which helped us contextualize her problems and understand how she opted to suffer in silence over an event she alluded to, but could not yet talk about. Complete acceptance is an important therapist attitude at this early stage of therapy, especially before an alliance develops. I felt that Violetta was in distress about the unspoken event and refrained from focusing on this immediately. The pace of the therapy process needs to be judged and regulated according to the therapist's perception and how much affective distress they believe the client can tolerate at any given moment. If in doubt, it is best to wait rather than become too intrusive and risk shutting down the client. As I listened to her background history, I tried to identify significant events in her life from as far back as she could remember, explore the nature of her relational patterns with important others, identify her strengths and sore points to help me establish the nature and severity of early trauma, and assess to what extent the client's strengths can help her to tolerate and work through core conflicts.

Violetta spoke of her estranged relationship with her father, her anger towards him for abandoning his family to set up home in another town with her mother's best friend. Although she visited her father occasionally, she felt jealous of his relationship with her half-brother, five years her junior and could not bear to be around her stepmother. She described her father as selfish and irresponsible. Her attitude towards her mother on the other hand, was positive. She described her as a dedicated and loving mother and dreaded the thought of failing her studies and disappointing her.

My initial working psychological formulation was that Violetta's attachment style was ambivalent, both craving closeness with father, while at the same time distancing herself from him. The separation of her parents and her father moving many miles away from home created feelings of being abandoned and not worthy of father's attention. She was very close to her mother, but felt protective of her, wanted to please her, was frightened of disappointing her and compensated for her guilt that she would burden her mother by being 'the good girl'. It takes considerable focus, observation, engagement and much detective work to develop a clear formulation, but a therapist needs to start from somewhere, then build on it as therapy progresses and the process deepens.

A deepening phase of therapy

In subsequent sessions, Violetta followed a pattern of silence for the first ten minutes then attempted to speak the unspoken, finding it too difficult and reverting to talk of worry and anxiety about her exams. In the eighth session, she arrived late, slumped into her chair and started to cry. I asked what it was that was bringing up her feelings.

Violetta: I didn't want to come to therapy this morning… I had one of those nights, drunk loads of alcohol, had some cocaine and ended up having sex with this creep that I don't even fancy. It was horrible. He was so aggressive it made me feel like a whore (cries). My flatmate was asleep when I got home in the early hours of the morning and I worried she might hear the noise from my bedroom. I asked him to leave. He got up, put his clothes on and disappeared with a grin on his face. My eyes were fixed on this pair of scissors, I don't know what came over me but I felt disgusted, so I took the scissors and cut my legs and my arms…there was blood everywhere. (She lifted her sleeves to show me the wounds). (I felt sadness and concern for her but remained calm).

Therapist: Well I'm glad you came for your session today despite feeling ambivalent and I'm sorry you feel so upset (pause). Have you self-harmed before?

Violetta: (Takes a big breath, while making direct eye contact). No, this was the first time. It was such a relief. It calmed me down. But I started to ruminate for a few hours. Couldn't sleep. This is difficult for me. I haven't told anyone before but last year…(sobs). Sorry.

Therapist: It's OK, take your time.

Violetta: Last year we had a family holiday at my grandparents' summer house. I remembered something that upset me a lot. After our father left us, our mother had to work and our grandparents looked after us. My granddad would take us to the park after school then he bought us sweets. We used to go to the summer house with him and I remember (pause, then she cries uncontrollably); he … I think he abused me. I'm not sure, but it all started to come back whilst at the summer house. I'm scared to tell mum. She'll think it's all her fault. People might think I made it all up.

Therapist: Do you mind telling me what kind of abuse?

Violetta: Sexual (she looks away). I wouldn't blame you if you think I'm disgusting (sobs).

Therapist: It's helpful that you've shared such painful memories with me. It takes courage to talk about something so painful. It seems these memories left you feeling disgusted with yourself, believing that I would be disgusted with you. You were a child. What happened is not your fault.

Violetta smiled in the midst of tears to my comment. She seemed relieved that she managed to speak about her traumatic memories as well as surprised at my response. The grandfather whom she loved and trusted had betrayed her. As she relayed her memories, she re-experienced the little girl's fear and depression. However, this had been a turning point in her life. She finally began to trust me, voice her pain, and the developing understanding about the abuse of trust had provided respite from persecutory self-blaming thoughts. At the same time, the traumatic memories crowding her mind and her fear of bringing shame upon her family posed the risk of more self-harming behaviour. The impact on her self-esteem had been considerable.

Two months into therapy, Violetta found the courage to disclose what she had been hinting at for several weeks. She had been a victim of sexual harassment by a

22-year-old student she met at college who originated from the same country as
Violetta. At first, she thought he was great. They dated for a few weeks and Violetta
referred to him as her boyfriend. She planned to tell mum her good news until one
day another female student told her some shocking news. Apparently Violetta's
boyfriend had video recorded them having sex and texted this to a group of students
at the university and friends from back home. He also uploaded it onto the Internet.
As she described this Violetta was in severe distress. She explained that since this
terrible exposure and humiliation she could not sleep, suffered from rumination,
constantly re-living the event, then wishing herself dead. This was a double betrayal.
First, the grandfather she trusted and now the boyfriend she doted on. It was evident
that she had been suffering from symptoms of post-traumatic stress.

Violetta: It was so horrible…I felt so ashamed. How could he do this to me!
Therapist: You felt betrayed, humiliated and ashamed?
Violetta: I felt so angry, then didn't know what to do. I just wanted to hide. The
    shame was too much; it affected my sleep; I could not concentrate on my
    studies. I wanted to die. I swallowed a handful of pills and thought, that's it.
    When my flatmate found me, she called for help. At the hospital, they were
    kind to me and recommended I see someone for therapy. I was angry and
    helpless. The images of me naked having sex with him and other people
    watching and laughing kept going around my head; I am so stupid. Why did I
    trust him? What will the other students think of me? I feel dirty, disgusting and
    worthless (she sobs). Can't bear to talk about it. I've been skipping classes and
    feel so dirty, I keep washing myself. Life is a struggle nowadays; I keep thinking
    what's the point of carrying on.
Therapist: Do you continue to have suicidal thoughts?
Violetta: Yes… (crying).
Therapist: I am so sorry you had to go through such pain. You are in touch with
    overwhelming feelings now and it's painful. You don't have to carry your
    feelings alone now. I'm here to help. Take your time. We can explore this again
    when you feel you can manage what's coming up. It is normal for you to feel
    the way you do.
Violetta: My mum doesn't know. She would be devastated if I told her.
Therapist: Is J still on the course?
Violetta: Yes. We do some modules together and every time I see him I feel like
    screaming, I can't concentrate and missed quite a few classes. But a part of me
    doesn't want to let him win.
Therapist: Have you spoken to student services or a tutor about this?
Violetta: No, I feel ashamed that I trusted him. They will think I'm stupid. He and
    his friends laugh at me now.
Therapist: Well, I don't think you are stupid. It can't be easy after what happened
    to you to encounter J in class. It may be worth thinking about possible ways of
    avoiding sharing lectures with him. A tutor might be able to help you with this.

This had been a betrayal of trust, an aggressive act against her entire being. It was a betrayal she could not comprehend, nor digest. Violetta felt she would never be able to have a sexual relationship again, as she felt violated and betrayed. As Trowel *et al.* (2002) showed 'the impact of the penetration, of threatened and actual violence, and of the transgression of normal expected boundaries, leaves the abused child vulnerable' (p. 242). Sexual bullying can also have devastating consequences for the victim's ability to continue in intimate relationships.

Violetta made it clear during the sessions that she was highly anxious about getting involved in an intimate relationship and opted instead for casual encounters. She was deeply upset during the first six months of our work, but her growing trust in me helped her to talk through her feelings. The more Violetta allied herself to me the more our therapeutic relationship was charged with feelings. At times my own feelings guided me in reaching out to Violetta, allowing myself to be touched by her despair and helped me find ways to listen and understand the depth of her experience.

Sexual harassment is prevalent in real and virtual environments, causing significant psychological harm to victims (Barak 2005). Sexual bullies take advantage of the vulnerability in the victim and exploit it to their own advantage. According to the study by Pryor and Stoller (1994), 'Men who are high risk in sexually harassing women perceive a connection between sexuality and social dominance'. Drawing from these findings, we can see how Violetta's humiliation was a perverse triumph for the man she trusted and who now degraded her. The harasser not only betrayed her trust, but also violated her sense of self-worth. Feeling ashamed, humiliated and degraded, Violetta developed obsessive symptoms that interfered with her functioning, management of her studies and negatively affected her self-esteem. This traumatic experience had also been a catalyst of sexual abuse in childhood. In such instances, the victim is flooded with overwhelming emotions and can resort to self-destructive behaviours as a way of fending off psychological pain. Cutting and OCD were coping mechanisms Violetta had adopted to manage negative emotions.

Psychological interventions

The initial approach to therapy with Violetta was to help her begin to voice her distress in a safe and containing therapy environment. To enable client disclosure of distressing experiences, the therapist needs to judge the client's ability to tolerate emotional pain from recounting traumas. My aim initially was to negotiate the tension between encouraging client deep level emotional re-experiencing, which would deepen the process, while monitoring the client's responses and pacing the work accordingly. As therapy progressed, Violetta's reported symptoms of OCD intensified. Behaviours such as hand-washing, checking lights, compulsive cleaning of her flat became all-consuming. Her avoidance of social situations remained the same but was greatly troubling her. I had warned Violetta in the early stage of our work that therapy could bring up intense and sometimes unbearable feelings. By pre-empting what could be expected, it helped normalize any intense feelings emerging during therapy. It is good practice to provide this information to clients, who sometimes expect positive change immediately, and feel shocked and anxious in discovering how painful therapy can be. By containing powerful feelings and helping Violetta process them, the therapy provided her with a sharpened awareness of how she used destructive mechanisms to rid herself of these feelings.

As the process of sharing and understanding was firmly established between us, Violetta's shame, self-disgust, betrayal, anger and fear also began to settle. Careful not to collude with her judgmental attitude to herself, especially the self-deprecation, her self-blame softened. People sexually abused in childhood often turn shame and humiliation against themselves, having not learned how to channel these feelings constructively. Together we explored Violetta's perspective while I focused on gently challenging her to consider alternative perspectives, or at least think about them. She recognized how the childhood sexual abuse and associated betrayal had an impact on her self-esteem, leaving her vulnerable. She felt that the betrayal by her boyfriend opened a 'Pandora's box' with primitive feelings from childhood sexual abuse surfacing and threatening her psychological equilibrium. Soon she got in touch with her anger but felt powerless and weighed down by it. She began to channel her anger by refusing to be defeated by her ex-boyfriend and attended the same course of study as the harasser. Given that she felt this was the only available avenue open to her, she entered into a double bind where by being strong she was placing herself in a threatening environment causing her to feel vulnerable again. During sessions, she was reluctant to use the toilet as she feared it would take her hours to come out. I encouraged her to time herself and spend no more than ten minutes, reminding herself that whatever she felt she could bring it to the session for us to process it together. This exposure technique in a controlled environment helped Violetta take control of her delusions that scissors were flying around aiming for her genitalia and she eventually managed to spend less time in bathrooms. We discussed the symbolic meaning of her delusions about sharp objects and arrived at the idea that they represented her experience of being penetrated during sexual abuse. She resonated with this idea and reported how it mediated in her achieving more control of her body.

After a year in therapy, Violetta had dealt with the intense debilitating feelings that she came to therapy for. By encouraging her to voice her feelings, think about them and contextualize them, she felt empowered. The previously reported one-night stands were attempts to discharge unwanted emotions. Although providing temporary relief from her negative feelings, such behaviour simultaneously fuelled her low self-esteem. She used the understanding she gained from therapy to refrain from this and other self-destructive behaviours, feeling levelled and more psychologically resolved. She benefitted through my normalizing of her distress and self-chastisement, felt more grounded and able to own her power. She was no longer besieged by anxieties and fear and the shame gradually began to recede. Destructive behaviours became less prominent in her life, her suicidal ideation was no longer present, and she felt worthy of a trusting relationship. Her decision to move to another university was part of her need to free herself from the ghost of the double betrayal.

My therapy approach with Violetta was inter-personal, actively involving her in constructing understandings, thinking through dialogue and jointly reflecting on the process of therapy while evaluating its effectiveness in helping her manage her distress. The therapeutic relationship is a very important consideration in inter-personal therapy where a spirit of collaboration, the establishment of a working alliance and shared responsibility on how therapy progresses create the cornerstone for a positive therapeutic climate. Clinical experience is valuable in sharpening understandings. Mine guided me through some negative phases, especially when Violetta's symptoms intensified. Violetta's trust in me was withering during these phases. Rather than avoiding addressing her doubts, as some inexperienced therapists might do, I opened exploration and invited Violetta to think about what was negatively impacting on our work and process it.

Discussion

Sexual bullying causes significant psychological harm to victims. It is used by some perpetrators to exercise control and dominance, a perverse triumph in the face of suffering in the victim. In cases where sexual bullying takes place within a current or previous intimate relationship, it is a betrayal of trust. Victims betrayed in this way become mistrustful of intimate relationships, fearing further exposure and humiliation. To cope, victims resort to isolation and avoidance, strategies aimed at managing their distress. However, isolation can cause depression and prevent victims from leading a normal life. As we have seen in this chapter, Violetta's studies were compromised, her mental health deteriorated and more crucially, the sexual bullying by her boyfriend was a catalyst of early childhood trauma. Left untreated, her condition could compromise her life.

Young people are at higher risk of suicidal ideation and 'participation in bullying increases the risk of suicidal ideations and/or behaviors in a broad spectrum of youth' (Kim and Leventhal 2008, p. 133). This makes it more pertinent that universities provide supportive services, including counselling and therapy by experienced clinicians. Cost cutting forces some university counselling services to rely on honorary or inexperienced therapists for the provision of student therapeutic support. While many students benefit from the service, it is fundamental that those harassed or sexually bullied are assigned experienced therapists, or at least referred on to experienced clinicians in other services.

Strategies for managing sexual bullying

Universities could do more to create a safe environment for all bullied students. For victims of sexual bullying to feel safe and able to focus on their studies, they need to be listened to by their university. Taking allegations of sexual bullying seriously and investigating further is fundamental to showing a no-tolerance attitude to sexual bullies, whilst supporting victims. Normally students who are bullied turn to lecturers or support services staff they trust for guidance. It is therefore essential that staff receive appropriate training to help them listen and offer appropriate support. Support may require making a referral to student counselling if such a service exists within the university, or external counselling services.

Ongoing emphasis in educating university students to understand appropriate behaviours is important. More active ways of educating students, such as making policies explicit during induction sessions, are likely to be more successful. In addition, by developing harassment policies to tackle perpetrators, universities would demonstrate that they are serious about tackling harassers. Personal tutorials tend to focus on academic problems. A victim of harassment may be deterred from raising a confidential disclosure about personal experiences that interfere with academic progress. Personal tutors are in a good position to advise or refer students to student support services if their role includes pastoral care. Ensuring the message that the university does not tolerate sexual bullying is accessible to all students and staff can create a safer environment for all students. Sexual harassment is traumatic for victims. Therefore, student-counselling services must consider allocating appropriately experienced psychological clinicians to work with victims of sexual bullying.

References

Barak, A. (2005). Sexual harassment on the Internet. *Social Science Computer Review*, 23(1): 77–92.

Bindel, J. (2005). The Life Stealers. *The Guardian*, Saturday, 16 April 2005. Available at http://www.theguardian.com/uk/2005/apr/16/ukcrime.weekend7.

Espelage, D. L. and Swearer, S. M. (Eds.). (2011). *Bullying in North American Schools* (2nd ed.). New York: Routledge.

Pryor, B. J. and Stoller, M. L. (1994). Sexual cognition processes in men high in the likelihood to sexually harass. *Personality and Social Psychology Bulletin*, 20: 163–69.

Trowel, J., Kolvin, I., Weeramanthri, T., Sadowski, H., Berelowitz, M., Glasser, D. and Leitch, I. (2002). Psychotherapy for sexually abused girls: psychopathological outcome findings and patterns of change. *British Journal of Psychiatry*, 180: 234–37.

Kim, S. Y. and Leventhal, B. (2008). Bullying and suicide: A review. *International Journal of Adolescent Medicine and Health*, 20(2): 133–54.

Walker, S., Sanchi, L. and Temple-Smith, M. (2011). Sexting and Young People. *Youth Studies Australia*, 30(4): 8–16.

12

POLICIES AND PROCEDURES TO ADDRESS BULLYING AT AUSTRALIAN UNIVERSITIES

Marilyn Campbell

Introduction

While bullying is often researched in children and adolescents and in the workplace, there is limited research in the emerging adult population, especially in students at university. This is perhaps due to the fact that bullying generally declines as children and young people become older (Nansel *et al*. 2001; Wang *et al*. 2009). Although this may indeed be the case, it is apparent that bullying does not completely abate when students graduate from high school. The plethora of literature evidencing workplace bullying clearly shows that bullying continues beyond the school years (Hoel *et al*. 2001; Privitera and Campbell 2009). With the advent of cyberbullying in the last decade it has been shown that this particular form of bullying may not decrease with age as does traditional bullying (Kowalski and Limber 2007; Raskauskas and Stoltz 2007). In addition, we know there is a spike in prevalence rates during the transition from primary to high school (Pellegrini *et al*. 2010), so it is possible that new university students are at an increased risk of victimization due to this being a transition period. This has led to some interest in examining the prevalence of bullying in the emerging adult population at universities (Chapell *et al*. 2004; Pontzer 2010; Wensley and Campbell 2009).

We know there are many negative consequences of bullying, such as long-term psychological problems including increased levels of anxiety, depressive symptoms, poor self-worth, social isolation and loneliness, psychosomatic complaints, suicidal ideation and suicide attempts for students who have been victimized (Hawker and Boulton 2003; Neary and Joseph 1994). Perpetrators of bullying have also been found to be at a heightened risk of experiencing problems such as anxiety, depression, psychosomatic symptoms and eating disorders (Kaltiala-Heino *et al*. 2000), difficulties with school, psychosocial adjustment, externalising behaviours and delinquency in late adolescence and early adulthood (Nansel *et al*. 2001; Perren and Hornung 2005), substance abuse (Houbre *et al.* 2006) and psychiatric problems (Kumpulainen 2008). Bully-victims are at the greatest risk for adversity. Not only do they tend to share the aforementioned risk factors of both bullies and victim for anxiety, depression, psychosomatic symptoms, eating disorders, frequent excessive drinking and other substance use (Cook *et al.* 2010; Kaltiala-Heino *et al.* 2000), but also there is continued hostility and violence toward others, weapon-carrying and increased risk of incarceration (Malecki and Demaray 2003; Nansel *et al.* 2001).

One prevention and intervention strategy to reduce bullying in schools is the provision of anti-bullying policies and procedures. It has been shown that a formal whole-school anti-bullying policy is strongly associated with a reduction in reported bullying in Farrington and Ttofi's (2009) meta-analysis. Clear policies and procedures provide a valuable framework for schools (Pearce *et al.* 2011) to show commitment to the prevention and intervention of bullying, including cyberbullying, and to demonstrate and communicate its procedural response to the whole school community (Smith *et al.* 2008).

This chapter presents some research into policies and procedures of Australian universities. Implications for practice and future research are discussed.

Why have anti-bullying policies?

An anti-bullying policy is a framework to show an institution's commitment to the prevention and intervention of all forms of bullying (Smith *et al.* 2008). The main aim is to reduce bullying. The policy is used to demonstrate and communicate the institution's procedural response to bullying for the school or workplace. Policies offer regulation and are sometimes mandated by law. The creation of an anti-bullying policy by an institution indicates that the management of the institution is aware of the possibility of bullying occurring. If the policy is disseminated to students and employees then they are also aware of this behaviour, which is the first step in the prevention of bullying (Campbell 2005).

There are usually two reasons that institutions devise an anti-bullying policy. The first is that the bureaucracy has a vision for the school, university or workplace that is based on values of equity and a safe learning and working environment. The anti-bullying policy is therefore the communication of a vision that is operationalized. The second is a reaction to external pressure such as legislation requiring a policy or media attention to bullying issues (Glover, Cartwright, Gough, and Johnson 1998).

Policies are part of the conception of bullying from an ecological perspective not just from a dyadic relationship perspective between a student or employee who bullies and the one who is bullied. Policies emphasize the broad contextual and social factors which influence bullying (Hatzenbuehler and Keyes 2012). This ecological perspective is based on Bronfenbrenner's Social Ecological Theory of Human Development (Bronfenbrenner 1977, 1979), which focuses on the importance of the relationships between people and their environment and the interaction between the environment and the individual. The theory posits four nested structures. The *macrosystem* represents belief systems or contextual patterns within the society, which includes: cultural norms, language, legal, educational and political systems. The *exosystem* consists of mass media, and governance matters. The *mesosystem* comprises the relationship between the person and the setting. The *microsystem* represents individual factors (Bronfenbrenner 1977, 1979; Leonard 2011; Reifsnider *et al.* 2005). Policies therefore are situated in both the *macro* and *exosystem*.

A benefit of anti-bullying policies is to emphasize that bullying and harassment is not exacerbated or normalized. Just as the law formalizes what each society contends are its social norms, reflecting that society's morals and values (Vago 2009) so policies can formalize the institution's social norms. Polices can also be used to modify behaviour and influence these social norms by the sanctions and punishments the policy may contain. Thus, policies convey a normative, educative message 'symbolically announcing what society deems good and valuable' (Limber and Small 2003, p. 448). It is envisioned that anti-bullying policies will influence people's social norms so that all forms of bullying are seen as unacceptable by peers. As we know, bystanders to bullying behaviour are extremely influential in the social context and how they choose to act sustains the social norm (Craig *et al.* 2000). Therefore, the ultimate aim of an anti-bullying policy is to reduce bullying.

Different contexts

Bullying research to date has, as previously mentioned, usually been researched in schools and workplaces. Universities are however, a unique environment where students are neither school children nor in the workplace. Thus, there is an opportunity to provide a knowledge 'bridge' in the developmental trajectory of bullying behaviour from school to work. All institutions or organizations have both a corporate culture and an organizational structure that provides an environment for bullying to flourish or to wither.

Bullying research in school populations emphasizes the individual factors involved in this problematic social relationship (concentrating more on Bronfenbrenner's *meso* and *micro* systems) while workplace bullying research emphasizes the organizational ethos or systems involved (the *maxo* and *exo* systems) (Coleyshaw 2010). Perhaps a combination of these approaches to researching bullying in universities will provide a richer explanation in future research. Research into bullying at schools is seen as altruistic, to prevent harm to children, to discharge their duty of care and to teach students not to abuse their power. Workplace bullying is viewed more in economic terms with arguments such as staff turnover, loss of productivity and absenteeism used to justify research into reducing bullying (Duffy 2009). In this regard, universities have a dual role: first as educational institutions, seats of learning which have a duty to challenge homophobia, sexism, racism and other forms of social exclusion; and second, about preparing students as future leaders and innovators in the workplace. The study of university policies for prevention and intervention of bullying among students is important as there has been an increase in the Australian university population from an elite group in the 1970s to over a quarter of young people attending university at present (Australian Bureau of Statistics 2012). Increases in tuition fees are also leading to a more student focus where students are expecting value for money teaching (Naidoo 2003). Additionally, these students are the first digital natives (Prensky 2001) to go to university and because of their rich online lives; there is an increased risk of cyberbullying. Furthermore, the way the students are taught, often online only or blended with face-to-face teaching and the extensive use of group work and group assessment could be risk factors for bullying to occur (Coyne *et al.* 2004). There are also unique power dynamics and structural differentiation in universities. There are faculty and professional staff, fee-paying students and also students who are faculty members. All these factors impact on policies and procedures designed to prevent and intervene with bullying incidents among students at universities.

In the next section each of the three sectors, schools, workplaces and universities will be examined in terms of the existence of anti-bullying policies, their content and the effectiveness of the policies. We are looking at bullying among peers; leaving aside that schools and universities are also workplaces.

Policies for bullying

As mentioned previously, there is scant research on bullying among university students and no research has been found on anti-bullying policies in universities. Therefore, much of the discussion is necessarily focused on anti-bullying policies for schools and workplaces.

Schools

The first country to legislate for schools to have an anti-bullying policy was England in November 1999 (Department for Education and Employment 1988). To examine the extent to which this requirement was being implemented, a survey of 109 schools from 1995 and 148 schools from 2002 were compared regarding their anti-bullying policies. It was found that there was a steady increase in the number of schools reporting that they had a separate whole school anti-bullying policy; from 18 per cent before 1996 to 29 per cent after 1996, up to 49 per cent before 2002 and 67 per cent after 2002 (Samara and Smith 2008).

In Australia, the National Safe Schools Framework as implemented by the Australian government in 2003 was to provide a safe and supportive school environment for students and for preventing and managing aggressive behaviours such as bullying (Commonwealth Department of Australia 2005). This arose from a 1994 government national inquiry that recommended programmes and policies to reduce school bullying. By 2007 it was found that although 90 per cent of the 453 teachers surveyed throughout Australia reported their school had an anti-bullying policy, 25 per cent of the teachers did not know its contents (Cross *et al.* 2011). Furthermore, it was found that there was a lack of collaborative development of these policies especially not engaging students and parents. The NSSF was revised in 2010 and again updated in 2013 to include cyberbullying; however, no further large-scale studies have been conducted to ascertain schools' compliance with this framework.

A small study was conducted that examined nine schools' anti-bullying policies in three government and three non-government schools in Queensland, and one government and two non-government schools in South Australia (Butler *et al.* 2011), It was found that all nine schools had anti-bullying policies, although they were contained in various documents. There is merit, however, in providing one place where a single comprehensive anti-bullying policy can be found, not only for ease of access but also to demonstrate the institution's commitment to take action (Marsh *et al.* 2011).

There is also the issue of ownership of the policy or who should contribute to anti-bullying policies. Given that there will be conflicting values and opinions about the content of the policy, it is imperative that the policy is crafted collaboratively within each organization. To ensure a shared value system and consistency in administering the policy, this should include the whole school community, university or workplace (Brown *et al.* 2006). However, the voices of parents and especially young people are often silent in this process in schools and in universities (Woods and Wolke 2003). This is despite research findings that schools demonstrate more ownership of the policy if they develop it themselves, including all stakeholders in the process (Glover *et al.* 1998). One way to allow schools, universities or workplaces to comply with legislation while maintaining their individuality may be the use of a model policy or detailed framework, which provides information to promote in-depth discussion for each content area in the anti-bullying policy (Limber and Small 2003). If there is not ownership of an anti-bullying policy then there can be conflict between leaders of the institution, the staff's interpretation of the policy and the way students experience the policy (Glover *et al.* 1998). One way to ensure a student voice could be through the Students' Union or Guild at a university, representing student interests to formulate, advertise and implement an anti-bullying policy.

Workplaces

Most large workplaces in Australia are required to have an anti-bullying policy. However, no studies were located which have surveyed workplaces to ascertain whether there is such compliance.

Universities

A small study of the anti-bullying policies of 20 Australian universities was conducted for this chapter. The universities were chosen as the largest in student enrolment in each state for the full year of 2013. There were seven universities in New South Wales, six in Victoria, three in Queensland, one in South Australia, two in Western Australia and one multi-state university. The policies were sourced from the university websites. It was found that only seven of the universities' policies mentioned bullying among students specifically. Most policies only mentioned students with the phrase 'staff and students' or all members of the university community. Note was taken of how easy the policy was to find, if it was a separate anti-bullying policy or the policy was scattered through various documents and if available, how the policy was developed.

For some of the universities the anti-bullying policy was very prominent on their website, clearly articulated and in one place. However, for the majority of universities any mention of student-to-student bullying was difficult to find, scattered among workplace bullying policies, codes of conduct or responses to aggressive behaviour. Similar to schools and workplaces where it is difficult to find policies, this would seem to indicate that there is a lack of commitment to the real prevention and intervention of bullying among students. There was no mention in any of the policies of how they were developed.

What do the policies contain?

Anti-bullying policies should provide the institution's expectations for appropriate behaviour in conducting social relationships, and send a clear message that all forms of bullying are serious and unacceptable. If there is no policy in an institution or organization, then it is difficult to mandate the protection of those who are bullied and to implement change in the organization. In general, there are calls for strong and detailed policies with language that can be easily understood by both students and adults, outlining what bullying behaviours are, that they are unacceptable, the penalties involved, and how bullying is reported (Hinduja and Patchin 2011).

The first research on the content of school anti-bullying policies was analysed by Smith and colleagues (2008) with four main categories: definition of bullying behaviour; reporting and responding to bullying incidents; recording bullying, communicating and evaluating the policy; and strategies for preventing bullying.

Definition

The first part of any anti-bullying policy document is defining what that institution considers to be bullying, which ensures objectivity. One problem with policies is that they may not define bullying with sufficient precision. The nuances of words are important for effective prevention and deterrence, with policy enforcement requiring clarity and precision in language. Policies may be practically and legally ineffectual if the language used is too vague and does not address the foreseeable risk. A clear, precise and unambiguous definition is needed. However, in an effort to accomplish this, one must ensure that the complexities and subtleties of all forms of bullying are not lost, and simplistic solutions may not be appropriate in response to a simple definition (Campbell et al. 2010).

However, this is difficult as researchers, practitioners and lawyers have differing views on what bullying actually is (Langos 2012). It has been suggested that schools should use their own state's legal definition in their policies (Bandow and Hunter 2008). However, in Australia there is no actual law against bullying, although it is advised the policy should comply with all legal requirements. All forms of bullying should also be included such as physical, verbal, relational and cyberbullying. Homophobic bullying, racial, religious, disability and sexual bullying also need to be covered. Very few studies have analysed school anti-bullying policies. Those that have analysed school anti-bullying policies found that in England there was an increase of 77 per cent to 89 per cent in the definition of bullying in school policies from 2002 to 2008. There was also an increase of forms and types being defined, with 85 per cent of policies mentioning physical bullying, 83 per cent verbal, 63 per cent racial, 48 per cent sexual, 32 per cent cyberbullying and 25 per cent homophobic bullying (Smith *et al.* 2012). In Australia, Butler *et al.* (2011) found in a study of nine Australian schools' anti-bullying policies that definitions varied widely with some failing to specify that bullying features an intention to hurt, power imbalance and repetition of conduct. Only four of the nine schools referred to cyberbullying.

No studies were found which analysed workplace anti-bullying policies. Of the 20 university policies analysed for this chapter, 13 included a definition of bullying with seven of these using the workplace definition of bullying of 'the repeated and less favourable treatment of a person by another or others in the workplace, which may be considered unreasonable and inappropriate workplace practice.' Many other words were used interchangeably such as harassment, discrimination and intimidation with bullying usually being used as a subset of harassment.

Reporting and responding to bullying incidents

In the study by Smith *et al.* (2012), 64 per cent of school policies provided procedures on what victims should do and how staff should respond, 68 per cent stated sanctions, but only 23 per cent what to do if the bullying persisted. In Australia, Butler and colleagues (2011) found that all nine schools stated a process for handling complaints, but varied in degrees of detail. These authors advocated a systematic process with a consistent imposition of sanctions. However, only 6 per cent of the nine schools set out the penalties that may be applied to bullying behaviour in their policies.

While there is advice about reporting in the workplace in policies (Bandow and Hunter 2008) and advocacy for such an approach (Bartlett and Bartlett 2011), to date there are no published studies that have analysed these policies to ascertain their compliance. In the analysis of the university study policy, it was found that there were well-developed grievance procedures shown in most university policies. Given the workplace nature of most of these anti-bullying policies it is not surprising that any bullying among students is treated similarly to either workplace grievances or academic complaints of students regarding marking. In the rare cases of universities specifying procedures for bullying among students, the procedures were often extremely vague, such as staff should appropriately manage student complaints.

Reporting of bullying

Central to the procedures contained in anti-bullying policies are the intentions of people who have been victimized to report the bullying. If there is no reporting then the policy cannot be enacted. We know that sometimes children report instances of bullying to people in authority in primary school (Cassidy *et al.* 2009). However, many do not, fearing the retaliation of the students bullying them (Rigby 1997); that adults would make the situation worse or it stays the same (Cross *et al.* 2009; Sticca and Perren 2013), or that if they report cyberbullying the technology would be taken away from them (Addington 2013; Campbell 2005). School age students also fear that adults may view their reporting behaviour as childish and tell them just to ignore the bullying (Perren *et al.* 2012). As young people enter adolescence, reporting to authorities lessens (Dowling and Carey 2013; McQuade *et al.* 2009). Older students feel they should be able to manage by themselves if they are bullied (deLara 2012). Similarly, in workplaces it has been found that employees who did report to authority figures were unhappy with the outcome, and experienced increased levels of anxiety (Bilgel *et al.* 2006). And similar to school-aged students in a workplace-bullying study, respondents reported that 62 per cent of employers either ignored the bullying complaint or made the situation worse (Yamada 2000). Thus, while most advice on coping with bullying is to tell authorities (Cassidy *et al.* 2009) without teacher, lecturer, or manager training in taking appropriate action, this advice is meaningless and can have unintended harmful consequences.

One strategy some schools have applied to overcome this has been the training of peers to refer bullied students to teachers (Soutter and McKenzie 2000). In addition, there should be clear and transparent steps describing what will happen after the reporting. An explicit process for investigating complaints needs to be articulated and all parties need to be confident that it will be followed.

In a recent study, 282 Australian university students aged between 18 to 25 were administered an online survey asking about cyberbullying experiences in the last 12 months. They were then presented with a ten-item scale, which referred to barriers that may prevent students from reporting future cyberbullying incidents to the university authorities. It was found that this sample of university students had high levels of confidence in dealing with cyberbullying incidents themselves, and most would not intend to report to university personnel. This could be because of a need for autonomy, as emerging adults perceive they should be able to manage problematic situations independently (Rickwood *et al.* 2005). However, another reason was that 75 per cent of this sample stated that they were uncertain of how to report cyberbullying to the university. Students could be unsure of what the universities' responsibilities are in this situation. Furthermore, there could be confusion over whom to report to, as the structure of authority figures is more complex in a university compared to a school or workplace. Additionally 58 per cent of the students reported that they would report future incidents of cyberbullying only if they had confidence that an authority figure within the university would be helpful. School-based cyberbullying research demonstrates that cyber victims are more likely to cope by seeking help from teachers, when these individuals are perceived to be supportive, knowledgeable about cyberbullying, and can offer adequate assistance (Cassidy *et al.* 2012; Perren *et al.* 2012). Therefore, emerging adult cyber victims may have an expectation that university lecturers will have the necessary knowledge and skills to resolve cyberbullying situations, particularly if cyberbullying is occurring on a university platform (e.g. online class discussion board).

Other data from this research sample examined the coping strategies these emerging adults at university intended to use for future incidents of cyberbullying. The study also explored the influences of victimization status on coping strategy intentions. An important finding was that cyber victims (14.5 per cent of this sample) were more likely to seek help from a university lecturer compared to non-victims. This is surprising given that adolescents are reluctant to report to teachers (Cassidy *et al.* 2013; Hoff and Mitchell 2009). However, the finding that cyber victims would seek help from a university lecturer indicates that emerging adults may not have the same concerns as adolescents, and this could be associated with developmental maturity (Zimmer-Gembeck and Skinner 2011).

Recording, communicating and evaluating

The study by Smith *et al.* (2012) found that 76 per cent of school anti-bullying policies said the reporting of bullying would be recorded, 65 per cent mentioned periodic review and updating of policy while only 35 per cent intended to evaluate the policy. In Australia, all nine schools disseminated the policy but no mention was made in the article about review or evaluation of policies (Butler *et al.* 2011). Advice about recording, communicating and evaluating workplace bullying policies is plentiful but with no research to date. In the university study, there was no mention of recording of bullying incidents in any of the policies. However, most of the policies maintained written records in grievance or complaints procedures. There was also no mention of evaluation of policies; however, most policies had a review date.

Strategies for preventing bullying

Although sanctions should be part of a school's anti-bullying policy, the policy will only serve as a reactionary measure to unwanted behaviour if sanctions are the main emphasis. These types of policies alone will not be as successful as those which also include preventative strategies such as promoting a positive school climate, fostering students' connectedness to school and educating them about bullying (Shariff 2008). Unfortunately, in developing anti-bullying policies, many schools seem to take a punitive view regarding the problem, similar to how the law is regarded in curbing bullying. Reactive measures were found to be much higher on the agenda for primary schools' anti-bullying policies than those that are preventative (Woods and Wolke 2003).

In England apart from 86 per cent of policies mentioning encouraging cooperative behaviour, most other policies did not include prevention type activities (Smith *et al.* 2012). The Australian study focusing on the legal perspective did not include an analysis for prevention strategies (Butler *et al.* 2011). Similarly, there were no studies found on workplace strategies for preventing bullying. Only two universities of the 20 Australian universities in the study provided detailed harassment and bullying guidelines.

Effectiveness of policies

Most studies on bullying, either at school or in the workplace advocate a policy or give advice as to what an effective policy would contain, but there is relatively little research on the effectiveness of these policies. However, the ultimate aim for any institution's policy is a reduction in bullying. It is difficult, however, to measure the effectiveness of policies in reducing bullying as the degree of dissemination and the fidelity of implementation need also to be measured. Difficulties of determining baseline bullying data before the policy implementation, the use of consistent and valid measures of bullying with definitions or not, global versus specific behavioural questions, time periods of a lifetime or a few weeks, frequency of response – once, twice daily – all contribute to the methodological problems of assessing the reduction of bullying. Furthermore, the difficulty of isolating the mediating and moderating variables is considerable.

It is unsurprising that although many prevention and intervention efforts to curb bullying have been implemented in schools since Olweus' work in 1993, not many of these have been evaluated and fewer still have an evidence-base gained from using a rigorous research methodology. In secondary schools with detailed and consistently applied anti-bullying policies, rates of bullying have reduced slightly (Glover *et al.* 1998). However, primary schools in England with detailed anti-bullying policies were compared to schools with low-scoring policies (Woods and Wolke 2003) and no relationship was found between direct bullying and anti-bullying policies. However, a higher incidence of relational bullying was found in those schools with detailed anti-bullying policies. The authors give several explanations for this finding, but conclude that anti-bullying policies are not well-implemented, and could be addressing general aggression and anti-social behaviour rather than bullying (Woods and Wolke 2003). The findings may also indicate that there is a vast gap between what was written in the policies and their daily integration in the life of the school.

Ttofi and Farrington's (2011) meta-analysis examined the effectiveness of school-based programmes to reduce bullying and the effectiveness of the programme components. It was found by examining the important elements in the programmes that decreased bullying perpetration by 20 to 23 per cent and victimization by 17 to 20 per cent, that having a whole school policy was the seventh most successful strategy. However, establishing a whole-school policy was only significantly related to effect sizes for perpetrators but not for victimization. That is, while students at schools with an anti-bullying policy reported less bullying behaviour there was no reduction in students reporting being bullied.

One large study of almost 32,000 eleventh-grade students in the United States found a positive effect, where victimization was less likely to occur in the schools of counties with inclusive anti-bullying policies (Hatzenbuehler and Keyes 2012). A very interesting finding from this study was that those school anti-bullying policies where the policy explicitly included the phrase 'sexual orientation' as a protected class significantly reduced suicide attempts in the lesbian, gay and bisexual respondents (1,413 students) but not in the heterosexual sample.

There seem to be no published studies on the effectiveness of anti-bullying policies in the workplace. However, one study in 2010 noted that in a random sample of 45 litigated cases of workplace bullying in the United States, in two-thirds of the court cases there was no policy banning bullying (Martin and LaVan 2010), with 15.6 per cent of employers referring to a code of conduct for their organization, but only 11.1 per cent referring to a bullying and/or disruptive behaviour policy. There were no studies on the effectiveness of university policies found, which could be a time bomb waiting to explode if a student takes a university to court for failure to take action over bullying.

Future research

As can be seen, more research on anti-bullying policies in universities is urgently needed. Not only do we need research on the effectiveness of anti-bullying policies, including the components of the policy, we also need intervention research so that policies are framed so that they achieve their intended outcomes as policies, as any other strategy for reducing bullying cannot be considered in isolation. While most Australian universities would have some vision for their institution, anti-bullying policies are piecemeal. Mostly they are difficult to find and are not well disseminated to students. It seems anti-bullying policies in Australian universities are part of health and safety, and are much more workplace policies dealing with employed staff than with student-to-student bullying. There seems to be no acknowledgment that peer bullying can be harmful, not only to the individual students but also to the culture of the university and the learning environment.

References

Addington, L. A. (2013). Reporting and clearance of cyberbullying incidents: applying 'offline' theories to online victims. *Journal of Contemporary Criminal Justice*, 29: 454–74.

Australian Bureau of Statistics (2012). *Education Difference Between Men and Women. Australian Social Trends (4102.0).* Canberra.

Bandow, D. and Hunter, D. (2008). Developing policies about uncivil workplace behavior. *Business Communication Quarterly,* 23: 103–06.

Bartlett, J. E. and Bartlett, M. E. (2011). Workplace bullying: An integrative literature review. *Advances in Developing Human Resources,* 13: 69–84.

Bilgel, N., Aytac, S. and Bayram, N. (2006). Bullying in Turkish white-collar workers. *Occupational Medicine,* 56: 226–31.

Bronfenbrenner, U. (1977). Toward an experimental ecology of human development. *American Psychologist,* 513–30.

Bronfenbrenner, U. (1979). *The Ecology of Human Development.* Cambridge: Harvard University Press.

Brown, K., Jackson, M. and Cassidy, W. (2006). Cyber-bullying: developing policy to direct responses that are equitable and effective in addressing this special form of bullying. *Canadian Journal of Educational Administration and Policy,* 57: 1–36.

Butler, D., Kift, S. M., Campbell, M. A., Slee, P. and Spears, B. (2011). School policy responses to cyberbullying: an Australian legal perspective. *International Journal of Law and Education,* 16(2): 7–28.

Campbell, M. A. (2005). Cyberbullying: An old problem in a new guise? *Australian Journal of Guidance and Counselling,* 15: 68–76.

Campbell, M. A., Cross, D., Spears, B. and Slee, P. (2010). *Cyberbullying: Legal Implications for Schools.* Occasional paper 118. Melbourne: Centre for Strategic Education.

Cassidy, W., Brown, K. N. and Jackson, M. (2012). 'Under the radar': educators and cyberbullying in schools. *School Psychology International,* 33: 520–32.

Cassidy, W., Faucher, C. and Jackson, M. (2013). Cyberbullying among youth: comprehensive review of current international research and its implications and applications to policy and practice. *School Psychology International,* 34: 575–612.

Cassidy, W., Jackson, M. and Brown, K. N. (2009). Sticks and stones can break my bones, but how can pixels hurt me? Students' experiences with cyberbullying. *School Psychology International,* 30: 383–402.

Chapell, M., Casey, D. and de la Cruz, C. (2004). Bullying in college by students and teachers. *Adolescence,* 39: 53–64.

Coleyshaw, L. (2010). The power of paradigms: a discussion of the absence of bullying research in the context of the university experience. *Research in Post-Compulsory Education,* 15: 377–86.

Commonwealth Department of Australia (2005). *Report on the National Safe Schools Framework Best Practice Grants Programmes (2004-2005).* Canberra: Australian Government Department of Education, Science and Training.

Cook, C. R., Williams, K. R., Guerra, N. G., Kim, T. E. and Sadek, S. (2010). Predictors of bullying and victimization in childhood and adolescence: a meta-analytic investigation. *School Psychology Quarterly,* 25: 65–83.

Coyne, I., Craig, J. and Smith-Lee Chong, P. (2004). Workplace bullying in a group context. *British Journal of Guidance and Counselling,* 32: 301–17.

Craig, W. M., Pepler, D. and Atlas, R. (2000). Observations of bullying in the playground and in the classroom. *School Psychology International,* 21: 22–36.

Cross, D., Epstein, M., Hearn, L., Slee, P. and Shaw, T. (2011). National Safe Schools Framework: policy and practice to reduce bullying in Australian schools. *International Journal of Behavioral Development,* 35: 398–404.

Cross, D., Shaw, T., Hearn, L., Epstein, M., Monks, H., Lester, L. and Thomas, L. (2009). *Australian covert bullying prevalence study (ACBPS)*. Western Australia: Report prepared for the Department of Education, Employment and Workplace Relations (DEEWR).

deLara, E. W. (2012). Why adolescents don't disclose incidents of bullying and harassment. *Journal of School Violence*, 11: 288–305.

Department for Education and Employment (1998). *Section 61(4): School Standards and Frameworks Act 1998*. London: HMSO.

Dowling, M. J. and Carey, T. A. (2013). Victims of bullying: Whom they seek help from and why: An Australian sample. *Psychology in the Schools*, 50: 798–809.

Duffy, M. (2009). Workplace mobbing and bullying with effective organizational consultation, policies, and legislation. *Consulting Psychology Journal: Practice and Research*, 61: 242–262.

Farrington, D. P. and Ttofi, M. M. (2009). How to reduce school bullying. *Victims and Offenders: An International Journal of Evidenced-based Research, Policy and Practice*, 4: 320–26.

Glover, D., Cartwright, N., Gough, G. and Johnson, M. (1998). The introduction of anti-bullying policies: do policies help in the management of change? *School Leadership and Management*, 18: 89–105.

Hatzenbuehler, M. L. and Keyes, M. (2012). Inclusive anti-bullying policies and reduced risk of suicide attempts in lesbian and gay youth. *Journal of Adolescent Health*, 53: 21–26.

Hawker, D. S. and Boulton, M. J. (2000). Twenty years' research on peer victimization and psychosocial maladjustment: a meta-analytic review of cross-sectional studies. *Journal of Child Psychology and Psychiatry*, 41: 441–45.

Hinduja, S. and Patchin, J. (2011). Cyberbullying: a review of the legal issues facing educators. *Preventing School Failure: Alternative Education for Children and Youth*, 55(2): 71–78.

Hoel, H., Cooper, C. L. and Faragher, B. (2001). The experience of bullying in Great Britain: the impact of organizational status. *European Journal of Work and Organizational Psychology*, 10: 443–65.

Hoff, D. L. and Mitchell, S. N. (2009). Cyberbullying: Causes, effects, and remedies. *Journal of Educational Administration*, 47: 652–65.

Houbre, B., Tarqinio, C., Thuillier, I. and Hergott, E. (2006). Bullying among students: its consequences on health. *European Journal of Psychology of Education*, 21: 183–208.

Kaltiala-Heino, R., Rimpela, M., Rantanen, R. and Rimpela, A. (2000). Bullying at school: An indicator of adolescents at risk for mental disorders. *Journal of Adolescence*, 23: 661–74.

Kowalski, R. and Limber, S. (2007). Electronic bullying among middle school students. *Journal of Adolescent Health*, 41: 22–30.

Kumpulainen, K. (2008). Psychiatric conditions associated with bullying. *International Journal of Adolescent Medicine and Health*, 20: 121–32.

Langos, C. (2012). Cyberbullying: The challenge to define. *Cyberpsychology, Behavior, and Social Networking*, 15: 285–89.

Leonard, J. (2011). Using Bronfenbrenner's ecology theory to understand community partnerships: A historical case study of one urban high school. *Urban Education*, 46: 987–1010.

Limber, S. P. and Small, M. A. (2003). State laws and policies to address bullying in schools. *School Psychology Review*, 32: 445–455.

Malecki, C. and Demaray, M. (2003). Carrying a weapon to school and perceptions of social support in an urban middle school. *Journal of Emotional and Behavioral Disorders*, 11: 169–78.

Marsh, L,. McGee, R., Hemphill, S. A. and Williams, S. (2011). Content analysis of school anti-bullying policies: a comparison between New Zealand and Victoria, Australia. *Health Promotion Journal of Australia,* 22: 172–77.

McQuade, S. C. III., Colt, J. P. and Meyer, N. B. B. (2009). *Cyber bullying: protecting kids and adults from online bullies.* Westport, CT: Praeger.

Martin, W. and LaVan, H. (2010). Workplace bullying: a review of litigated cases. *Employment, Responsibility and Rights Journal,* 22: 175–94.

Naidoo, R. (2003). Repositioning higher education as a global commodity: opportunities and challenges for future sociology of education work. *British Journal of Sociology of Education,* 24: 249–59.

Nansel, T. R., Overpeck, M., Pilla, R. S., Ruan, W. J., Simons-Morton, B., and Scheidt, P. (2001). Bullying behaviours among US youth: Prevalence and association with psychosocial adjustment. *Journal of the American Medical Association,* 285: 2094–100.

Neary, A. and Joseph, S. (1994). Peer victimization and its relationship to self-concept and depression among schoolgirls. *Personality and Individual Differences,* 16: 183–86.

Olweus, D. (1993) *Bullying at School: What We Know and What We Can Do.* Oxford: Blackwell.

Pearce, N., Cross, D., Monks, H., Waters, S. and Falconer, S. (2011). Current evidence of best practice in whole-school bullying intervention and its potential to inform cyberbullying interventions. *Australian Journal of Guidance and Counselling,* 21: 1–21.

Perren, S. and Hornung, R. (2005). Bullying and delinquency in adolescence: Victims' and perpetrators' family and peer relations. *Swiss Journal of Psychology,* 64: 51–64.

Perren, S., Corcoran, L., Cowie, H., Dehue, F., Garcia, D., McGuckin, C., Sevcikova, A., Tsatsou, P. and Völlink, T. (2012). Tackling cyberbullying: Review of empirical evidence regarding successful responses by students, parents, and schools. *International Journal of Conflict and Violence,* 6: 283–93.

Pellegrini, A .D., Long, J. D., Solberg, D., Roseth, C. and Dupuis, D. (2010). Bullying and social status during school transitions. In S. R. Jimerson, S. M. Swearer, and D. L. Espelage (Eds.), *Handbook of Bullying in Schools: An International Perspective.* New York: Taylor and Francis. pp. 199–210.

Pontzer, D. (2010). A theoretical test of bullying behaviour: Parenting, personality, and the bully/victim relationship. *Journal of Family Violence,* 25: 259–73.

Prensky, M. (2001). Digital natives, digital immigrants. *On the Horizon,* 9(5): 1–6.

Privitera, C. and Campbell, M. A. (2009). Cyberbullying: The new face of workplace bullying? *CyberPsychology and Behavior,* 12: 395–400.

Raskauskas, J. and Stoltz, A. D. (2007). Involvement in traditional and electronic bullying among adolescents. *Developmental Psychology,* 43: 564–75.

Reifsnider, E., Gallagher, M. and Forgione, B. (2005). Using ecological models in research on health disparities. *Journal of Professional Nursing,* 21: 216–22.

Rickwood, D., Deane, F. P., Wilson, C. J. and Ciarrochi, J. (2005). Young people's help-seeking for mental health problems. *Australian E-Journal for the Advancement of Mental Health,* 4: 218–51.

Rigby, K. (1997). What children tell us about bullying in schools. *Children Australia,* 22(2): 18–28.

Rigby, K. and Slee, P. (1993). Dimensions of interpersonal relations among Australian children and implications for psychological well-being. *Journal of Social Psychology,* 133: 33–42.

Samara, M. and Smith, P. K. (2008). How schools tackle bullying, and the use of whole school policies: Changes over the last decade. *Educational Psychology,* 28: 663–76.

Shariff, S. (2008). *Cyber-bullying: Issues and Solutions of the School, the Classroom and the Home.* London: Routledge.

Smith, P. K., Smith, C., Osborn, R. and Samara, M. (2008). A content analysis of school anti-bullying policies: Progress and limitations. *Educational Psychology in Practice,* 24: 1–12.

Smith, P. K., Kupferberg, A., Mora-Merchan, J. A., Samara, M., Bosley, S. and Osborn, R. (2012). A content analysis of school anti-bullying policies: A follow-up after six years. *Educational Psychology in Practice,* 28: 47–70.

Soutter, A. and McKenzie, A. (2000). The use and effects of anti-bullying and anti-harassment policies in Australian schools. *School Psychology Review International,* 21: 96–105.

Sticca, F. and Perren, S. (2013). Is cyberbullying worse than traditional bullying? Examining the differential roles of medium, publicity, and anonymity for the perceived severity of bullying. *Journal of Youth and Adolescence,* 42: 739–50.

Ttofi, M. M. and Farrington, D. P. (2011). Effectiveness of school-based programs to reduce bullying: A systematic and meta-analytic review. *Journal of Experimental Criminology,* 7: 27–56.

Vago, S. (2009). *Law and Society.* Upper Saddle River, NJ: Pearson Prentice-Hall.

Wang, J., Iannotti, R. J. and Nansel, T. R. (2009). School bullying among adolescents in the United States: Physical, verbal, relational, and cyber. *Journal of Adolescent Health,* 45: 368–75.

Wensley, K. and Campbell, M. A. (2009). Heterosexual and non-heterosexual young university students' involvement in traditional and cyber forms of bullying. *Cyberpsychology, Behavior and Social Networking,* 15: 649–54.

Woods, S. and Wolke, D. (2003). Does the content of anti-bullying policies inform us about the prevalence of direct and relational bullying behaviour in primary schools? *Educational Psychology,* 23: 381–401.

Yamada, D. C. (October, 2000). *Is There a 'Business Case' for Workplace Bullying Legislation?* New Workplace Institute Work, Stress, and Health Conference, San Juan, Puerto Rico.

Zimmer-Gembeck, M. J. and Skinner, E. A. (2011). Review: The development of coping across childhood and adolescence: An integrative review and critique of research. *International Journal of Behavioral Development,* 35: 1–17.

13

CYBERBULLYING AND RAPE CULTURE IN UNIVERSITIES

Defining the legal lines between fun and intentional harm

Shaheen Shariff and Ashley DeMartini

Introduction

In this chapter, we highlight the prevalence of misogyny and rape culture among university students (Olson 2014; Burnett *et al.* 2009), and its increasing prevalence online. We draw attention to the blurred legal boundaries concerning online communication, and the resulting legal and public-policy dilemmas that confront university administrators and government policymakers. We conclude with recommendations for educational, legal, and policy approaches that show promise in clarifying the boundaries between free expression, safety, privacy, protection, and regulation. We suggest that these approaches outlined in this chapter could offer sustained guidance to policymakers and young people in lieu of the over-reactive legal frameworks currently emerging across North America that attempt to control non-consensual distribution of intimate images and cyberbullying. We propose that to reduce harmful online communication among young adults, it is essential to first understand the root causes that inform such behaviors.

As chapter 1 of this book indicates, there is currently a dearth of research on cyberbullying among university students. Despite two decades of research focused on bullying and cyberbullying behavior among children and adolescents (Menesini *et al.* 1997; Craig and Pepler 1998; Keltner *et al.* 2001; Smith *et al.* 2004; Hymel *et al.* 2005; Perren and Gutzwiller-Helfenfinger 2012), minimal attention has been paid to similar behaviors among university students. This gap in research could be due to societal assumptions about young people being adults by the time they attend university, who have likely outgrown their tendency to bully others. Regrettably, this is not the case. Elsewhere, we (Shariff 2004, 2008) argue that this assumption not only ignores the roots of bullying and its online forms, but also fails to recognize the impact of negative models of adult behavior within popular culture, news, and entertainment media. We have made little progress in reducing bullying or cyberbullying across generations because we overlook dominant ideologies that focus on symptomatic behaviors as opposed to systemic influences, and uses of hegemonic forms of language and communication (Ttofi and Farrington 2011; Vreeman and Carroll 2007). We have always maintained (Shariff 2004–14) that bullying and cyberbullying behaviors are merely symptoms of discriminatory and hegemonic societal attitudes and beliefs. These are often deeply rooted in sexism, homophobia, racism, and fear of difference. These perspectives and attitudes can influence and shape the adult personalities of post-secondary students, as they navigate their way through university life, and establish long-term partnerships, careers, and social relationships.

Therefore, if we are to better understand the cyberbullying behavior of university students, it is important to consider discriminatory roots as reflected in misogynist and homophobic forms of online communication among young adults. Such an understanding would better inform public policy and legal responses that are more effective in balancing free expression, safety, and privacy rights. This knowledge would also enhance young people's awareness of their rights and responsibilities, and the legal risks they confront when they post insults or risqué videos and photographs online.

To date, we observe that cyberbullying and online distribution of non-consensual images have resulted in legal and policy responses that attempt to 'control' and 'stop' such behaviors, rather than addressing its roots with a view to preventing it. Examples include the Canadian government's endorsement of the WITS program (www.witsprogram.ca), which encourages victims of bullying or cyberbullying to 'walk away' from the bullying. The reality is that it is not possible to 'walk away' from relentless online bullying, threats or harassment, and when ostracized from one's peer group, or when demeaning photographs are distributed online affecting one's reputation, 'walking away' is not a viable solution. A similar government sponsored program is the Stop Bullying website by the United States government (www.stopbullying.gov/cyberbullying). Canadian provincial laws such as Nova Scotia's *Cyber-safety Act* (2013), Quebec's Bill 56 (2012) and Ontario's *Accepting Schools Act* (2012), and California's Seth's Law (2011) have emerged to address cyberbullying. Most of these laws primarily target schools and parents of children and teens, placing greater responsibility on those stakeholders. The legal boundaries as they relate to cyberbullying at the university level are less clear. Our goal is to highlight legal and educational responses that are grounded in, and informed by *substantive* legal principles (such as human rights and constitutional law). We suggest it is essential to look to the law for guidance in developing sustainable educational and preventative approaches (Van Praag 2005, 2007; Eltis 2011; Altobelli 2010) that respect young people's rights, while providing a frame of reference that enhances socially responsible and inclusive forms of online communication and digital citizenship at all ages.

To that end, we recommend a practical starting point that would enhance public legal education and critical media literacy. In 1973, then Chief Justice Bora Laskin of the Supreme Court of Canada argued that public legal literacy was long overdue, and that this lack of public knowledge would eventually have a significant negative impact on Canadian society. Unfortunately, little was done to address that gap in public knowledge across Canada in response to his warning, and today we find ourselves grappling with enormous policy dilemmas as the Internet presents unprecedented legal challenges. As society becomes increasingly immersed in online communication, it is essential that people are better apprised of their legal rights and responsibilities, and of the emerging legal risks to their privacy and safety. As we present our discussion of rape culture and slut-shaming in this chapter, it should also become quickly apparent to readers why it is important for girls and women to become better apprised and equipped with knowledge about their legal rights both on- and off-line. For example, legal literacy would play a key role in raising young people's awareness about issues of consent in cases of sexting. Legislation needs to address issues of misogyny, homophobia, sexism, racism and other forms of discrimination within society, and their influence on perpetuating cyberbullying and related online sex-related offences. Otherwise, the policy vacuum will be sustained.

Before proceeding to the legal discussion, we begin with examples of sexism and misogyny (as it plays out through cyberbullying) in university environments. Within the context of these examples, we introduce a discussion about *rape culture* and *slut-shaming*. In brief, *rape culture* rests upon the assertion of heterosexual male sexuality whereas *slut-shaming* is a policing apparatus of the culture that regulates ideas around female sexual agency. The examples presented below illustrate the kind of social environment we have begun to outline above as well as the blurred social and legal lines that university students find themselves negotiating.

Blurred lines between on- and off-line sexism on university campuses

The lines between on- and off-line sexual harassment have become increasingly integrated across universities. Consider the example we have provided elsewhere (Shariff, in press) of the recent wager and proposed rape scenario of the University of Ottawa's student council female president by her male colleagues. Below is an excerpt (a pseudonym is used) from that exchange as reported in the blog, *The Belle Jar*:

> Student A [a non-elected [male] student]: *Let me tell you something right now: the 'tri-fluvienne' [nickname for someone from Trois-Rivières, Québec] president will suck me off in her office chair and after I will fuck her in the ass on [D.M.'s] desk.*
>
> Student B [male VP Social for the Criminology Student Association]: *Someone punish her with their shaft.*
>
> Student C [male member of the Board of Directors of the Student Federation of the University of Ottawa]: *Well Christ, if you fuck [female president's name] I will definitely buy you a beer.*

The above excerpt is only one of numerous examples of young adult males glorifying acts of heteronormative violence – a kind of violence that polices sexuality and gender roles, and hinges on the assertion of the sexual dominance of the alpha, hetero-male. We want to thank Jailyn Hanson, an undergraduate student from the University of Winnipeg, for bringing our attention to this idea of heteronormative policing of sexualities when she spoke insightfully about her experience as living as a trans person. Other disturbing incidents include the reports of FROSH (or freshers, as it is known in the UK) chants endorsing non-consensual sex at the University of British Colombia and St. Mary's University (CBC News 2013a, b). To add to this disturbing event is the video in the St. Mary's incident, which shows girls chanting these violent lyrics alongside their male counterparts. Rape culture is not only limited to heterosexual dominance over females, but also is used to control and regulate sexualities that diverge from this hetero-male norm. For example, in 2005, senior members of McGill University's football team used a broomstick to sexually assault a male freshman player (Kryk 2013). This latter incident speaks to the functions of rape culture: the assertion and maintenance of power and dominance.

Rape culture as a power differential

Sexist and misogynist attitudes are rampant online. As the example of the female student president illustrates, when women claim coveted positions of leadership or professional spaces, they challenge traditional and underlying assumptions about public space as heterosexual male space (Hess 2014). These assumptions are not new to North American society, but online forums amplify and intensify the spread of sexist reactions to women who challenge them. Elsewhere, Shariff (in press) notes that when women in positions of cultural or political influence assert themselves in online forums, and express informed opinions and/or feminist perspectives, they often threaten insecure males, who in turn, assail them online with violent threats to their life. These forms of harassment can be devastating, and the humiliation can affect women's health, academic success, and careers. Some of these deep-seated and discriminatory societal attitudes are emerging as normative forms of online communication among young adults who have grown up in the digital age. For example, consider the increasingly popular activity known as sexting – the sharing of intimate or nude images online, which is an acceptable online activity when it takes place between consenting adults within adequate online privacy settings. However, problems arise when a person sends intimate images to a trusted friend via sexting, and these are subsequently distributed online without consent by the recipient. Not only does non-consensual distribution of intimate images breach the privacy of individuals, who initially engage in it as part of a consensual and private communication, but also, it makes underage youth vulnerable to online sexual predators. Due to these safety risks, sexting among children and teens has become a public policy concern (Unruh 2014). Although minimal data is available regarding the extent of sexting among university students, the ensuing risks are similar. Thus, it is important to consider the potential legal dilemmas that might confront young adults in this regard. In the upcoming section, we highlight the tensions between an individual's right to assert their sexuality via private sexting and the double standards that exist within society and popular culture once that privacy has been shattered.

Sexting and slut-shaming: a double standard in assessing harm

As noted, sexting occurs when sexual or sexually suggestive images or videos, nude or semi-nude, are sent and received through cell phones and social media apps (Poltash 2013). Snapchat, an app that was developed by university-aged young adults has quickly become the social media application favored as a forum for sexting among young adults. This app allows users to take images, record videos, and then send them to their recipients with a limited time to view. The platform's appeal rests on a false sense of impunity for users while sending data to recipients. The app's users might think they can act without accountability due to the design of the app, but in fact, their actions are traceable. Although Snapchat deletes the files from the recipients' and the application's server, recipients can take screenshots of the image sent by the social media app. In a matter of seconds, those risqué images sent in privacy can now be disseminated online and across the world.

The phenomenon of sexting is deeply gendered, especially because of the higher levels of risk involved for young women and girls (Bailey and Hanna 2011; Bailey and Steeves 2013; Ybarra *et al.* 2006). Young girls who have trusted male peers and sent risqué photographs online have sometimes paid the heavy price of public humiliation, ruined reputations, and blame for bringing it on themselves through slut-shaming. What these largely young women are not necessarily aware of is the broader set of normative values in a society shaped by male hegemony, misogynist attitudes, and the sexual objectification of women that shape the kind of negative responses to women and girls who sext; such as slut-shaming, harassment, and sexual violence (Ringrose and Renold 2012; Hirschman *et al.* 2006).

Key to understanding the pervasiveness of rape culture, and by extension, how to address it at its roots, is to understand the function of slut-shaming as a policing apparatus of the culture itself. Commenting on how society views female victims of sexual violence, Poole (2013, p. 242) argues, 'peers, adults, media and courts all give attention to how much make-up a girl uses, the type of clothing she wears, how late she stays out, and how she acts towards males'. Poole's statement addresses the deeply entrenched gender norms in North American society around female sexuality. Slut-shaming is a way to control a female's sexual agency (Poole 2013). It functions to regulate the extent to which women, and adolescent girls, can express their sexual agency before enduring scorn from society. Policing female sexuality creates a double standard between males and females, and ultimately marks female sexuality as deviant (Attwood 2007).

For example, in the well-publicized Steubenville rape, young men were found guilty of the rape of a drunken 16-year-old girl at a party. As noted elsewhere

(Shariff, in press), the act itself was shocking enough as images of the rape in progress surfaced online (Welsh-Huggins 2013). Equally shocking, however, was the slew of online comments from the public (Binder 2013). A Tumblr user collected a series of these comments and posted them to his site in an effort to bring attention to the public's backlash towards the girl. These comments included, 'Shouldn't they charge the lil' slut for underage drinking?' or, 'I honestly feel sorry for those boys in that Steubenville trial, the whore was asking for it' (Binder 2013, n.p.). Interestingly, women made many of these posts.

One of the many unsettling features of slut-shaming is that women slut-shame each other, and in effect, regulate themselves in accordance with long-standing patriarchal norms that govern Western societies. A quick etymological glance at the term, *slut,* reveals that even in the late-eighteenth century, middle-class women used the term to pejoratively refer to female domestic servants as a means to distinguish women-of-means from women of the working classes (Attwood 2007; Blackwell 2004). Highlighting the way women participate in dominant narratives serves to underscore the way in which a rape culture is produced and reproduced within society, and more so, why women struggle to navigate these harmful messages.

While slut-shaming itself is not new, its foray onto the Internet provides a context for opinions to spread rapidly and widely, amplifying the shame felt by girls who fall victim to this cruel behavior. Women (and girls) continue to police each other by vilifying and shaming females who assert themselves beyond what society deems acceptable. For instance, Poole (2013, pp. 241–2) examines the viral Tumblr post, 'Hey Girls. Did You Know?' The initial post paired photos of women's exposed breasts with the phrase, 'Hey Girls. Did You Know... that uhm, your boobs go inside your shirt'. Although taken down by Tumblr, spin-offs included posts, such as 'Hey Girl. Did you know? That you spread Nutella... not your legs' (Poole 2013, p. 241–2). A large number of people posting slut-shaming content were also female users. Poole's discussion reveals how sexist and misogynist norms regulate and govern online spaces. To date, the majority of research on cyberbullying does not pay sufficient attention to the conflicting messages that young people receive from the adult world of news media and popular culture. Research needs to address the impact of society's conflicting messages on the development of youth's sexual identities, and *how* in the midst of this, young people mimic and begin to internalize detrimental attitudes of homophobia and misogyny.

A site of contradiction: messages in popular and rape culture

Feminist scholarship has highlighted the contradictory messages women and girls encounter on a daily basis. On the one hand, they are encouraged to take on leadership roles and positions of power traditionally held by males. On the other hand, popular culture also depicts as powerful, female celebrities such as Lady Gaga, Rihanna, Madonna, Miley Cyrus, and Beyonce, celebrity icons who often perform in overtly sexualized costumes, sometimes reflective of dominatrix attire with leather, whips and bondage paraphernalia. Publicists, record companies, and the artists themselves carefully craft a branded image of the artist as an icon that markets a message of sexual independence. The marketization of the *modern woman* – strong and sexually assertive – has been dominating popular culture storylines across the music, film, advertising and television industries (Chen 2013). Suddenly, 'high-heeled shoes are emblematic of confident, powerful femininity' (Gill 2008, p. 37). These trends in popular culture are more indicative of consumer choice and market supremacy, than the actual liberation of women's bodies from traditional, passive and subjugated positions (Chen 2013; Gill 2008).

Neoliberal marketing spins notions of agency and independence as a part of a sexually-liberated woman's choice to voluntarily self-objectify (Chen 2013). For instance, Rihanna's music video, 'Pour It Up,' portrays the pop star as a stripper-pimp. The character in the video has power and influence, using her sexualized body to make money and obtain status. Miley Cyrus' video, 'Wrecking Ball,' shows the young singer naked while provocatively straddling a swinging wrecking ball as she sings about a troubled relationship. 'Today, the body is portrayed in advertising and many other parts of media as the primary source of woman's capital' (Gill 2008, p. 42). These sexually explicit pop-music videos, occurring within a predominantly heteronormative economy, significantly influence the socialization of young females (Zhang *et al.* 2010; Levande 2008). To what extent young university students understand that these pop stars are doing this as a business is unclear; particularly, a business occurring within a larger economy, which positions power, pleasure, and agency in relation to heterosexual relationships while streamlining what kind of bodies (read race and body type) are seen as beautiful (Gill 2008). The reality is that when university students post sexually risqué images online, they risk ridicule.

We are currently embarking on the next stage of our five-year research project with a view to address the gap in knowledge regarding the online practices of post-secondary students. The participants in our upcoming research will comprise university undergraduate and law students at Canadian and American universities. The qualitative research will help us determine the extent to which the experience of female university students differs from those of girls in high school. For example, in Shariff's (2014) Facebook Report, data collected on adolescents' communication style on social media revealed that out of 522 students surveyed, 46.47 percent of students between the ages of 13 to 18 believed that when a girl posts or sends an intimate image of herself online, she no longer has the right to object to it being shared. One participant wrote, 'once you send something to a friend, they can do what they want with that information' (Shariff 2014, p. 29). Students tended to place the burden of blame on girls for incidents of sexting gone awry. One student remarked, 'I think it's 60 percent the girl's fault and then 40 percent the guys fault because she starts the whole process of it being sent to everyone' (Shariff 2014, p. 25). There is not much difference between the age of 18 and 19. Pending the gathering of empirical data to confirm whether 19-year-old university students and those between the ages of 19 to 30 share the same perspectives as the high school student group, it would not be unreasonable to assume that those perspectives would not undergo significant change at the university level. The next phase of research for Define the Line's Projects, headed by Shariff, will build on what we know about rape culture and the 'up for it' and 'asking for it' notions surrounding female sexuality.

Rape culture: 'up for it' and 'asking for it' notions around female sexuality

In recent years, a trend involving young males and young adult males has emerged where videos and images of rapes-in-progress have been posted on social media sites. Such was the case in the Steubenville rape; the Nova Scotia case of RP (currently under a publication ban), which sadly ended with RP taking her own life; the Maple Ridge Case; and in Chicago, three young men raped a 12-year-old girl, after luring her into one of the boy's home, and days later, posted the act on Facebook (Williams 2013; Ford 2013). In the Maple Ridge case, the female victim was drugged and gang-raped at a rave party while a 16-year-old male watched the rape conducted by older students, videotaped the incident, and passed it to an older friend to post on Facebook (Shariff, in press). The public's reaction to many of these cases reveals how rape culture erodes some people's abilities to make compassionate connections to the victims of sexual violence – and, that it desensitizes people to the devastating emotional effects that the victims experience when the events are available for repeated viewings and widespread distribution online.

In the Maple Ridge case, once the rape video went viral, there was sustained discussion on social media as to whether the girl who was raped had 'asked for it,' and whether the images in the video made it look as though she 'enjoyed' it. Similarly, in the Steubenville rape, discussion over social media forums contained comments that blamed the victim by naming her a 'slut' and 'whore' as though she was, *asking for it*. We return to this notion of *asking for it* momentarily as it provides a nuanced way to think about rape culture and its relationship to adolescent males' notions of female sexuality. To do so, we first return to our earlier discussion on neoliberal marketing of modern femininity as the sexually empowered woman within popular culture and advertising. By doing so, we begin to understand both how adolescent females negotiate their identities amidst society's contradictory messages as well as how adolescent males negotiate their understandings of female sexuality amidst sexist and misogynist portrayals of women and girls. Parts of this section also appeared in our chapter in 'eGirls, eCitizens: Putting Technology Theory and Policy into Dialogue with Girls' and Young Women's Voices'. We include them here because they underpin our nuanced reflections of how female and male university students negotiate notions of sexuality, consent, and misogyny as they define the line between fun and cyberbullying. More so, it serves in part as a theoretical framework to interpret our data from the next research phase with the Define the Line Research.

A new figure of femininity has been constructed over the past decade within media and advertising: 'A young, attractive, heterosexual woman who knowingly and deliberately plays with her sexual power and is always "up for it" (that is, sex)' (Gill 2008, p. 41). To think about the ways popular culture, advertising, and film construct this femininity, is to also think about the ways that male sexual fantasy perpetuates this notion of the sexually voracious female figure, and what Evans *et al.* (2010) call this 'up for it' femininity. Examples of this 'up for it' femininity, offered by these authors, include the popular re-emergence of pole-dancing and burlesque dance classes. Neoliberalism's impact on the feminist ideals of sexual agency, empowerment, and revolution have produced a sexy kind of 'feminism lite' – a non-revolutionary form of feminism that is non-threatening to the patriarchal norms governing the political and economic relations within mainstream society (Gill 2008). This kind of 'feminism lite' creates a market (from pop and film icons, to car advertisements) that cultivates a popular belief among consumers that women live in an era where feminism is no longer relevant in contemporary society.

However, Gill (2008) argues it is precisely this template production of the idea of the sexually voracious female, 'made real' by male sexual fantasy, that convince women as if these attitudes were authentically their own. It is important to note that our examination of women does not presume them to be passive, but as active subjects that are also subjected to intricate belief systems and norms that are sexist and misogynist. Perhaps a weakness in Gill's analysis, as Evans, Riley and Shankar (2010) point out, is her homogeneous portrayal of women's engagement with neoliberal marketization of the modern woman. Even as we discuss the ways in which sexist views intertwine with popular culture, we must keep in mind that women's experiences of neoliberal marketing depend on their varying positions within society.

Of interest to our discussion here, is Gill's (2008) consideration of the work of Janice Turner (2005). Turner examines how 'straight porn' has moved from the realm of fantasy to mainstream society, conveniently coinciding with the emergence of the 'up for it' female figure in popular culture and advertising. The following excerpt appeared in Gill (2008), but we sourced it from Turner's (2005) article:

> Once porn and real human sexuality were distinguishable. Not even porn's biggest advocates would suggest a porn flick depicted reality, that women were gagging for sex 24/7 and would drop their clothes and submit to rough, anonymous sex at the slightest invitation. But as porn has seeped into mainstream culture, the line has blurred. To speak to men's magazine editors, it is clear they believe that somehow in recent years, porn has come true. The sexually liberated modern woman turns out to resemble – what do you know! – the pneumatic, take-me-now-big-boy fuck-puppet of male fantasy after all.

The potency of Turner's (2005) observation is that she addresses both the underlying influences behind the post-feminist femininity as well as the purpose that the 'up for it' female figures plays for the enjoyment of the hetero-male consumer. With the barrage of messages young males receive from popular culture and advertising, a significant amount of their understanding on female sexuality likely comes from music, movies, advertisements and television. Thus, if there is a tendency in entertainment and advertisement marketing to portray women as always 'up for it' alongside the materialization of male-fantasy-straight-porn come true, then there are grounds to think about the ways young adult males view young adult females who also try to mimic these examples of 'up for it' via their latest female pop culture icon. In short, as young adults negotiate the boundaries of consent in their sexual lives, the lines between 'up for it' femininity and the females who are 'asking for it' blends within popular culture and mainstream entertainment. Given that most young women establish their long-term relationships and sexual partnerships between high school and approximately 30 to 35 years of age, and that this is the time many of them attend university, it is important to consider the emerging policy frameworks that attempt to address the line between sexting and the distribution of non-consensual images that border on pornography, and what young people, including young adults, think of as simply 'fun'.

Policy attempts at defining the lines between cyberbullying and online fun

Policymakers have come under significant pressure to develop and implement legislation with harsher punishment for young offenders who engage in the non-consensual distribution of images. It is unlikely that many policymakers are knowledgeable about the complex social contexts we describe above. Consequently, police in Canada initially responded in a fashion similar to law enforcement in the United States – by applying child pornography laws to arrest and charge youth as young as 11 years of age (Kimber 2014; Schwartz 2013). Court rulings confirm the opinions of many U.S. judges that applying these laws to youth behaviour is like attempting to 'fit a square peg in a round hole'.

Child pornography laws would only apply to university-aged young adults if a minor were involved in the abuse. Such laws would not be applicable to sexting and cyberbullying that took place between university-aged students with no minor involved (as in the University of Ottawa student union case). As explained elsewhere (Shariff, in press; Shariff and DeMartini, in press) the patterns we found in our Define the Line Research with children and youth, indicate that often, there is a lack of *criminal intent*. The students are simply acting out established adult social norms of misogyny and homophobia with an absence of criminal intent (legal term *mens rea*). Since *mens rea* must be established in a court of law, criminal convictions of children and teens will likely be difficult and rare. However, university students are deemed to be adults and are thus subject to criminal laws that govern adult behavior. It is important for research to establish whether university students are more capable than high school students, of defining the lines between harmless fun and teasing – and harmful and intentionally offensive forms of online expression that carry the risk of criminal liability. We are sceptical that it shifts substantially, and here is why. It is important to remember that young adults between the ages of 18 to 25 have grown up in a very different world from older generations. For the first time ever, this generation of young adults has been significantly immersed in digital and social media. When these unprecedented social experiences are combined with the confusing messages in popular culture – it is likely that young adults in this generation might be 'caught between omissions' or caught in transition, as society and the law grapple with how to define the increasingly blurred boundaries of communication between real and virtual worlds. It is essential that we obtain empirical evidence that confirms whether or not university students, which society views as adults, also have difficulty discerning the difference between harmful forms of communication and playful jests.

Between 2006 and 2009, Shariff collected media reports on over 100 highly publicized cases involving cyberbullying and sexting. Despite the fact that news media often sensationalize, and the reports may not always have been accurate, it was nonetheless useful and interesting to identify patterns in the reported cases that confirmed a lack of motivation or intent to commit a criminal act. What stood out more clearly in all these cases was the intention of the young participant to 'have fun,' 'entertain friends and make them laugh' and 'just joke' with friends. What is notable is the recurrence of responses such as: 'I was just joking' or 'It was just a prank' (Shariff 2008–9; Shariff, Wiseman and Crestohl 2012; Retter and Shariff 2012). This preliminary research indicates that *mens rea*, or criminal intent, would be difficult to establish with university students in a court of law. Pending completion of the next phase of our research, Shariff's preliminary findings indicate that university students can be as impulsive in their online postings as teens and children. Consider the following case examples that involved young adults and/or university students who claim to be joking, venting, and/or welcoming students to university FROSH activities and football teams respectively:

- *David Abitbol:* The case of David Abitbol, a 28-year-old who lived at home with his parents. In the fall of 2010, Abitbol posted threats against his former high school teachers online, showing photographs of himself with five guns ready to shoot (Shariff 2011). The Montreal police could not find his name on a gun registry and obtained a search warrant of his parents' home. The search disclosed five unregistered guns under his mattress. What resonated was his parents' insistence that he was 'just joking' and would never kill anyone. However, there is an assumption here that anything goes as a joke, and the belief that people who make these comments are incapable of harm – when in fact they could be quite dangerous.
- *Ravi Dhuran and Tyler Clementi:* Similarly, in the well-publicized case of Ravi Dhuran and Tyler Clementi at Rutgers University in New York, Ravi filmed his classmate Tyler Clementi in a same-sex relationship and posted the

video online. Clementi committed suicide as a result of the video and homophobic cyberbullying online. Dhuran was criminally charged and maintained he did not *intend* any harm to Clementi. Moreover, he argued that he regrettably sought to entertain his friends by distributing the video, without foreseeing its impact on Clementi, and least of all the tragic suicide. The judge found that Dhuran had seriously flawed judgment in posting the video, but agreed that he lacked the *mens rea* for Clementi's suicide. Dhuran was given a one-month jail sentence and community service (Retter and Shariff 2012).

- *Frustrated Tweeter:* The third example involves a McGill University student who disagreed with the views of a political panel at a seminar. As he listened to the panel and became angrier, he Tweeted that he wished he had an M-16 shotgun so that he could kill everyone on the panel, and one female participant in particular. When asked to explain his intentions, he insisted that he had no actual intention to kill the panelists. He was frustrated and merely expressing his frustrations online. The form of discipline he received for his impulsive Tweets is not known.

- *Misogynist and homophobic student association blogs and FROSH songs:* We quoted from the student association blog at the University of Ottawa where male student reps joked and wagered about the potential rape of the female student union representative (Belle Jar 2014). We highlighted concerns regarding FROSH (fresher) songs containing vulgar and demeaning language sung by both male and female FROSH participants at Canadian universities.

The objective of FROSH (fresher) and intimidating activities are to help new students settle into their new universities, but clearly in the examples provided, the lines can be easily crossed from simply having fun to becoming seriously abusive and intimidating. These undefined boundaries between impulsive postings and those intended to victimize will be the focus of courts as they consider the issue of *mens rea* in each case on its own merits. However, legislators in North America are succumbing to lobbyists who call for stricter laws and harsher penalties for those who engage in cyberbullying, no matter how old they are. Post-secondary students convicted of engaging in such activities risk everything. They could receive jail terms and prison sentences if convicted, which would in turn affect their family relationships, friendships, their potential for career success, and ultimately, their financial situation. University years are critical in shaping the long-term futures of students. Suspensions, expulsions and criminal convictions for impulsive, sexist, homophobic and thoughtless online postings can result in years of hardship.

New legislation designed to update the Canadian *Criminal Code* for the digital age, and target cyberbullying and the non-consensual distribution of intimate images, is pending as a result of significant controversy over several of its provisions. Canadians are concerned with the broad discretionary powers provided to police and other law enforcement agencies within Bill C-13, which could result in serious breaches of citizens' online privacy. Moreover, the bill concerns many legal academics and educational policymakers who believe it does not address cyberbullying. Although its amendments to Section 162 of the existing *Criminal Code* address the non-consensual distribution of intimate images (Non-Consensual Distribution Provisions), expert witnesses who presented to the House of Commons Committee (Shariff 2014; Bernstein 2014; Aftab 2014) expressed concern that the five-year sentence, if applied against young adults, would be too harsh.

We argue that the Non-Consensual Distribution Provisions cannot be expected to change misogynistic attitudes that are deeply ingrained in society. Nor will this clause deter paedophiles or young males who intentionally coerce young women and girls into sending intimate images in trust. More importantly, 'big stick sanctions' (Kift *et al.* 2009) will not work without educational support to help young people understand the lines between harm*less* and harm*ful* forms of online expression that carry the potential for criminal sanctions. Furthermore, the *Youth Criminal Justice Act* protects children and teens from retaining a criminal record after the age of 18. At age 18, criminal records for youth to that date are erased in Canada. However, university students convicted under the Non-Consensual Distribution Provisions of Bill C-13 once it passes into law can expect to carry a criminal record for the rest of their lives.

Conclusion and implications

We have highlighted well-publicized cases of cyberbullying, and sexting at the university level, and discussed those cases within the context of the literature on rape culture, popular culture and emerging legal and policy frameworks. There is no question that cyberbullying, and sexting as a form of cyberbullying, present complex and nuanced challenges for policy development and implementation of regulatory and educational responses to address them. We have stressed that the lack of success in reducing cyberbullying could be partly due to the reluctance by researchers to address its discriminatory and misogynist roots. We have argued that in addition to addressing its behavioral symptoms, it is essential to consider systemic and societal influences that are rooted in several generations. In the absence of focused empirical research on how university students define the lines between fun and criminal intent to harm, we have looked to the data obtained from high school students up to age 18, and compared those findings with publicly reported cases of sexualized cyberbullying at universities. The similarities suggest that university students may be as impulsive as high school students in posting offensive and sexualized forms of expression, without considering the immediate and long-term impact on those they target. We are currently embarking on empirical research at the university level to verify our preliminary findings. As we have explained earlier in this chapter, women and girls are especially vulnerable to the gendered dimensions of online harassment. Cyberbullying and the non-consensual distribution of images are rooted in a widespread culture of rape enforced through the policing apparatus of slut-shaming. It is these roots that the law needs to address – not the online behaviors, which are merely symptoms.

Improve public legal education

Our research indicates that there remains significant public ignorance about the differences between positivist laws like the Criminal Code and substantive human rights and constitutional frameworks that provide the balance between free expression, safety, privacy, protection and regulation (Bailey *et al.* 2014). Without sufficient knowledge about human rights and the fundamental constitutional principles of our Canadian *Charter of Rights and Freedoms*, university professors, student resident dons, student deans and university administrators may be too quick to apply punitive measures. Mentioned at the outset of this chapter, then Chief Justice Bora Laskin of the Supreme Court of Canada noted that implementing legislation without adequate public legal knowledge was risky, because ignorance often results in reactive and harsher responses. His insight and predictions three decades ago are proving to be accurate as we grapple with unprecedented legal challenges in an increasingly digitized society that is immersed in social media.

Assumptions about youth by justice system officials

There are also concerns over erroneous assumptions that police, prosecutors and judges may bring to their application of this law if they lack sufficient awareness about rape culture and the contradictory messages young adults receive from older generations of adult society. In this regard, additional research currently underway with the Define the Line Projects (2014–2017) involves the review of case law, scholarly literature, and qualitative research to assess these officials' perspectives about youth and their uses of digital and social media. We are particularly interested in the judicial assumptions of judges who will be required to consider legal sanctions and appropriate sentencing in cases of sexting and cyberbullying.

As noted in our introduction, there is currently an overemphasis on positivist (punitive) types of legal responses, which criminalize children, adolescents and young adults, for behavior we do not entirely understand in the adult world. It is therefore essential to question what other legal frameworks (substantive), such as human rights, constitutional, tort law, and emerging provincial legislation, might better apply to cyberbullying, which may be more appropriate for addressing legal breaches related to the non-consensual distribution of images among youth (see list of relevant legislation at the end of this chapter).

The Canadian government argues that in conjunction with Bill C-13, it is also undertaking and/or supporting important educational initiatives. It is disappointing to note that one of the few programs it has chosen to finance is out-of-touch with the realities of cyberbullying, particularly WITS, which has been identified by government as an educational support for Bill C-13. The program advocates 'walking away' from the abuse, but as discussed in this chapter, it is impossible for victims of cyberbullying to 'walk away' when their nude or intimate images appear across the Internet or, equally horrifying, when videos and images of the victim's rape are filmed and distributed online. Questions that must be considered by legislators and public policy developers include:

- How well are the social online norms and perspectives of adult society, which influence young people's behavior, understood by prosecutors, judges, law enforcement, university student deans, administrators and counselors?
- What assumptions about young people will these stakeholders bring to their application of law to charge, convict or sentence those involved in cyberbullying?
- Along with the proposed Bill C-13, will there be sufficient resources provided by provincial governments to help university professors, student deans, and administrators to understand young peoples' online expressions?

Until these questions are addressed in a thoughtful, informed, educational and non-arbitrary manner, we will be no further ahead in reducing the non-consensual distribution of intimate images or cyberbullying. If we seek to clarify legal boundaries, we need to ensure that cohesive and coordinated efforts are made to update all legal frameworks that apply, rather than piecemeal and overly broad amendments to criminal legislation. Until we address the roots of misogyny within our societal, legal and institutional structures, we will not make progress. Sadly, we will unfairly continue to scapegoat and criminalize our children with contradictory messages that they receive from adults.

In closing, it is important to consider that the law can play two roles: it can protect and guide civil society, or it can punish. So long as we choose to focus only on the latter role, we will continue to unleash a Pandora's box of legal challenges in a rapidly evolving digital age. Thus, as part of the communications recommendation, it is important that universities engage their students in policy development on digital and social media. Engagement in the development of codes of conduct would provide students with increased awareness, legal literacy and opportunities for leadership. Legally literate students would more easily understand their rights, responsibilities and the legal risks before posting forms of expression they may not express in a face-to-face situation. At McGill University, we have begun to offer courses on Public Policy and the Internet. Ultimately, university students are the future leaders of society. Thus, it is imperative we provide young adults with the capacity and agency to effectively address the culture of rape, and lead society towards a more inclusive, supportive and caring global society.

References

Aftab, P. (2014). Testimony as expert witness to Canadian House of Commons Committee on Bill C-13: *Protecting Canadians from Online Crime Act*. Unpublished testimony, April 3.

Altobelli, T. (2010). Cyber-abuse – a new worldwide threat to children's rights. *Family Court Review*, 48(3): 459–81.

Attwood, F. (2007). Sluts and riot girrrls: Female identity and sexual agency. *Journal of Gender Studies*, 16: 233–47.

Bailey, J. and Hanna, M. (2011). The gendered dimensions of sexting: assessing the applicability of Canada's child pornography provision. *Canadian Journal of Women and The Law*, 23: 405–41.

Bailey, J., Mishna, F., MacKay, A. W. and Slane, A. (2014). Submission to Canadian House of Commons Committee on Bill C-13. House of Commons. Unpublished.

Bailey, J. and Steeves, V. (2013). Will the Real Digital Girl Please Stand Up? In H. Koskela and M. Wise (Eds.), *New Visualities, New Technologies: The New Ecstasy of Communication*. London: Ashgate Publishing. pp. 41–66.

Belle Jar, The (2014). Rape Culture at the University of Ottawa. *The Belle Jar [online]* 28 February. Available at http://bellejar.ca/2014/02/28/rape-culture-at-the-university-of-ottawa [Accessed on 10 April 2014].

Bernstein, M. (2014). Testimony as expert witness to Canadian House of Commons Committee on Bill C-13: *Protecting Canadians from Online Crime Act*. 3 April, unpublished testimony.

Blackwell, B. (2004). How the jilt triumphed over the slut: the evolution of an epithet, 1660–1780. *Women's Writing,* 11: 141–61.

Binder, B. (2013). Public Shaming: Tweets of Privilege [blog] 19 March. Available at http://publicshaming.tumblr.com/day/2013/03/19 [Accessed on 28 April 2014].

Burnett, A., Mattern, J. L., Herakova, L. L., Kahl Jr., D. H., Tobola, C. and Bornsen, S. E. (2009). Communicating/muting date rape: A co-cultural theoretical analysis of communication factors related to rape culture on a college campus. *Journal of Applied Communication Research*, 37(4): 465–85.

CBC News (2013a). UBC investigates frosh students' pro-rape chant: Chant condoned non-consensual sex with underage girls. *CBC News British Columbia,* [online] 7 September. Available at http://www.cbc.ca/news/canada/british-columbia/ubc-investigates-frosh-students-pro-rape-chant-1.1699589 [Accessed on 8 April 2014].

CBC News (2013b). Saint Mary's University frosh chant cheers underage sex: Frosh week leaders, student union executive sent to sensitivity training. *CBC News Nova Scotia* [online] 4 September. Available at http://www.cbc.ca/news/canada/nova-scotia/saint-mary-s-university-frosh-chant-cheers-underage-sex-1.1399616 [Accessed on 13 April 2014].

Chen, E. (2013). Neoliberalism and popular women's culture: Rethinking choice, freedom and agency. *European Journal of Cultural Studies,* 16: 440–52.

Craig, W. M. and Pepler, D. J. (1998). Observations of bullying and victimization in the school yard. *Canadian Journal of School Psychology*, 13(2): 41–59.

Eltis, K. (2011). The Judicial System in the Digital Age: Revisiting the Relationship between Privacy and Accessibility in the Cyber Context. *McGill Law Journal*, 56(2): 289–316.

Evans, A., Riley, S. and Shankar, A. (2010). Technologies of sexiness: theorizing women's engagement in the sexualization of culture. *Feminism and Psychology,* 20: 114–31.

Ford, L. (2013). Prosecutors: 3 teens posted taped sex assault of girl, 12, Facebook. *Chicago Tribune* [online] 17 May. Available at: http://www.chicagotribune.com/news/local/breaking/chi-3-teens-posted-taped-sex-assaults-of-girl-12-on-facebook-20130517,0,4873584.story [Accessed on 8 July 2014].

Gill, R. (2008). Empowerment/sexism: Figuring female sexual agency in contemporary advertising. *Feminism and Psychology,* 18: 35–60.

Hess, A. (2014). Why Women Aren't Welcome on the Internet. *Pacific Standard* [online] 6 January. Available at http://www.psmag.com/navigation/health-and-behavior/women-arent-welcome-internet-72170/ [Accessed on 7 May 2014].

Hirschman, C., Celeste, E. and Schooler, D. (2006). Dis/embodied voices: What late-adolescent girls can teach us about objectification and sexuality. *Sexuality Research and Social Policy*, 3: 8–20.

Holman, R. (2013). She's a homewrecker: the website where women expose 'infidelity'. The Internet just ate itself. *The Telegraph* [online] 15 November. Available at http://www.telegraph.co.uk/women/womens-life/10452482/Shes-A-Homewrecker-the-website-where-women-slut-shame-each-others-infidelity.-The-internet-just-ate-itself.html [Accessed on 10 April 2014].

Hymel, S., Rocke-Henderson, N. and Bonanno, R. A. (2005). Moral disengagement: A framework for understanding bullying among adolescents. *Journal of Social Sciences*, 8(1): 1–11.

Keltner, D., Capps, L., Kring, A. M., Young, R. C. and Heerey, E. A. (2001). Just teasing: a conceptual analysis and empirical review. *Psychological Bulletin*, 127(2): 229–48.

Kift, S., Campbell, M., and Butler, D. (2009). Cyberbullying in social networking sites and blogs: Legal issues for young people and schools. *Journal of Law, Information and Science*, 20(2): 60–97.

Kimber, S. (2014). Why are we using child pornography laws to charge children? *Rabble* [blog] 14 January. Available at http://rabble.ca/blogs/bloggers/skimber/2014/01/why-are-we-using-child-pornography-laws-to-charge-children [Accessed on 3 March 2014].

Kryk, J. (2013). Target in 2005 McGill hazing horror speaks out. *The Toronto Sun* [online] 9 November. Available at http://www.torontosun.com/2013/11/09/target-in-2005-mcgill-hazing-horror-speaks-out [Accessed on 12 March 2014].

Levande, M. (2008). Women, pop music, and pornography. *Meridians: Feminism, Race, Transnationalism*, 8: 293–321.

Menesini, E., Eslea, M., Smith, P. K. and Genta, M. L. (1997). Cross-national comparison of children's attitudes towards bully/victim problems in school. *Aggressive Behaviour*, 23: 245–57.

Olson, L. J. (2014). Transforming Rape Culture on a College Campus: Using Peer Advocacy for Social Change. In: S. White, J. M. White, and K. O. Korgen (Eds.), *Sociologists in Action on Inequalities: Race, Class, Gender, and Sexuality*. Thousand Oaks, CA: SAGE Publications.

Perren, S. and Gutzwiller-Helfenfinger, E. (2012). Cyberbullying and traditional bullying in adolescence: Differential roles of moral disengagement, moral emotions, and moral values. *European Journal of Developmental Psychology*, 9: 195–209.

Poltash, N. (2013). Snapchat and Sexting: A snapshot of bearing your bare essentials. *Richmond Journal of Law and Technology*, 19: 14.

Poole, E. (2013). Hey girls, did you know? Slut-shaming on the Internet needs to stop. *USFL Review*, 48: 221–60.

Retter, C. and Shariff, S. (2012). A delicate balance: defining the line between open civil proceedings and the protection of children in the online digital era. *Canadian Journal of Law and Technology*, 10(2): 232–62.

Ringrose, R. and Renold, E. (2012). Slut-shaming, girl power and 'sexualisation': thinking through the politics of the international SlutWalks with teen girls. *Gender and Education*, 24: 333–43.

Schwartz, D. (2013). The fine line between 'sexting' and child pornography: Criminal Code may be too blunt an instrument to stop the practice of young people sharing sexually suggestive images. *CBC News* [online] 13 August. Available at http://www.cbc.ca/news/canada/the-fine-line-between-sexting-and-child-pornography-1.1367613 [Accessed on 5 March 2014].

Shariff, S. and DeMartini, A. (in press). Defining the Legal Lines: E-Girls and Intimate Images. In: J. Bailey and V. Steeves (Eds.) *eGirls, eCitizens: Putting Technology Theory and Policy Into Dialogue with Girls' and Young Women's Voices*. Ottawa: University of Ottawa Press.

Shariff, S. (2004). Keeping schools out of court: Legally defensible models of leadership. *The Educational Forum*, 68(3): 222–33.

Shariff, S. (2008). *Cyber-bullying: Issues and Solutions for the School, the Classroom and the Home.* New York: Routledge.

Shariff, S. (2009). *Confronting Cyberbullying: What Schools Need to Know About Misconduct and Legal Consequences.* New York: Cambridge University Press.

Shariff, S. (2011). Adolescents Unclear of When Joking and Venting Become Criminal Threats. Available at http://www.internetsafetyproject.org/articles/adolescents-unclear-when-joking-and-venting-become-criminal-threats [Accessed on 24 March 2014].

Shariff, S. (2014). Submitted to House of Commons Committee on Bill C-13 in support of invited testimony as expert witness [unpublished policy brief], 3 April.

Shariff, S. (2014). *Facebook Report*. Montreal: Define The Line. Available at http://definetheline.ca/dtl/define-the-line-facebook-report/ [Unpublished report].

Shariff, S. (in press) *Sexting and Cyberbullying: Defining the Line on Digitally Empowered Kids.* New York: Cambridge University Press.

Shariff, S. and Churchill, A. H. (Eds.) (2010). *Truths And Myths of Cyber-Bullying: International Perspectives on Stakeholder Responsibility and Children's Safety.* New York: Peter Lang Inc.

Shariff, S., Wiseman, A. and Crestohl, L. (2012). Defining the Lines between Children's Vulnerability to Cyberbullying and the Open Court Principle: Implications of A. B. (Litigation Guardian of) vs. Bragg Communications Inc. *Education and Law Journal*, 21(3): 231–62.

Smith, P. K., Pepler, D. and Rigby, K. (Eds.) (2004). *Bullying in Schools: How Successful Can Interventions Be?*, New York: Cambridge University Press.

Ttofi, M. M. and Farrington, D. P. (2011). Effectiveness of school-based programs to reduce bullying: A systematic and meta-analytic review. *Journal of Experimental Criminology*, 7(1): 27–56.

Turner, J. (2005). Dirty Young Men. *The Guardian* [online] 22 October. Available at http://www.chicagomanualofstyle.org/tools_citationguide.html. [Accessed on 8 June 2014].

Unruh, B. (2014). Nearly ½ of Teens: Sexting is 'Part of Everyday Life'. *WND Education* [online] 22 August. Available at http://www.wnd.com/2014/08/nearly-12-of-teens-sexting-is-part-of-everyday-life [Accessed on 28 August 2014].

Van Praagh, S. (2005). Adolescence, autonomy and Harry Potter: The child as decision maker. *International Journal of Law in Context*, 1(4): 335–73.

Van Praagh, S. (2007). 'Sois Sage'– Responsibility for Childishness in the Law of Civil Wrongs. In: J. W. Neyers, E. Chamberlain and S. G. A. Pital (Eds.). *Emerging Issues in Tort Law*. Oxford: Hart Publishing. pp. 3–84.

Vreeman, R. C. and Carroll, A. E. (2007). A systematic review of school-based interventions to prevent bullying. *Archives of Pediatrics and Adolescent Medicine*, 161(1): 78–88.

Welsh-Huggins, A. (2013). Ohio football players guilty in rape of 16-year-old girl, face year-plus in jail. *National Post* [online] 17 March. Available at http://news.nationalpost.com/2013/03/17/ohio-football-players-guilty-in-rape-of-16-year-old-girl-face-year-plus-in-jail [Accessed on 14 April 2014].

Williams, M. E. (2013). Horrifying New Trend: Posting rapes to Facebook. *Salon* [online] 20 May. Available at http://www.salon.com/2013/05/20/worst_horrifying_new_trend_posting_rapes_to_facebook [Accessed on 24 June 2014].

Ybarra, M.L., Mitchell, K.J., Wolak, J. and Finkelhor, D. 2006 Examining characteristics and associated distress related to internet harassment; findings from the second youth internet safety survey, *Journal of the American Academy of Pediatrics*, 118, 1169–1177.

Zhang, Y., Dixon, T. L. and Conrad, K. (2010). Female body image as a function of themes in rap music videos: A content analysis. *Sex Roles,* 62: 787–97.

Relevant Canadian and International Legislation

Accepting Schools Act (Bill 13), S. O. 2012 c. 5.

Act Concerning the Strengthening of School Bullying Laws (2011) SB 1138.

Anti-Bullying Bill of Rights Act (2011) P. L. 2010, c. 122.

An Act to prevent and stop bullying and violence in schools (Bill 56), 2012.

Canadian Charter of Rights and Freedoms, Part I of the *Constitution Act, 1982,* being Schedule B to the *Canada Act 1982* (UK), 1982, c. 11.

Convention of the Rights of the Child, Can T. S. 1992.

Criminal Code, R. S. C. 1985, c. C-46.

Cyber-safety Act, SNS 2013 c. 2.

PART VI

Reflections

14

COMMENTARY

Awakening and harnessing the sleeping dragon of student power

Keith Sullivan

Introduction

For many years, I have been a participant-observer in the lived-culture of universities. My journey has taken me geographically from Canada to the USA, England, New Zealand, the South Pacific and Ireland. I started as a first year student of 16, and 50 years on have run the gauntlet of progression and promotion within the academic and administrative dimensions of my various universities to become a full professor, a head of department, a head of school and a dean of faculty. During this time, with colleagues and students alike, I have experienced and witnessed a gamut of experiences from the highs of world class creativity found in exceptional programmes and inspirational research to the troughs of destructive and cruel manifestations of the dark, often hidden, underbellies that universities can nurture. Being intimately familiar with the culture and the politics of universities, I am both shocked but not at all surprised by the worrying findings as described in *Bullying Among University Students: cross-national perspectives*. As well as providing an excellent compendium of important issues, this fine array of international scholars and researchers have laid down a marker and made an implicit demand that universities acknowledge their failure to protect their students from the predation of bullying on both their university campuses and in the other arenas where university life takes place. It is a matter of urgency that they fix this life-destroying problem.

Although neglectful, even outrageous, this absence of effective action does, however, present us with an almost blank canvas upon which to develop creative and effective responses to bullying among university students. In this respect, we can learn much from how schools have effectively addressed bullying (Cowie and Sharp 1996, 1994; Craig and Pepler 1995; Rigby 2007; Salmivalli 2010; Sullivan 2011; Sullivan, Cleary and Sullivan 2004). Research into school bullying has examined the nature of school bullying: what forms it takes; what roles are taken on by all in the bullying dynamic; what harm it does; how to address it in a pragmatic, empowering and problem-solving fashion; what is required to stop the perpetrators; meeting the immediate and ongoing needs of the victimized and empowering the bystanders. All of these issues are as appropriate for the university context. Making a general comparison of the cultures and physical settings within which school and university bullying takes place is a useful starting point for considering bullying among university students.

The school context and bullying

1   **At schools, you have a more or less uniform context.** At the primary and secondary levels, students are essentially carrying out the same curriculum and in secondary schools pupils choose their curriculum from the same subject base and prepare for the same final exams.
2   **At school, students are largely present all day.** Generally, students and teachers have set routines for the school day throughout the school year and are mostly on site all day.
3   **As well as providing an education, teachers have a duty of care.** Students are largely minors and teachers have *in loco parentis* responsibilities (although this can decrease in practice when older students are becoming responsible young adults in their last years of secondary school).
4   **Bullying is a major issue for students.** Bullying can occur both at school and outside of school hours, particularly with the advent of cyberbullying.
5   **Student power is limited.** Although schools may have student councils, their power is limited both by the schools' administration and because they are minors.
6   **A whole school approach is best for dealing with bullying.** The administrative structures of schools are such that when an issue, such as bullying, occurs, the administration, teachers, parents, students and the wider community can work together to create, put into practice, and carry out anti-bullying policies and processes.
7   **Bullying is an issue for school staff.** Although the main focus is bullying among students, the bullying of staff also occurs and needs addressing.
8   **Bullying is not restricted to the school, its grounds and school hours.** Bullying can occur both in and outside of school, in real space and time (which I have called rstbullying) and in virtual space and time (cyberbullying). Former secondary school principal, Mark Cleary (Sullivan, Cleary and Sullivan 2004), stated that if bullying occurred outside of school space and time but related to school-based relationships/incidents, it was his responsibility to deal with it. Although it could be argued that this stance was inappropriate because it was outside of his remit and jurisdiction, his response to this argument was that the safety of his students was his primary concern and that furthermore, if not

firmly dealt with, this 'out of school' bullying would almost certainly have repercussions at school.

9 **Bullying can be difficult to address.** Although it may seem illogical and unacceptable, the culture of students can dictate, for instance, that 'ratting on other students' is worse than bullying and it therefore often goes unreported. Students also fear (often from experience) that reporting bullying will only make matters worse.

The university context and bullying

1 **At university things are more complex.** There are a vast range of subjects, courses and levels (within a context of undergraduate and postgraduate programmes) and there is usually a larger and more diverse student and staff population. University-related activities, both academic and social, occur both on and off campus.

2 **At universities, students come and go within a much more fluid context.** Students attend lectures, tutorials, research supervisions etc. and have access to libraries, computer suites and a large number of places for working and/or socializing. They come and go according to individual needs and choices.

3 **Universities are highly political places** and students need to understand how power and politics work in their particular university so as to be heard when requesting/challenging that issues such as bullying, be appropriately and fully addressed.

4 **At university, students are mostly 18 or older, qualify as adults and have greater rights and potential power than they realize.** If explored, understood and if they choose to exercise them, students' rights are potentially far more likely to influence the running of universities in areas that affect them than is the case at school. Both as adults and consumers, they can more easily demand that their right to be physically, sexually, psychologically and intellectually safe is upheld.

5 **University's duty of care.** Although most students are legally adults, the university still has a duty of care towards them not only in terms of their education but also for the provision of a safe place to study and grow. Students could demand that this is part of their implied contract of basic rights within the university. Also, as consumers, they pay fees from which the university benefits and also their enrollment can bring secondary financial benefits to the university in the form of government subsidies in support of their studies. They therefore have strong grounds for making demands upon the university, such as, at the very least, to be safe from being bullied.

6 **Bullying is a major issue for university students.** Both on and off the university campus, students are being bullied and intimidated physically, psychologically, virtually, sexually and criminally.

7 **Bullying is also a major issue for university staff** (Hodgins 2004).

Bullying among university students can be either/or/and rstbullying (bullying in real time and space) and cyberbullying and this can occur both on and off campus. Bullying is destructive for the individual and can create a feeling of unsafeness for individuals and within the student population as a whole. It is crucial that university authorities address this malignant phenomenon by creating effective anti-bullying policies and practices for halting and addressing bullying and its effects. The role of a university's CEO in dealing with bullying is similar to that articulated by former secondary school principal Mark Cleary. When bullying was visited upon his students, whether at school or outside of school space and time, he stated that it was his responsibility to fully address the bullying with clarity, commitment and strength of purpose. His response also entailed providing appropriate support to those victimized (such as through counselling and psychological referrals). His underlying premise was that if bullying were not adequately dealt with, it would settle in and create long-term, even devastating, effects upon those targeted. In effect, he was not prepared to give bullying 'a place to hide'. He knew that if not addressed it could result in loss of self-confidence, inability to function effectively, and lead to self-harm, even suicide for those being victimized. He was also aware that an ineffective response could give the perpetrators of bullying an inordinate sense of power and a feeling that they could act with impunity. Addressing student bullying is not only part of the institution's duty of care, be it a school, a university or any other type of educational organization, it is also a basic human right not to be intimidated and physically, mentally and sexually assaulted. It is also in everybody's best interests to have a transparent and healthy environment to live and work within.

Developing a healthy university culture, which includes effectively addressing the destructive phenomenon that is bullying is logical, appropriate and goes hand in hand with the positive encouragement of educational dynamism, creative thinking, boundary breaking programmes and world-class research.

To address the bullying of university students, five crucial commitments need to be undertaken by the university's CEO and her/his administration:

1 To establish unequivocally the right of students not to be bullied in any way, shape or form and to thereby have their health fully safeguarded.
2 To identify the nature of student bullying in universities, the various forms it takes, whom it affects and who is responsible for it.
3 To create and establish long-term policies, processes and practices to effectively address university bullying among university students both on and off campus.
4 The university, through its CEO, should accept full financial and moral responsibility for addressing bullying among university students. This would also mean, as appropriate, enlisting support from administrative, academic and counselling staff as well as various appointed governing body members, and experts and interest groups from the wider university community (e.g. parents, alumni, anti-bullying experts, counsellors, psychologists, the police etc.).

5   In addressing the bullying of university students, students themselves need to be central to identifying the nature of the bullying that occurs and the creation of effective and empowering policy and practice to counteract it.

6   Dealing with the bullying among university students should be fully committed to by the university's administration on an ongoing basis, not just to provide an initial response to a high profile and publicly embarrassing issue and to then abandon it when 'hysteria' dies down and the next high profile issue emerges to take its place. What is required instead, is to develop a creative and intelligent process for addressing this often complex, multi-faceted, humiliating and ongoing process through confidentially building up case-knowledge and adopting/creating effective problem-solving processes.

My concern that institutional thinking can be ill-considered and lacking depth rather than being based on experiential intuition and social intelligence was brought home to me when I visited a secondary school I'd worked with in relation to bullying. A year prior to the visit in question, the school's administration had responded intelligently and appropriately to the worries of teachers and parents about the damage being caused by bullying. They supported the development of an excellent whole-school anti-bullying programme. Much to my surprise, however, a year later, rather than fine tuning their excellent initiative, they mistakenly concluded that the brief intervention had solved the problem (despite the fact that there was a new cohort of students in need of being educated about: i. the nature of bullying; ii. being encouraged not to initiate it; iii. being told how to safely get help if you were being bullied; and iv. learning about the nature and dynamics of bullying). Instead, they enthusiastically trumpeted their success and informed me that they had 'moved on' and were now using their resources to focus on truancy. Although it was important to address truancy, it seemed shortsighted to think that bullying no longer needed their attention. In my experience, however, such ill-considered and incomplete thinking is not uncommon. In order to avoid falling on the swords of 'shifting sands', poor decision-making, power game interferences, the culture of university politics etc., bullying among university students needs to be better understood, anticipated and guarded against.

In order to provide a starting point for more effectively addressing bullying among university students, I have adapted a six-step anti-bullying template that I originally created for schools (Sullivan 2011) as a foundation for addressing bullying among university students, as follows:

An anti-bullying initiative for universities

Part I planning

Step 1. Preliminary explorations

•   Defining the underlying philosophy and getting started. Although the aim of the intended programme is to stop bullying, from a practical point of view, it is crucial to participate in the discussions and decision-making so that people are agreed upon and clear about what the thinking underlying subsequent actions is.

The aims of step 1 are:

- To clarify the university's philosophy, both generally and also in terms of the rights and expectations of staff and students concerning the handling of bullying;
- To arrange an initial meeting to discuss the initiative publicly and making sure that all interested parties have the opportunity to be party to what is decided;
- An appropriate agenda is created and a skilled facilitator appointed to keep things on track. A knowledgeable guest speaker with expertise in bullying could be included to provide a short introductory lecture/discussion to focus the meeting.

Step 2. The first meeting 'What are we going to do about bullying?'

- The purpose of the meeting is explained.
- What we know about bullying is discussed.
- 'What can we do about bullying?' is put to the group.
- An appropriately representative anti-bullying committee is established.
- The terms of reference of the committee are created.
- A timeframe for preparing and rolling out an initiative is created.

The aims of step 2 are:

- To introduce the topic with clarity and enthusiasm;
- To provide opportunities for all to participate;
- To form an anti-bullying committee and develop its terms of reference;
- To create a preliminary plan that will include a draft policy statement, a programme for dealing with bullying, plus a timeline.

Part II Developing policies and programs

Step 3. The anti-bullying committee gets to work

- Carrying out a SWOTSS analysis (identifying what strengths, weaknesses, opportunities and threats to the effective running of an anti-bullying initiative there are and what strategies and solutions to the problem are appropriate for dealing with these challenges.) (See Sullivan 2011, chapter 8).
- Carrying out a bullying survey provides an initial statement about the extent and nature of the bullying in the university and can provide details that identify needs and immediate priorities.

- Writing a draft anti-bullying policy.
- Developing a strategy for dealing with bullying.
- Consolidating findings.

The aims of step 3 are:

- To examine the issues surrounding bullying and come up with an action plan for developing an anti-bullying policy in line with an underlying philosophical foundation;
- To report on the university's current strengths and weaknesses in dealing with bullying (ibid chapter 8);
- To provide a survey and identify the nature of bullying at the university;
- To write a draft anti-bullying policy (ibid chapter 9);
- To make recommendations about what programmes to adopt (preventative and interventionist). For example, see Sullivan 2011 for ideas (peer mentoring, for example), and the excellent peer counselling processes developed by Cowie and Sharp (1994 and 1996). These two tools (and others) would be useful strategies to adapt for the university context.
- To recommend other resources, such as videos, books and reports that should be acquired as a reference base (shortlists could be made and after discussions choices made so that the most useful resources are acquired).
- To provide a short report containing this information both to put things on the record and as a reflective review before making decisions (an important consideration is that in developing a deep, effective and uncluttered process, less can sometimes be more).

Step 4. Presenting a plan to students, staff and key administrators

The aims of step 4 are to:

- Present the plan and its recommendations;
- Debate the document between the key 'players';
- Consolidate policy;
- Plan for the implementation of the programme.

Step 5. Implementing the initiative

- The initiative is put in place.
- The policy is widely disseminated (and should be considered as a living document to be refined on an on-going basis as appropriate).
- Effective practice is gradually established.

The aims of step 5 are:

- To establish the policies and programmes and put them into practice;
- To inform all concerned parties that this is happening.

Step 6. Evaluation and maintenance of the initiative

The aims of step 6 are:

- To maintain and modify the adopted anti-bullying processes and programmes on a regular basis and as appropriate. When an initiative has been undertaken, the experience of addressing a variety of situations provides a further opportunity for refining and improving policy and practice.
- To make sure the anti-bullying initiative is explained to new students and staff. As each new cohort of students and staff arrive, details of university bullying policies, such as who can be contacted when bullying occurs etc. needs to be provided.

Three central elements intended to assist long-term success underpin this initiative. They are as follows:

- *Inclusivity* – This requires that all those with an interest in making the initiative work need to be involved.
- *Ownership* – There needs to be a sense that things have been thoroughly and jointly thought through, discussed, argued about and decided upon by all of the stakeholders, as it is necessary for all participants to believe in and therefore support what has been developed, both in theory and practice. Furthermore, as a 'living process', fine-tuning and changes will be made, as appropriate, in response to the lived experiences that arise from applying the program in practice.
- *Agreement* – The various stakeholders need to be clear about what is intended and agree with what is decided and to argue and debate over contentious issues with a concern to solve problems/issues being addressed.

Addressing bullying by awakening the sleeping dragon of student power

The potential of student power

Student unions are funded largely from student fees, meaning they are not there as a gift from the university, but are a student-funded resource. Realising this means that an equal rather than a deferential relationship needs to be negotiated and claimed. If confident and prepared to respond authoritatively to university pressures and any reactionary responses from within the student body itself, students can claim their power and demand that universities deal with bullying in an empowering and more effective fashion than is currently the case. Such a response was taken by students internationally in the 1960s and 1970s whereby university students bravely and assertively influenced politics in relation to civil rights, the Vietnam War, the nature of how universities are run, challenging the rights of government to exert, even abuse, their powers without adequate accountability etc. in the US, Europe, Canada, Australia and New Zealand. The context is different today, but the latent power to deal with human rights issues in general, and the right of students to be safe from being bullied while attending university specifically, are reasons to awaken the sleeping dragon of student power, not to create havoc and desolation but rather to unleash its latent power for the protection of students from this life-destroying phenomenon of bullying.

Universities are very political places. If bullying is to be treated seriously, students need to establish their credibility and publicly declare that not to address this issue fully is irresponsible. This should put universities under 'appropriate' pressure and, if done coherently and convincingly with passion and intelligence, it would make a clear statement to the powers that be that it is crucial to address this fundamental human right. My sense of the moral right and the potential courage of students, both individually and in a unified response, is that there are 'sleeping dragons' waiting to be awakened. They are potentially in a position of great strength and could make a coherent and morally appropriate case to their particular university, and if agreement and strong support from the university is forthcoming, there should be no need to use the lethal arrows 'in-waiting' to bring Smaug administrators crashing down to earth!

One of the most compelling of ways that students can help to address university bullying is through peer processes (see Cowie and Sharp 1994 and 1996 in relation to peer counselling) and peer mentoring (Sullivan 2011). University counselling services and psychology departments (perhaps through their clinical programs) may be interested in developing research and practical clinical work opportunities for their students. Although often over-worked, university counselling services are also an excellent and potentially key resource for effectively addressing the bullying of university students.

The potential for university staff as allies

When carrying out research into workplace bullying (Sullivan 2010), I became aware that the issue of university staff being bullied was a major one. Hodgins' (2004) research into the bullying of staff in my own university provides worrying reading. In contradiction of the fine words of the human resources department's anti-bullying policies, the reality of staff concerns and experiences painted a different picture and demonstrated that creating effective problem-solving policy and programmes were needed or such well-articulated intentions became empty rhetoric. Claiming their power and working in partnership with university administrations, students may find that they have excellent allies within the university staff (academic and administrative) and their often clued-in unions, and that working in tandem with them to address the bullying of both university staff and students would be very constructive, and could make a stronger case for addressing bullying as a whole within the university context.

Conclusion

In conclusion, I reiterate the need to harness the potential power possessed by student bodies and the academic and administrative staff of a university in mounting a case to protect its members from internal and external bullying. Any particular university should find it to be in its best interest to deal with bullying based on the knowledge generated by this book's authors and with solutions proposed and implied in this and other chapters.

References

Cowie, H. and Sharp, S. (1994). Empowering pupils to take positive action against bullying. In P. K. Smith and S. Sharp (Eds.) *School Bullying: Insights and Perspectives*. London: Routledge.

Cowie, H. and Sharp, S. (Eds.) (1996). *Peer Counselling in Schools: A Time to Listen*. London: David Fulton.

Craig, W. M. and Pepler, D. J. (1995). Peer processes in bullying and victimization: an observational study. *Exceptional Education Canada*, 5: 81–95.

Espelage, D. L. and Swearer, S. M. (2004). *Bullying in American Schools: A Social-Ecological Perspective on Prevention and Intervention*. Mahwah, NJ: Erlbaum.

Hodgins, M. (2004). *Perceptions of Anti-Bullying Policy and Practice in NUI*. Galway: Centre for Health Promotion Studies, NUI, Galway.

Rigby, K. (2007). *Bullying in Schools and What to Do About It*. Revised and updated. Australia: ACER.

Salmivalli, C. (2010) Bullying and the peer group: a review. *Aggression and Violent Behavior*, 15(2): 112–20.

Sullivan, K. (2010). Bullying in the Irish Workplace: a Cause for Concern. In K. Österman (Ed.), *Indirect and Direct Aggression*. Oxford: Peter Lang Inc. Available at http://www.peterlang.com/download/datasheet/53087/datasheet_260028.pdf.

Sullivan, K. (2011). *The Anti-Bullying Handbook* (2nd ed.). London: Sage Publications. Available at http://www.uk.sagepub.com/books/Book234440.

Sullivan, K., Cleary, M. and Sullivan, G. (2004). *Bullying in Secondary Schools: What it Looks Like and How to Deal With it*. London: Sage. Available at http://www.uk.sagepub.com/books/Book225571.

15

COMMENTARY

What universities can learn from workplace bullying research

Iain Coyne

Firstly, congratulations to all contributors for constructing an informative and, at times, quite shocking synopsis of bullying in a university context. While a fledgling research area, this book demonstrates a collective drive and expertise to understand and reduce such abusive behaviour. Secondly, given the unique status of university students as neither children nor employees (Aziz; Campbell, this volume), the inclusion of parallel commentary chapters from a school (Sullivan) and work perspective should help to offer further insight into this new, yet growing research topic.

This commentary shall consider the previous chapters and map them to extant research within workplace bullying. It will commence with a short debate on defining bullying, followed by a discussion of the antecedents and shall culminate in a framework for interventions to address bullying within a university context.

Defining bullying

It is beyond the scope of this chapter to delve into a profound discussion of defining bullying; however, it is worth noting that some of the 'key criteria' often mooted within workplace bullying are highlighted in this volume. These include the notion of bullying as an abuse of power (Aziz; Simmons; Campbell; Shariff and DeMartini); frequency and repetition (Cowie and Myers; Björklund); and victim perceiving the act as bullying (Simmons *et al.*). By contrast specific acts of homophobic and transphobic abuse (Rivers), stalking and violence (Björklund) and sexual abuse (Pearce) tend to be viewed as harassment and not bullying within a work context – largely because these acts can be a one-off incident. Yet, in agreement with Hershcovis (2011), rather than restricting our understanding of abusive behaviour by generating a proliferation of conceptually similar constructs with supposedly different defining criteria, we should conceptualize the area within a superordinate construct of aggression. Specific 'criteria' (e.g. repetition) are then seen as moderators in a causal path between aggression and outcomes. The diversity of acts presented in this volume goes some way to achieving this aim and moves us away from our silo mentality.

Antecedents of bullying

The work environment hypothesis has played a dominant role in explaining antecedents of workplace bullying. Bullying has been shown to be promoted in organizational environments that are: strained and competitive (Vartia 1996); undergoing change (Harvey *et al.* 2006); conducive to bullying (Archer 1999); and populated by poor leadership (Hauge *et al.* 2007). Salin (2003) conceptualized a three-process model of organizational antecedents: 'precipitating processes' (organizational changes) that provide the trigger mechanism for bullying processes to evolve; 'motivating processes' (competitive work environments and organizational norms that justify bullying), which present the individual with a rationale to engage in bullying; and 'enabling processes' (power imbalances, poor social climate and poor management style/skills), which provide the conditions that facilitate bullying. Applying this model to university bullying, the transition (change) to university (Campbell) provides the trigger for bullying to evolve and the competitive environment (e.g. Aziz; Simmons *et al.*) which normalizes abusive behaviour (e.g. Pearce; Rivers) provides the motivation to engage in bullying. When these are coupled with a lack of clear policies on bullying and power differentials (e.g. Shariff and DeMartini), you have the right environment for bullying to occur. Notably, if at least two processes are not present then bullying will not occur. Intervention-wise, if we can remove two of these processes the outcome should be a reduction in abusive behaviour in universities.

Additionally, individual level explanations of workplace bullying also emerge. Aquino *et al.* (1999) and Coyne *et al.* (2000) point to the notion of submissive/vulnerable victims or provocative victims based on a dispositional hypothesis. The submissive victim notion marries well with the targeting of vulnerable peers as a feature of university bullying (Cowie and Myers, Björklund and Giovazolias and Malikiosi-Loizos, this volume). Additionally, unrealistic self-esteem, low-emotional control, low empathy and need for power (Zapf and Einarsen 2003) have been offered as characteristics of perpetrators that promote their engagement in bullying. Again, this is reflected in this volume by Aziz, Arıcak and Giovazolias and Malikiosi-Loizos.

Perhaps where current university bullying research is limited is in terms of developing a theoretical framework that considers both individual and situational antecedents of bullying. Bowling and Beehr's (2006) victim-perspective model could be of use to researchers in university bullying. This model includes organizational culture and climate, HR-systems, perpetrator characteristics and victim characteristics as antecedents of bullying. An attribution process of the causes of the bullying will result in different fairness perceptions and behaviours based on whether the cause is attributed to the self, the perpetrator or the organization. While, in this volume both Aziz and Rivers intimate unfairness/ injustice perceptions in their discussions, they are not explored theoretically. Notions of fairness and social exchange have been hypothesized in workplace bullying research, specifically in terms of violation of dignity and the psychological contract (Parzefall and Salin 2010). Models focusing on fairness, attributions and social exchange could be a fruitful area for helping to understand university bullying.

Workplace bullying interventions: how can they apply?

Combining the extant research on bullying antecedents, Coyne (2011) conceptualized a framework reflecting preventative, supportive and remedial interventions at the organizational, group and individual level. The organizational level considers initially identifying risk factors for bullying, through ultimately developing a culture of dignity and respect where bullying is not tolerated. Group level interventions focus on changing group norms and values, and individual level interventions include providing training, informal and formal support mechanisms, and support. An overarching society level captures the national context in terms of social values and provides a macro perspective on the extent that bullying is tolerated.

This framework could be adopted within a university context and focused at all stakeholders (staff and students). To some extent, we can see levels of this framework represented in this volume. For example, Giovazolias and Malikiosi-Loizos highlight training victims and perpetrators (individual-prevention level) and peer support (group-supportive), and Luca illustrates the role of the therapist (individual-remedial).

At the organizational-preventive level, to develop a culture of dignity and respect, all stakeholders in the university context need to understand and adhere to the culture. A whole-university policy becomes an important piece in this intervention jigsaw because (as Campbell outlines) it sends the message that the university is committed to preventing bullying, the university supports a culture of dignity and respect, and emphasizes that bullying is not normalized behaviour (an issue various authors in this volume highlight). A policy promoting dignity and respect should help to foster positive social exchange relationships, perceptions of fairness and a positive psychological contract. However, a word of caution from the workplace bullying arena; policies are limited in their effectiveness (Beale and Hoel 2011) and mistrust can emerge in enactment of the policy (Harrington *et al.* 2012). Should this occur the psychological contract will be broken and negative social exchange relationships follow.

As eloquently portrayed by Shariff and DeMartini, societal attitudes appear to normalize abusive behaviour in a university context. It becomes accepted practice for laddish and rape cultures to emerge. Therefore, the society intervention level becomes increasingly important as it provides a barometer of what is acceptable behaviour. Student and staff unions, national political bodies, charities and professional associations all need to cooperate to set the wider society agenda in this topic area. Clearly, this may be difficult to achieve top-down, but as some of our university graduates will become the next leaders of industry and politics, by ensuring the university sector is one that supports and promotes dignity and respect, one would hope this ethos follows these students into their working lives. From a bottom-up process, this should start to change the norms within society more towards treating people with dignity and respect in any social exchange context.

References

Aquino, K., Grover, S. L., Bradfield, M. and Allen, D. G. (1999). The effects of negative affectivity, hierarchical status, and self-determination on workplace victimization. *Academy of Management Journal,* 42: 260–72.

Archer, D. (1999). Exploring 'bullying' culture in the para-military organization. *International Journal of Manpower,* 20: 94–105.

Beale, D. and Hoel, H. (2011). Workplace bullying and the employment relationship: exploring questions of prevention, control and context. *Work, Employment and Society,* 25(1): 5–18.

Bowling, N. A. and Beehr, T. A. (2006). Workplace harassment from the victim's perspective: A theoretical model and meta-analysis. *Journal of Applied Psychology,* 91(5): 998–1012.

Coyne, I. (2011). Bullying in the workplace. In C. P. Monks and I. Coyne (Eds.), *Bullying in Different Contexts.* Cambridge: Cambridge University Press. pp. 157–84.

Coyne, I., Seigne, E. and Randall, P. (2000). Predicting workplace victim status from personality. *European Journal of Work and Organizational Psychology,* 9(3): 335–49.

Harrington, S., Rayner, C. and Warren, S. (2012), Too hot to handle? Trust and human resource practitioners' implementation of anti-bullying policy. *Human Resource Management Journal,* 22(4): 392–408.

Harvey, M. G., Treadway, D., and Heames, J. T. (2006). Bullying in global organizations: A reference point perspective. *Journal of World Business,* 41: 190–202.

Hauge, L. J., Skogstad, A. and Einarsen, S. (2007). Relationships between stressful work environments and bullying: Results of a large representative study. *Work and Stress,* 21: 220–42.

Hershcovis, M. S. (2011). Incivility, social undermining, bullying... oh my!: A call to reconcile constructs within workplace aggression research. *Journal of Organizational Behavior,* 32(3): 499–519.

Parzefall, M-R. and Salin, D. M. (2010). Perceptions of and reactions to workplace bullying: A social exchange perspective. *Human Relations,* 63(6): 761–80.

Salin, D. (2003). Ways of explaining workplace bullying: a review of enabling, motivating and precipitating structures and processes in the work environment. *Human Relations,* 56(10): 1213–232.

Vartia, M. (1996). The sources of bullying – psychological work environment and organizational climate. *European Journal of Work and Organizational Psychology,* 5: 203–14.

Zapf, D. and Einarsen, S. (2003). Individual antecedents of bullying. In S. Einarsen, H. Hoel, and C. Cooper (Eds.), *Bullying and Emotional Abuse in the Workplace: International Perspectives in Research and Practice.* London: Taylor and Francis. pp. 165–84.

16

EPILOGUE

What can be done?

Helen Cowie and Carrie-Anne Myers

At present, universities would appear to react to bullying when it is brought to the attention of the authorities and respond in a piecemeal, slapdash manner, if at all. Evidence from the authors of this book highlights the strong need to have systems in place to provide a framework within which each university as an organization should demonstrate its commitment to the prevention of bullying and the provision of interventions to support potentially vulnerable individuals and groups. Taking the argument a step further, a policy consistent *across* universities should be designed and implemented along the lines of whole school policies adopted across the school sector. University lecturers need heightened awareness of the problem, and training in knowledge of its legal and social aspects and in confidence on how to address bullying when they encounter it, either directly or through referral on to relevant experts. Specific strategies and detailed guidelines are provided by Sullivan in chapter 14 and by Coyne in chapter 15. The important role of student unions is also discussed, as is the value of peer support systems for empowering bystanders to challenge bullying when they encounter it on campus. There is also an urgent need for research to evaluate the effectiveness of a range of policies and practices.

As this book demonstrates, the problem is endemic and extends from undergraduate students through Masters and postgraduate programmes. Some individual students are more prone to be bullied through their previous experiences at school, which they bring with them to university. As Pörhöla points out in chapter 4, there is considerable continuity in abusive peer relationships from school to university. In this context, she proposes peer community integration theory as an explanatory model for understanding the quality of students' relationships with one another and for giving insight into the processes through which individuals integrate (or fail to integrate) with the networks in their community. The long-term suffering that continuing victims bring with them to university – e.g. loneliness, difficulty in making friends, lack of peer interaction skills – points to the need for counselling and other forms of social support, particularly on entry to university. Student health services and counselling centres are places where staff must be alert to the impact of bullying on the emotional health and well-being not only of the targets of bullying but also of the perpetrators.

Luca (2015), from the perspective of a university counsellor, points out that the victims of sexual bullying often fear to tell anyone through shame and guilt about what happened to them. Giovazolias and Malikiosi-Loizos in chapter 9 also indicate the important role of professional counselling as well as peer support in alleviating the suffering of bullied students. Studies of school and workplace bullying document the catastrophic impact that bullying can have on the mental health of those involved. There are many negative consequences of bullying, including long-term psychological problems such as chronic anxiety, depressive symptoms, suicidal ideation and suicide attempts on the part of victims. Perpetrators have also been found to be at heightened risk of anxiety, depression, psychosomatic symptoms and eating disorders, as well as anti-social behaviour. Therefore, it is of paramount importance that university authorities take action to protect the students in their care from such risks to their emotional health and well-being and their capacity to study.

At the same time, some groups are particularly vulnerable to attack. Racism, homophobia, sexism, and prejudice against those with disabilities have an impact on certain students regardless of their individual vulnerabilities. Such discrimination has the effect of normalizing social exclusion. As Pörhölä argues, the members of particular groups have the power to determine the extent to which certain people can be included or excluded and even to decide what they can or cannot do within the group, and the position they have within that group. The outcome can be the removal of victims' fundamental right to socialize, to study and feel positive about themselves and their values and beliefs. Whether they like it or not, such individuals are forced by the group into the role of outsider, and often silenced or even banished in the process, or forced to live in terror, as documented by Björklund in chapter 6 in the context of the victims of stalking, and by Rivers in chapter 5 in the context of LGBT students. This is further illustrated in chapter 8 where Simmons, Bauman and Ives discuss membership of sororities and fraternities – the Greek life of USA universities. It is not surprising that some minority students band together in their own sororities and fraternities as a way of asserting their own sense of identity. Others deny their group identity; many bullied students remain silent. There are also broader cultural factors that either promote or reduce bullying among students, as indicated in the cross-cultural research discussed in chapter 10.

Universities seem to be very far from celebrating diversity and difference. The experiences reported by Aziz in chapter 3 indicate that the bullying culture at university is present among staff as well as students. Aziz sums this up as 'an unfriendly and hostile environment'. Sullivan in chapter 14 refers to 'the dark and often hidden underbelly universities can nurture'. We cannot ignore the social context within which the bullying is taking place. The immediate social environment is the university itself and the discrimination against individuals and groups is unlikely to go unnoticed by the undergraduate population who must observe it in their classes, lectures, seminars and tutorial groups. At institutional level, there need to be strong policies in place to address the problem. Not only do tutors and lecturers need to be trained to be alert to this issue and to have knowledge about how to deal with it directly when it occurs, for example, during a lecture or seminar, but also visiting lecturers and guest speakers need to have support mechanisms in place. Staff also need to know how and when to refer the situation on to relevant support agencies, either within the university (for example, to the student counselling service) or outside it (for example, to the police), as Shariff and DeMartini so graphically indicate in chapter 13. Mindful of the fact that students are young adults, when does the law take over from the rules and regulations of the university? As shown, stalking, hate crime and harassment are all criminal offences in society. So how do we define the grey area between bullying and crime?

Students' Unions have a key role to play and, in fact, have been pioneering in commissioning reports and research into the phenomenon of bullying and discrimination on campus. Pearce, NUS President at the time of writing, indicates in chapter 2 the helplessness felt by some students in the face of persistent denigration on the grounds of their sexual orientation with worrying data on the impact on these students' well-being and on their studies. There is very little information on the extent to which this kind of discrimination undermines student grades or even causes them to drop out of university altogether. Fellow students are in a unique position of being able to offer interventions, such as peer support, that have already been shown to be effective in school contexts with younger students. They can also actively promote positive recognition of minority groups.

But at organizational level, as Coyne indicates in chapter 15, universities need to be considerably more proactive in demonstrating their commitment to inclusion, the promotion of tolerance and the celebration of diversity – all underlying ingredients in the make-up of bullying. The presence of bullying and social exclusion on campus undermines the role of universities as places where ideas are explored though dialogue and debate, not violence and discrimination. Authors in this book emphasize the urgent need for universities to have effective policies on bullying with strong action on the implementation of these policies and clear sanctions for those who engage in this form of violence against fellow students. It cannot be right that behaviour and attitudes grounded in prejudice and stereotyping so often remain unchallenged on campus. When extreme bullying happens at school, students can be permanently excluded. Should this kind of sanction be considered by universities? Policies and interventions provide an essential framework for addressing the issue. But ultimately the university should also be a place where values are openly explored and where difference is a matter for celebration not shame.

As indicated throughout this book, the corporatization of higher education is on the rise with its typical valuing of individualism and competitiveness. Not only can this promote 'laddish' values, it can also act as a powerful deterrent for apparently 'vulnerable' students to seek help when they experience social and emotional difficulties. Universities are increasingly signing up to market values with their concern for income from student fees and research grants taking priority. The danger is, that in the process, they lose sight of the campus as a learning community grounded in partnership, cooperation, mutual respect and the search for knowledge.

INDEX